Advancing Responsible Adolescent Development

Series Editor

Roger J.R. Levesque
Indiana University, Bloomington, IN, USA

For further volumes:
http://www.springer.com/series/7284

DISCARDED

Stephen M. Gavazzi

Families with Adolescents

Bridging the Gaps between
Theory, Research, and Practice

 Springer

Stephen M. Gavazzi
Department of Human Development and Family Science
The Ohio State University
Columbus, OH 43210
USA
sgavazzi@ehe.osu.edu

ISBN 978-1-4419-8245-2   e-ISBN 978-1-4419-8246-9
DOI 10.1007/978-1-4419-8246-9
Springer New York Dordrecht Heidelberg London

Library of Congress Control Number: 2011921348

© Springer Science+Business Media, LLC 2011

All rights reserved. This work may not be translated or copied in whole or in part without the written permission of the publisher (Springer Science+Business Media, LLC, 233 Spring Street, New York, NY 10013, USA), except for brief excerpts in connection with reviews or scholarly analysis. Use in connection with any form of information storage and retrieval, electronic adaptation, computer software, or by similar or dissimilar methodology now known or hereafter developed is forbidden.

The use in this publication of trade names, trademarks, service marks, and similar terms, even if they are not identified as such, is not to be taken as an expression of opinion as to whether or not they are subject to proprietary rights.

Printed in the United States of America

Springer is part of Springer Science+Business Media (www.springer.com)

This book is dedicated to the memory of Patrick C. McKenry, Ph.D.

Mentor, scholar, and friend.

Foreword

> "What we call the beginning is often the end. And to make an end is to make a new beginning. The end is where we start from."
>
> T. S. Eliot, *Little Gidding*

All books, like everything else in life, have a beginning and an end, reflecting a storyline that the author has chosen to follow. Selecting an end for the present book– in this case, a review of the most recent literature pertaining to families with adolescents that would be covered as part of this effort – was the easy part. The book contract from Springer called for the manuscript to be delivered no later than May 2010. So, no information from articles or book chapters published beyond this due date would make it into the present edition.

But what was the most appropriate starting point? There was reason enough to begin at the beginning; that is to say, at least some of the literature review would have to cover seminal material – and especially theoretical work – that helped to shape the study of families with adolescents, regardless of its publication date. On the other hand, research articles related to this area of inquiry had now reached massive proportions, stemming back many decades, with the prevention and intervention literature not far behind in terms of sheer volume. There literally was no way to deal with this entire body of work on empirical and applied topics related to families with adolescents, so some sort of decision about what to include and what to exclude was inevitable.

Providentially, the anticipated publication of this book was to coincide with the fifteenth anniversary of the release of *Vision 2010: Families & Adolescents* (McKenry & Gavazzi, 1994), a collection of articles published by the National Council on Family Relations (NCFR). I had been given the distinct honor of co-editing this *Vision 2010* monograph with Patrick McKenry, a colleague of mine at The Ohio State University who had been a prominent leader in the family science field for many years before his untimely passing five years ago (and to whom this book is dedicated). According to Sharon Price, the series editor, the primary purpose for the overall *Vision 2010* effort was "to increase awareness of the critical nature and role of families in our society and how major social, economic, and developmental life problems are affecting the core of our social fabric – our family life" (Price, 2004, p. *i*). Almost prophetically, 2010 had been selected as a year in the not-too-distant future that would be marked by economic calamity if our policymakers did not begin to make family issues a national priority.

This publication was a virtual "Who's Who" of luminaries in the field who had focused their attention on topics related to families with adolescents. For instance, Richard Gelles wrote a chapter on "Violence and abuse in the lives of adolescents," covering a number of topics concerning adolescent involvement in family violence. Jeanne Brooks-Gunn co-wrote chapters on the biological aspects of adolescence (with Julia Graber) as well as a chapter on the impact of poverty (with Greg Duncan). Richard Lerner wrote a chapter on the school context alongside a chapter by Brad Brown on peer effects. Michael Farrell and Grace Barnes co-wrote a piece entitled "Families and adolescent substance abuse," while Tom Gullotta compiled a chapter on prevention approaches. And so on.

The fact that a book on families of adolescents was now to be published in the year 2010 lent itself to the idea of compiling a literature review of studies conducted over the last decade and a half. Hence, the year 1995 was selected as this book's beginning point, at least in terms of the bulk of empirical and application work that would be covered throughout these pages. Although not its original intention, this book nonetheless serves as a "Pilgrim's Progress" of ideas and data stemming from the last fifteen years of work that has focused on families with adolescents.

As well, I wish to point out that the compilation of materials for this book was preceded by my invitation to contribute a chapter on families with adolescents for the third edition of the *Handbook of Marriage and the Family*. Entitled *Theory and Research Pertaining to Families with Adolescents*, the writing of this chapter opportunely became a "warm-up" exercise for the present book. As such, readers will discover that portions of the chapter have been used liberally throughout this book with the permission of Springer, the publisher of both of these works. I am grateful to editors Gary Peterson and Kevin Bush for their early guidance on the book chapter that would lay the groundwork for the more extensive treatment of material on families with adolescents in this book.

At the same time, the writing of this book also was preceded directly by my authoring a trade publication on families with adolescents entitled *Strong Families, Successful Students: Helping Teenagers Reach their Full Academic Potential* (Book Surge). The trade book served as an importance counterbalance to the present book you have in your hands, in that the relative success of any trade book hinges in large part on the ability to translate academic knowledge into a form that can be more readily accessed by the general public. As such, not only would I respectfully submit this *Strong Families Successful Students* book for the reader's inspection as one model for translating important scholarly information on families with adolescents, but I would also humbly suggest that it has allowed me to write about scholarly work in a decidedly more user-friendly format that can be appreciated by the widest possible audience.

Further, the revision of the first draft of this book coincided with my taking on a leadership role in the development of *Vision 2020: Families with Adolescents*, a follow-up to the original *Vision 2010* monograph discussed above. Instead of a printed publication, however, the *Vision 2020* effort has involved the development of a web-based platform for theorists, researchers, and application-based professionals to explore and discuss where the study of families with adolescents would be heading in the next ten years. In my capacity as series editor of this new NCFR informational database, I was given the responsibility of writing the inaugural *Vision 2020* article. I chose to focus attention on the field's need to recommit to the "triple threat" model of scholarship (cf., Olson, 1976) that seeks to unify theoretical, empirical and application-based efforts regarding families with adolescents. Readers will recognize a similar call for such scholarship integration in the final thoughts chapter of the present book.

Last but not least to be mentioned in terms of opening comments is the fact that the finalization of this book was greatly facilitated by the efforts of over 75 members of NCFR who had responded to an email inquiry that I had sent to the affiliates of all specialty sections. My request was for members to pass along any and all citations of material on families with adolescents that they had authored or co-authored over the past fifteen years. The fact of the matter is that, no matter how hard you search, you always end up overlooking extremely relevant material. Hence, this book is all the more rich and detailed because of the time that my colleagues took to respond to that inquiry.

Acknowledgements

First and foremost, I had no better teachers for this content area than my own sons. Their growing up experiences constantly forced me to examine what it was that I really knew about families with adolescents. Second, I have had the pleasure of mentoring quite a number of budding young scholars over the years. These dedicated professionals, who share my passion and interest in both basic and applied research regarding families with adolescents, are helping to advance the field through the direct utilization of the extensive knowledge base represented by this book's contents. Third, I am grateful to have had the privilege of working with hundreds of families with teenagers over the past two decades both through the programs I have developed and the clinical work I have conducted. Their stories and experiences are woven into the very fabric of the many examples of family situations that I have used to illustrate certain points throughout this book.

I owe much to Roger Levesque, the editor of the *Advancing Responsible Adolescent Development Series* within which this book appears. Dr. Levesque also is the editor of the *Journal of Youth and Adolescence*, and has written about the need to take books more seriously in the social sciences (Levesque, 2007). This scholar understands the important place that monographs such as the one you are now reading have in the dissemination of knowledge within the academic community. Happily, the family field continues to share this passion for books, as witnessed most recently by an editorial entitled "Books Still Matter" (Blume, 2009) published in the *Journal of Family Theory and Review*.

As well, Dr. Levesque has extended this commitment to books that apply such knowledge to real life situations and issues. This has resulted in critical reviews of books such as my own *Strong Families, Successful Students* (see Day, 2010), a strength-based and solution-focused approach to helping teenagers reach their full academic potential that was published just as I began to write this current book in earnest. I am sincerely grateful for the range of opportunities that continue to be made available to authors such as myself. Modifying the oft-used quote from Logan Wilson's *The Academic Man*, we either will publish our ideas or they will perish with us.

Finally, I wish to acknowledge the support and encouragement of my friends and colleagues both here at The Ohio State University and beyond. My appreciation extends first to those departmental, college, and university administrators who had a hand in approving the sabbatical that allowed me the opportunity to take on the task of writing this book. In turn, my thanks go out to those faculty members in Ohio State's Department of Human Development and Family Science – Suzanne Bartle-Haring, Michael Glassman, Julie Serovich, Sarah Shoppe-Sullivan, and Natasha Slesnick – who took precious time out of their busy schedules to review various portions of this book. As well, deep gratitude is reserved for Angie Shock-Giordano, one of the very best of my former doctoral students, who has provided me with thorough commentary, editing suggestions, and insights on the entire manuscript.

Contents

**Part I Introduction and Overview of Theoretical,
Research, and Application Topics**

1 Introduction... 3

2 Overview of Theory, Research, and Application Topics 9
   2.1   A Theoretical Overview 9
   2.2   Overview of Family-Based Research............................. 14
         2.2.1   Models for Conducting Research on Families 15
         2.2.2   Unit of Analysis Issues 18
   2.3   Overview of Family-Based Application Efforts................... 20

Part II Theorizing About Families with Adolescents

3 Family Development Theory 25
   3.1   Basic Family Development Theory Concepts...................... 26
   3.2   Reflections: Family Development Theory
        and Families with Adolescents 30

4 Family Systems Theory 33
   4.1   Basic Family Systems Theory Concepts 34
   4.2   Reflections: Family Systems Theory
        and Families with Adolescents 38

5 Ecological Theory 41
   5.1   Basic Ecological Theory Concepts 42
   5.2   Reflections: Ecological Theory
        and Families with Adolescents 45

6	Attachment Theory		49
	6.1	Basic Attachment Theory Concepts	50
	6.2	Reflections: Attachment Theory and Families with Adolescents	53

7	Social Learning Theory		57
	7.1	Basic Social Learning Theory Concepts	58
	7.2	Reflections: Social Learning Theory and Families with Adolescents	61

Part III Research on Families with Adolescents

8	Research on the Parent–Adolescent Dyad		67
	8.1	Selected Studies on Parenting Behaviors	70
	8.2	The Dimensionality of Parenting Behaviors	72
	8.3	The Cultural Relevance of Parenting Behaviors	74
	8.4	Summary of Research on the Parent–Adolescent Dyad	75

9	Polyadic Research on Families with Adolescents		77
	9.1	Selected Studies Regarding Family Distance Regulation	82
	9.2	Selected Studies Regarding Family Conflict and Family Problem-Solving	85
	9.3	Selected Studies Regarding the Influence of Siblings	87
	9.4	Summary of Polyadic Research	89

10	The Family's Impact on Adolescent Outcomes		91
	10.1	The Impact of Families on Delinquency and Conduct Disorders	94
	10.2	The Impact of Families on Adolescent Mental Health	96
	10.3	The Impact of Families on Adolescent Substance Use	99
	10.4	The Impact of Families on Adolescent Sexual Activity	101
	10.5	The Impact of Families on Adolescent Educational Issues	103
	10.6	The Impact of Families on Adolescent Social Competence	107
	10.7	Summary of Research Regarding Family Influences on Adolescent Outcomes	109

Part IV Application Topics Concerning Families with Adolescents

11 Family Therapy and Other Family Intervention-Based Efforts.... 113

    11.1 Specific Family Intervention Models............................ 116
            11.1.1 Brief Strategic Family Therapy 116
            11.1.2 Functional Family Therapy.............................. 117
            11.1.3 Multidimensional Family Therapy 119
            11.1.4 Multisystemic Therapy 121
    11.2 Other Family-Based Intervention Efforts 122
    11.3 Summary of the Family Intervention Literature 123

12 Family Prevention Programs... 125

    12.1 Characteristics of Effective Family Programs 127
    12.2 Examples of Specific Family-Based
           Prevention Programs... 130
    12.3 Web-Based Resources on Family Programs 134
    12.4 Summary of the Family Prevention Literature................... 135

Part V Summary and Future Directions

13 Outlook on Theoretical, Research, and Application Efforts to Date 139

    13.1 Outlook of Theoretical Efforts to Understand
           Families with Adolescents...................................... 140
    13.2 Outlook on Empircal Efforts to Understand
           Families with Adolescents...................................... 142
    13.3 Outlook on Application Efforts Targeting
           Families with Adolescents...................................... 147

14 The Need to Integrate Theory, Research, and Application Efforts 151

    14.1 Original Thoughts About the Need
           for a "Triple Threat" Model 153
    14.2 Key Factors That Serve as Barriers to Unification............... 155
    14.3 The Importance of Integration in the Study
           of Families with Adolescents................................... 157
    14.4 Coda... 158

References... 159

Index... 191

About the Author

Stephen M. Gavazzi, Ph.D., is Professor, Department of Human Development and Family Science at The Ohio State University, and Lead Director of the OSU Center for Family Research. During the past 20 years at Ohio State, Dr. Gavazzi has established a research program that identifies the impact of family dynamics on youth development, psychopathology, and problem behavior. This work has been supported by more than $4 million in grants from a wide variety of federal, state, and private sources. He also is a trained Family Therapist, thus bringing an applied clinical perspective to his work. Dr. Gavazzi has been involved in the development and evaluation of a number of family-based programming efforts, including a multifamily psychoeducational group for families containing children with mood disorders, as well as a strength-based program for families who have adolescents involved in some aspect of the juvenile court. Most recently, he has been involved in the development of the Global Risk Assessment Device, a web-based instrument designed to generate information that assists professionals in making appropriate service referrals for at-risk youth and their families.

Part I
Introduction and Overview of Theoretical, Research, and Application Topics

Chapter 1
Introduction

> *The secret of all victory lies in the organization of the non-obvious.*
>
> Marcus Aurelius, *Historia Augusta*

Abstract This first chapter serves as an introduction to the basic format of this book. Brief descriptions are given in each of the three main parts of this book in terms of coverage of theoretical, research, and application topics concerning the study of families with adolescents. Three questions are raised that correspond to each of the three main parts of this book: (1) where do we get our ideas about the families within which adolescents grow and develop? (2) what actual data do we have that informs us about the families of adolescents? and (3) what is our knowledge base about how to prevent problems in families with adolescents or otherwise how do we intervene with adolescents and their families when difficulties arise? The natural overlap between the theoretical, empirical, and practical parts of the book is discussed as well. Further, the intended audience of this book is delineated, including most importantly those students and instructors of both family-based and adolescent development courses. The secondary audience of professionals working directly with adolescents and their families is also identified.

Families matter: The available empirical evidence strongly supports the notion that the impact of family members on the lives of adolescents is both profound and lasting. In fact, this body of research findings directly challenges the general public's view that peers are the most important influence in the lives of adolescents. While peers, without doubt, play a progressively more important role in adolescent well-being, the family environment remains the first and most significant social context within which adolescents grow and develop.

As researchers continue to generate evidence regarding the immense power and influence that families exert in the lives of adolescents, more and more social scientists have become interested in including family variables in their theoretical, empirical, and application efforts (Collins & Laursen, 2004). In parallel fashion, there has been heightened awareness of some noteworthy demographic shifts that have taken place within families over the last century (Hernandez, 1993, 1997, 2003). These factors include the following:

- Increased divorce rates
- Increased numbers of single-parent (and especially mother-headed) families
- Increased parent education levels
- Increased numbers of mothers in the workplace
- Decreased numbers of siblings
- Migration from rural to urban environments

Among other things, these changes provide the field with a historical context by which consumers of literature on families with adolescents can reflect on the representativeness of samples used to conduct research and build programs.

This first part of the book serves both as an introduction and an overview to all the topics that will be covered within the subsequent pages. As well, there is a final part that serves both as a review of the content of this book and as a springboard for future directions in terms of scholarship on families with adolescents. In order to provide coverage of the resulting knowledge base that has been created over the past 15 years, however, this book is organized further into three main parts related to the field's current understanding of families with adolescents: theory, research, and application topics. Separately, these parts are meant to describe different aspects of how we understand, observe, and work with families containing adolescent members. At the same time, however, there is a natural overlap between these three main parts that will be explored wherever possible. For example, when empirical studies are based on specific family theory approaches or premises, these linkages will be discussed in the research portion of this book. As well, the empirical work that is based upon prevention and intervention efforts will be presented in the application portion. Hence, the three main parts of this book are thought to be distinct and yet interrelated with components, of the field's overall acquired wisdom, about families with adolescents.

This overlap here is portrayed as "natural" because these intersections reflect the reality of how both science and research-based applications typically are practiced. The theory involves a set of ideas about the way that things work (in this case, families with adolescents). Research aims to test those ideas, which generate supportive evidence in some cases and less than supportive data in others. Applications are then built based on those ideas and data that are most compelling in terms of their ability to explain and predict phenomena.

Taken together, the three main parts of this book draw evenly from a broad cross section of social science disciplines, providing an integrative and concise approach to the interdisciplinary nature of work being conducted in this area of inquiry. These three main parts are further broken down into subdivisions that organize the content of adolescents and their families, and illustrate the basic themes of each subdivision contained in this book.

The most important point about the scope of this monograph that may not be immediately obvious to the casual reader is that this book centers on the families of adolescents, not on the adolescents themselves. Hence, the topics that are covered throughout this book – and especially in the research part – pertain to those areas that are family-focused in their orientation. This is why the opening portion of the book is titled as "Families *with* Adolescents" and not "Adolescents *and* their Families." The former implies concentration on the family as a whole, whereas the latter makes the adolescent as the central point of focus. Therefore, instead of the typical biological (puberty and physical development) and individual developmental (identity, cognitive growth, and emotional maturity) issues found in texts on adolescents, this book shines a spotlight on subject matter such as family processes, family structure, family conflict, and family problem solving, as well as focuses on variables that reflect interactions within and among different dyads in the family such as the parent–adolescent, interparental, and sibling subsystems.

The first main part of this book (Part 2) involves efforts to theorize about families with adolescents. In essence, we will be attempting to answer this question: Where do we get our ideas about the families within which adolescents grow and develop? The reader will be exposed to a variety of theoretical frameworks from the field of human development and family science, including family development theory and family systems theory. Due to the interdisciplinary nature of this book, however, we also will be examining theories coming from other fields that have been used to understand families with adolescents, including ecological theory, attachment theory, and social learning theory.

The second main part of this book (Part 3) focuses on family research topics. Here, we want to answer the question: What data do we have that informs us about the families of adolescents? As noted in the foreword, this book covers the empirical literature on families with adolescents conducted over the last 15 years. Particular attention has been given to articles in family-focused journals such as *Journal of Marriage and the Family, Family Relations, Family Process,* and *Journal of Family Psychology*. Information on family issues published in more adolescent-oriented journals such as *Journal of Youth and Adolescence, Journal of Adolescent Research, Journal of Research on Adolescence,* and *Journal of Early Adolescence* also are extensively covered. And again, because of the interdisciplinary scope of this book, articles concerning families with adolescents contained in other journals from fields related to health, psychology, psychiatry, counseling, and social work also are included wherever applicable.

In these journals, while covering empirical material about how the families of adolescents operate, attention also is paid to the research literature concerning the family's impact on adolescent-oriented outcomes. That being said, this is not an exhaustive review of studies pertaining to the role of families in all aspects of adolescent development and well-being. Instead, systematic attention is given to a core set of outcome indicators – delinquency, mental health, substance use, sexual activity, education, and social competence – that are believed to be representative of the family's influence on the positive (and not so positive) outcomes of its adolescent members.

The third main part of this book (Part 4) concerns application topics, and our question to answer is this: How do we prevent problems and intervene with families of adolescents when difficulties arise? In the family intervention chapter, we will focus on family-based work that targets many of the same issues covered in the empirical portion of this book, especially problem behaviors related to adolescent delinquency, mental health, and substance abuse. Other family-based interventions that deal with multiple problem behaviors will also be covered. In the family prevention chapter, our focus will turn to family strengthening programs that reflect a primary prevention (or universal) focus. As well, however, those initiatives that fall into realm of selective prevention will also be covered, meaning that more at-risk families are targeted.

Once again we will confine our review largely to those works published over the last decade and a half, and also cover information contained in most of the same journals. On an as-needed basis, books and book chapters published during the same time period also will be referenced. And once again, the emphasis is on family-based work rather than mere individual-oriented approaches to the adolescents themselves.

Throughout the book, assistance will be provided to readers in the integration and utilization of each part's contents. The intent here is to allow some back and forth movement between academic literature, and real life situations and issues. For instance, every theory covered in the first main part of this book (Part 2) will begin with a vignette. Each of these brief scenes is meant to provide an illustration of how a family with adolescents would be viewed through the lens of that particular theoretical framework.

The second main part (Part 3) contains straightforward examples of how researchers can measure variables related to family dynamics and adolescent outcomes. Here, the reader will be able to examine items taken directly from various measures, including, but not limited to domains embedded within the Global Risk Assessment Device (GRAD), a risk and needs instrument developed by a team of researchers at The Ohio State University for use with adolescents, their family members, and those professionals who work with these youth and families.

Finally, the third main part (Part 4) provides descriptions of families that the author has worked with over the past 2 decades, altered only enough to protect the identities of the family members. These case examples are meant to present readers with some realistic illustrations of the kinds of issues and concerns that are routinely faced by families with adolescents.

Closing out this book is a capstone part (Part 5) that serves as both a summary and discussion of future directions for scholars interested in families with adolescents. Beyond a chapter that reviews all of the theoretical, empirical, and application-based material covered in this book, readers will be exposed to deliberation about how the current state of literature on families with adolescents tells us something about where the field should be headed in the future. Hence, in the last chapter, particular consideration will be given to the *intersection* of theoretical, empirical, and application issues. The viewpoint of students who are attempting to integrate all of this information on families with adolescents is kept firmly in the forefront throughout this final chapter. For that reason, this closing chapter begins with a vignette that is focused on graduate students themselves. While hypothetical, the topics covered within the conversation that ensues is one that occurs with some regularity among the students I have known and taught over the years.

Taken together, the parts of this book have been compiled for a wide audience of students and professionals interested in and working with the families of adolescents. Instructors of courses that specifically focus on families of adolescents, often as not, must either decide among several books that cover portions of theory, research, and application material, and/or must work hard to compile a course packet made up of those articles and book chapters that "fill in" what those books do not cover. Expectantly, students in those classes will appreciate the ability to have one primary text that contains sufficient and necessary material for mastery in this area of study.

For instructors of more straightforward adolescent development courses, it is anticipated that this book becomes the perfect companion to the primary text that has been selected, allowing students to experience a much wider breadth and depth of topics surrounding families with adolescents. And finally, for professionals working directly with adolescents and their families, this book is meant to provide "one stop shopping" in terms of serving as a reference guide to the theoretical, empirical, and applied work being conducted in this burgeoning field.

Chapter 2
Overview of Theory, Research, and Application Topics

If you wish to converse with me, you must first define your terms.
Voltaire, *Dictionnaire Philosophique*

Abstract This second chapter serves as an overview of the three main parts of this book: theorizing about families with adolescents, research on families with adolescents, and application topics concerning families with adolescents. Theoretically, an intergenerational nurturing definition of families with adolescents is advanced in order to provide parameters around the literature covering two theoretical frameworks most associated with the field of human development and family science – family development theory and family systems theory – as well as three additional theories that claim more individual psychological origins: ecological theory, attachment theory, and social learning theory. The empirical overview offered in this chapter presents a number of heuristic models that help readers to understand the ways in which the direct and indirect effects of family factors are measured by researchers, as well as discussing unit of analysis issues that help to define both dyadic and polyadic efforts to understand families with adolescents. Finally, the application overview sets the stage for a review of both prevention and intervention efforts targeting families with adolescents. Here, our intergenerational nurturing definition regarding families with adolescents is used as a litmus test to determine which initiatives actually "do" something that is *family*-oriented.

2.1 A Theoretical Overview

Where do we get our ideas about the families within which adolescents grow and develop? In order to answer this question, indeed to undertake an examination of any type of phenomena, we must develop and adopt definitions of terms that describe our central focus of inquiry. For present purposes, the task at hand is to define what it means to study "families with adolescents." Despite the assertion that this book concerns family phenomena and not individual developmental issues, the fact that family life cycle stages are predicated on the developmental phases of its offspring necessitates a delineation of what the term "adolescent" implies.

A brief exercise can be done with a blank piece of paper in order to help us accomplish this initial task. At the top of the paper, draw three boxes in a row and label them sequentially with the following words:"Child," "Adolescent," and "Adult." Next, draw lines in between each of the boxes in order to make three columns that stretch from the top to the bottom of the paper. Your paper should look like Table 2.1 below.

Next, use the left hand column to write down all of the words you can think of that can be used to describe someone who is a child. When you have filled out that column, move to the right hand column and write down all of the words you can think of that can be used to describe someone who is an adult. Now comes the interesting part of this assignment. Without using any of the words you have already written in the left and right hand columns of your piece of paper, use the middle column to write down all of the words you can think of that can be used to describe someone who is an adolescent.

If you experienced any sort of difficulty in completing the middle column, you are not alone. The complexity involved in defining adolescence is reflected in many books that focus on this developmental period. These texts typically contain a section that discusses the variety of ways that the adolescent developmental period can be defined. Steinberg (2007), for example, notes that there are various ways that definitions of adolescence can be constructed depending on the biological, cognitive, and/or social context criteria that are employed. For instance, chronological age can be used, resulting in a focus on *teen*agers (13–19 years of ages). Alternatively, there are legal definitions, with an emphasis on 18 as the "age of majority" signifying adulthood (although the age of 21 as the legal drinking age also can be employed). Also, there are definitions that surround physical development, usually emphasizing events such as puberty, the end of physical growth and the development of adult sex characteristics. Further, there are more psychology-based definitions that rely on markers of emotional and cognitive maturity. Finally, there are definitions that are based on social contexts and events, such as high school graduation.

Such variations in definitions also are reflected in differences of opinion regarding the period of time covered by adolescence. The general public tends to think only in terms of chronological age, thus making the terms "adolescent" and "teenager" synonymous. In contrast, developmental theorists and researchers employ a variety of timeframes to capture the adolescent period. For instance, some scholars divide

Table 2.1 First exercise in defining terms

Child	Adolescent	Adult

this developmental period into early adolescence and late adolescence (Cobb 2006; Santrock 2008). Here, early adolescence is marked by tasks related to the establishment of a group identify amongst one's friends, whereas later adolescence concerns the development of an individual identity. Others break down this developmental period into early, middle, and later adolescence, with an emphasis on the school environment (middle school, high school, and college respectively), as well as emphasizing an additional transitional period known as "emerging adulthood" (Arnett 2010).

As noted earlier, the present book goes beyond the individualized focus on adolescents in order to establish and describe the larger family context. At the same time, the complexity of describing the adolescent developmental period directly impacts the definition of terms regarding families with adolescents. To illustrate, a modification of the first exercise described above can be carried out by creating another sheet of paper that contains three columns (see Table 2.2 below). Using the left hand column, write down all of the words you can think of that describe a "family with young children" and, using the right hand column, write down all of the words that describe a "family with adult offspring." Are there any words left over that can be used to describe a "family with adolescents?" Write all of the words you can think of in the middle column.

Do not become unduly concerned if this exercise proves to be an even more difficult challenge in comparison to the activity that simply asked you to describe the adolescent family member. The chapters ahead are meant to provide assistance to you in this task, as the necessary and sufficient material regarding the conceptualization, research, and treatment of families with adolescents is covered in comprehensive detail.

At the same time, because there are differences of opinions regarding the beginning and ending points of this developmental period, the reader also must expect that definitions will vary regarding what constitutes a family with adolescents. This lack of unanimity is both embraced and used as a point of comparison wherever possible, such that the scholarship reviewed throughout this book makes explicit reference to the ages of adolescent family members wherever available in material regarding theories and research findings related to their families.

The theory chapters cover conceptual frameworks that directly impact our understanding of families with adolescents. In preparation, we might well ask

Table 2.2 Second exercise in defining terms

Family with young children	Family with adolescents	Family with adult offspring

the question: what is a theory? A theory – any theory – involves the use of a set of principles that are used to predict and explain some sort of phenomena. In turn, these principles are subject to scientific testing in order to determine their reliability and validity, meaning how consistent and convincing they are in accounting for the things that we observe and experience.

What then does it mean to say that we are interested in family theory? It would follow most simply that a family theory would involve scientifically supported ideas that help us to understand and explain certain phenomena about families. To follow this line of logic, however, some common ground must be developed regarding what our definition of family will be.

Dictionary definitions state that the term "family" references the most basic unit of a society that has as its main function – the raising of children. In most mainstream Western societies, families traditionally are thought to be made up of two parents rearing their offspring (Anderson & Sabatelli, 2006). In other societies, there is greater emphasis on the extended generations of a family, and therefore can include any number of additional members such as grandparents, aunts, uncles, cousins, and the like. Even in current American society, however, the consistently high divorce rates and large numbers of children being born to unmarried parents has given rise to the need to include different combinations of members that can be regarded as comparable to the traditional family form (Olson & DeFrain, 2006). Hence, single-parent headed households, custodial and noncustodial parents following a divorce, cohabiting couples with children, stepfamilies, and gay and lesbian parents together create a virtual kaleidoscope of diversity regarding family forms.

Given this rather tremendous variation in family membership, this book adopts what might best be described as an "intergenerational nurturing" definition regarding families with adolescents. The intergenerational component denotes that there is at least one adult and one adolescent present to count as a family. As well, the nurturing component of this definition implies that the adult or adults inside of this family have primary caregiving responsibilities for the adolescent.

The notion of intergenerational nurturing is thought to align well with frameworks offered by Bush and Peterson (2007) and others regarding the main influences that families have on their offspring. Here, major emphasis is placed on a family socialization process that views parents and other adult caregivers as assuming a central role in teaching their adolescents how to become useful members of the larger society in which they reside. The relative success of these parental efforts often is addressed in terms of the offspring's development of socially competent behavior (i.e., problem-solving skills, achievement orientation) as examples of positive outcomes on the one hand, and the manifestation of problematic behaviors (i.e., delinquent behavior, substance abuse) as instances of more negative outcomes.

This book reviews various family-based theories that fit well within the intergenerational nurturing framework. In the most general sense, White and Klein (2008) have asserted that there are two kinds of family theories. First, there are theories containing family concepts that are used to describe other phenomena. Second, there are theories that attempt to describe families themselves as an object of study. Extending this to our present purposes, we can see there are theories that use family concepts to describe how adolescents develop, and there are theories that describe families of adolescents as entities of their own. Often as not, the theories covered in this book chapter are utilized to accomplish both tasks; that is, these theories both describe the families themselves as well as their impact on the development and well-being of their adolescents.

The first two theoretical frameworks covered in this book are associated most often with the field of human development and family science: family development theory and family systems theory. In addition, three additional theories that are known more broadly throughout the social sciences are covered due to their critical focus on the larger social context within which these families with adolescents are situated (ecological theory) as well as the nature of the parent-offspring relationship itself (attachment theory and social learning theory).

Because five very different conceptual frameworks will be presented in the theoretical part of this book, there is reason to stop and ponder how readers will be able to evaluate the relative merits of each theory in terms of our efforts to understand families with adolescents. The White and Klein (2008) book on family theories utilizes 13 criteria that family scientists have endorsed for making judgments about the relative worth of a family theory in order to discuss the relative merits of the conceptual frameworks included in their text. As originally reported by Klein (1994), these criteria include: internal consistency, clarity/explicitness, explanatory power, coherence, understanding, empirical fit, testability, heuristic value, groundedness, contextualization, interpretive sensitivity, predictive power, and practical utility.

In a similar vein, but somewhat more parsimoniously, Knapp (2009) presents five functions of theory that also can be used to evaluate the assistance that different conceptual frameworks provide in terms of our knowledge base about families. These functions, which are thought to be generative in nature, include:

1. A descriptive function
2. A sensitizing function
3. An integrative function
4. An explanatory function
5. A value function

For present purposes, these functions will be adopted in order to launch a discussion of each theory's comparative contributions in this area of inquiry. Because these five functions are thought to be generative, they can be viewed as benchmarks for the production of knowledge about families with adolescents. As such, each chapter devoted to a theory will end with a reflective segment that will include commentary about the degree to which these five functions are reflected in that conceptual framework.

For instance, the focus on the "descriptive function" will allow readers to evaluate the ways in which each theory helps to depict the particular details regarding families with adolescents. In turn, the "sensitizing function" will help us to explicate exactly what each theory spotlights in terms of main concepts, as well as calling into question how sharply that conceptual framework brings families with adolescents into focus.

Further, an examination of the "integrative function" draws readers toward an understanding of how well a given theory helps to organize our overall thinking about families with adolescents. A focus on the "explanatory function" will help us to explore the degree to which the concepts embedded in each theory can help us to elucidate or otherwise give reasons for what is observed as occurring in these families. Finally, the "value function" will be used to draw out exactly what principles, standards, and ideals stand behind each theoretical framework covered in this book.

2.2 Overview of Family-Based Research

What data do we have that informs us about the families of adolescents? The Russian writer Leo Tolstoy wrote that "happy families are all alike; every unhappy family is unhappy in its own way." This quote from the novel *Anna Karenina* is thought to represent but one example of the many ways that people attempt to organize knowledge about families. In this case, the Russian author would have us believe that the path to "happiness" is pretty much the same for all families, whereas the state of "unhappiness" can come from almost limitless sources. Whether or not you agree with this sentiment can and should be a function of the evidence that you are given in support of such a statement. And to gain access to such evidence, we must examine the research literature on families.

It was noted earlier that White and Klein (2008) had classified family theories into one of two categories: theories containing family concepts used to describe other phenomena (for example, how well individual family members are functioning), and theories that describe families themselves as a whole (i.e. how the entire family is functioning). If this perspective were to be extended into the empirical realm, we could classify research efforts surrounding families with adolescents into two similar kinds of categories. First, there are efforts to use family concepts as independent variables in order to explain dependent variables associated with adolescent development and well-being. As well, there are efforts to study families with adolescents as the central theme of the empirical effort, where the family variables themselves, often as not, serve as the de facto dependent measures. In practice, many of the research studies in this area of inquiry represent a blend of both efforts, such that families with adolescents are both described and are used to explain variations in adolescent development and well-being.

In order to gain a sense of the different approaches that can be adopted within family-based research efforts, readers are presented with a brief overview of six different models that can be used to conduct research on families with adolescents. These models include: (1) the direct family effects model; (2) the mediated indirect family effects model; (3) the complex mediated family effects model; (4) the family as mediator model; (5) the family as moderator model; and (6) the transactional family effects model. This is followed by a discussion of "unit of analysis" issues, used here to describe different focal points that researchers can adopt when seeking to generate family-based data: (1) the single intergenerational dyad; (2) the adolescent's relationship to both parents; (3) the adolescent's family as a totality; and (4) the family with adolescents as the combination of various dyads.

This discussion is meant to provide a context for the review of studies in Part 3 of this book that focus on families of adolescents, covering empirical work in three main areas: (1) research on the parent–adolescent dyad; (2) polyadic (i.e. multiple dyad) research on families with adolescents; and (3) the family's impact on adolescent outcomes. In Part 3, the main topics that have been covered by researchers to date in each of these three main areas of inquiry are reviewed, and newer trends that are emerging out of this empirical work are discussed as well. Examples of studies within each of these three main areas are presented in order to provide readers with an understanding of the types of samples that are being employed, the empirical questions that are being addressed, and the methods that are being utilized by these researchers.

Readers are invited to evaluate the relative merits of the present state of research in each of these three main areas empirical areas through use of the information that is given about this collection of studies. For instance, the information about samples includes the age ranges of the study's participants, an important indicator of the boundaries or parameters that researchers are setting in terms of their definition of who is (and who is not) considered to be an adolescent family member. Information about empirical questions identifies not only what a given researcher is trying to document about families with adolescents, but also what is *not* being covered in that study. Finally, information about methods includes information about who exactly is being used to generate information that will be used in the study, among other things. In other words, this becomes critical information about precisely whose viewpoint "counts" in the eyes of a given researcher.

2.2.1 Models for Conducting Research on Families

Masten and Shaffer (2006) presented six basic models for understanding how families matter in terms of their impact on children and adolescents. Most simple and straightforward of all is the "direct family effects" model (see Fig. 2.1), where the influence of a given family variable has an immediate and undeviating impact on some factor related to the youth. For instance, we could hypothesize that family conflict is directly related to depression levels in adolescent family members. That is, as family conflict levels increase, so too does the amount of depressive symptoms reported by adolescents.

The "mediated indirect family effects" model (see Fig. 2.2) assumes that a third variable plays an intermediary role regarding the impact of the family variable.

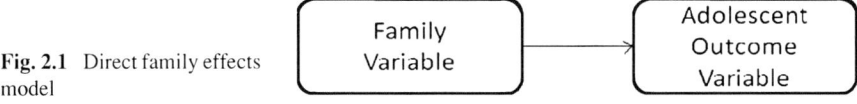

Fig. 2.1 Direct family effects model

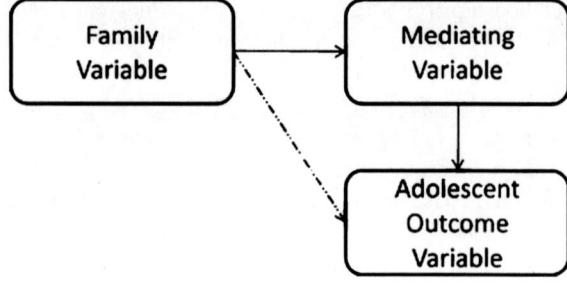

Fig. 2.2 Mediated indirect family effects model

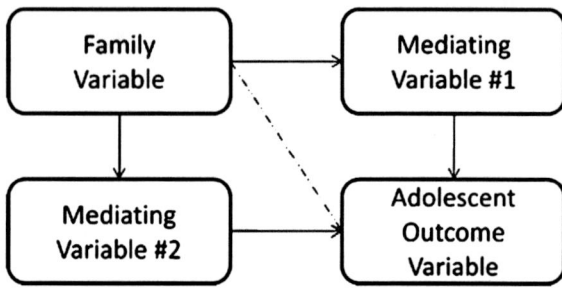

Fig. 2.3 Complex mediated family effects model

Extending our example above, the impact of greater levels of family conflict on adolescent depression levels may be buffered (mediated) by the amount of affection that is expressed in the mother-adolescent relationship. For instance, it might be the case that the impact of family conflict on adolescent depression is decreased by the presence of higher levels of mother-adolescent affection.

The "complex mediated family effects" (see Fig. 2.3) model elaborates how multiple variables might be employed in order to better understand the indirect influences of family factors on youth outcomes. Taking the example above one step further, the impact of greater levels of family conflict on adolescent depression levels may be mediated both by the presence or absence of a family history of depression in addition to the amount of mother-adolescent affection.

The "family as mediator" model (see Fig. 2.4) holds that certain family factors can mediate the influence of other variables on factors related to youth. Here, we might hypothesize that the relationship between gender and the type of problem behaviors experienced by adolescents – where girls are more likely to report internalizing problems (depression and anxiety) and boys are more likely to report externalizing problems (delinquency and aggressive behavior) – is mediated by the amount of family conflict reported by adolescents. When family conflict levels are high, for instance, boys are more likely to report internalizing problems and girls are more likely to report externalizing problems in addition to the more gender-specific findings that are present when family conflict levels are low.

The "family as moderator" model (see Fig. 2.5) holds that certain family factors can moderate the influence of other variables on factors related to youth. In the case

2.2 Overview of Family-Based Research

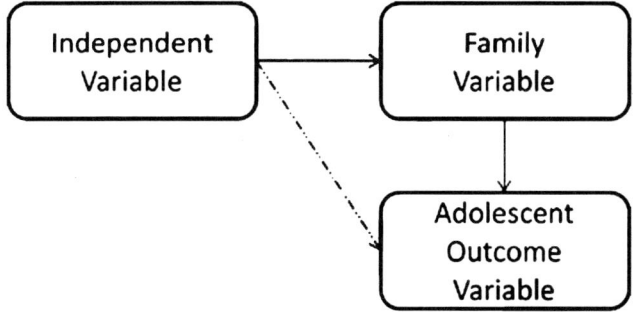

Fig. 2.4 Family as mediator model

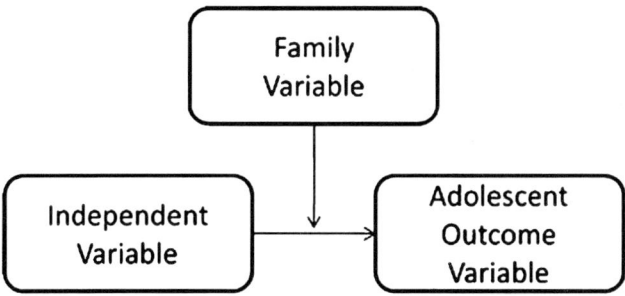

Fig. 2.5 Family as moderator model

of moderation, the family variable has a "conditional" influence on the relationship between some independent variable and adolescent outcomes. For example, we might hypothesize that the strength of the association between negative peer pressure and adolescent antisocial behavior is conditional on the amount of family support experienced by adolescents. Here, high amounts of peer pressure to become involved in delinquent activities may exert a substantial influence on the likelihood of an adolescent actually displaying antisocial behavior, when family support levels are low. Alternatively, however, in the presence of high amounts of family support, the strength of association between negative peer pressure and adolescent antisocial behavior may be sharply reduced.

Finally, the longitudinal and reciprocal impact of family and youth factors is represented by the "transactional family effects" model (see Fig. 2.6), whereby the bidirectional influence that parents and their offspring can have on each other are taken into account as they impact both present and future family member interactions across time. For example, we might hypothesize that the consistency of discipline displayed by parents both impacts and is impacted by the amount of antisocial behavior displayed by adolescents across several time points. In addition, we might further hypothesize that the amount of consistent discipline displayed by parents at Time 2 will be predicted by the amount of consistent discipline the parents displayed

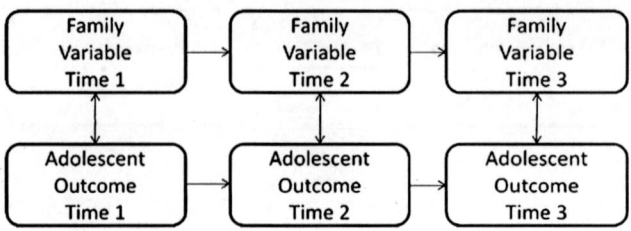

Fig. 2.6 Transactional family effects model

at Time 1, as well as hypothesizing that the amount of antisocial behavior displayed by adolescents at Time 2 will be predicted by the amount of antisocial behavior the adolescents displayed at Time 1. Here, the associations between the family and adolescent outcome variables are both bidirectional (reciprocal) at any one point in time, as well as being prognostic across time.

Studies have documented the critical role that family factors play in explaining a variety of outcome variables associated with adolescent development and well-being through use of a variety of models described above. In total, these studies have served to emphatically counter some recent arguments that the family environment plays a relatively inconsequential role when compared to the impact of other predictor variables such as peer groups and genetic susceptibilities (Clarke-Stewart, 2006). As well, this body of compelling evidence has given rise to many forms of family-focused treatment for families with adolescents that are evidence-based and contain objectives founded on the results of this body of family-focused research (Werner-Wilson & Morrissey, 2005). In fact, the overall literature base is thought to have been sufficiently well-developed for Hinde (2006) to pose the question: "are we not getting near to knowing enough for framing policies that will permit interventions where they are most needed and ameliorate the most urgent issues, and indeed for framing any policy that is likely to be implemented?" (p. 363).

2.2.2 Unit of Analysis Issues

In general, issues concerning the "unit of analysis" are thought to provide assistance in helping us to define exactly what we are attempting to think about, study, or otherwise impact (Sabatelli & Bartle, 1995). Regarding families with adolescents, there are at least two units of analysis that we could consider beyond the focus on any individual family member. One of these units of analysis concerns the dyad, or two-person system. In fact, there are a number of potential dyads that we can focus on within the family, including the parent–adolescent dyad, the marital dyad, and sibling dyads. The second unit of analysis would include triads and larger constellations of members (polyads) that are labeled as "family level" variables. These three-person

2.2 Overview of Family-Based Research

systems (and four-person systems, and five-person systems, etc.) can include triads such as mother–father–adolescent, for instance, mother–adolescent–sibling, father–adolescent–grandmother, and so on.

All of the dyads mentioned in the previous paragraph potentially exist within a family, and certainly are considered to be a part of the larger family system. However, typically these dyads are not considered to be *fully* representative of the family unit itself. At the same time, the parent–adolescent dyad (mother–adolescent, father–adolescent) is thought to be a distinctive dyad inside of the family. Unlike others mentioned, it is both intergenerational and is based on caring activities, thus satisfying the "intergenerational nurturing" definition of family adopted within this book.

As well, the parent–adolescent dyad has been the most extensively utilized unit of analysis to date, and often has been given the label of "family" research by others. Hence, there is a precedent for viewing these empirical efforts as family-based, even though this book maintains that such a dyadic approach is incomplete at best. Finally, not being able to label certain household compositions (i.e., a single parent and his/her adolescent offspring) as representing a family unit is fraught with all kinds of political and policy difficulties. In other words, if a given household consisted of an unmarried single mother and her teenage son, it would be indelicate to state that this dyad does not "count" as a family.

In all, Part 3 of this book contains examples of empirical work that reflect four distinct types of studies that have made contributions to the field's empirical understanding of families with adolescents (see Table 2.3). First, there are those studies that have focused on a single intergenerational dyad. Second, there are empirical efforts that have centered on the adolescent's relationship to both parents. Third, there are studies that have focused on the adolescent's family as a totality. Fourth, there are empirical efforts that have conceptualized the family with adolescents as the combination of various dyads.

Studies that have focused on an intergenerational dyad typically concern a single parent–adolescent relationship, but could include the adolescent's relationship to other caregivers such as a grandparent or a foster parent. Empirical work classified as focusing on the adolescent in relation to both parents concerns studies that do

Table 2.3 Types of Studies Focused on Families with Adolescents

Focus of the study	One intergenerational dyad	Adolescent and both parents	Family as a totality	Family as the combination of dyads
Example of the wording on an item used in this type of study	"My mother gives me the support I need"	"My parents give me the support I need"	"My family members give me the support I need"	"My mother gives me the support I need" *and* "My father gives me the support I need"

not make a distinction between the two caregiving adults (i.e., parents are treated as a single entity with questions such as "My parents..."), or ask about relationships to both parents, but conduct separate analyses for data pertaining to the mother–adolescent and father–adolescent relationships. Research findings generated from these first two types of studies will be reviewed below under the heading of "dyadic research on families with adolescents."

Studies focusing on the family with adolescents as a totality would involve research that makes no distinction among various members (i.e., family members are treated as a single entity with questions such as "My family..."). Finally, those studies that conceptualize the family with adolescents as being comprised of various dyads that exist within the family involve the combination of at least two reciprocal relationships such as adolescent–mother, adolescent–father, and/or adolescent–sibling. In these cases, data pertaining to the dyadic relationships are handled as "relational family data" (Fisher et al., 1985), meaning that the appropriate statistical analyses are employed in order to examine the interrelated nature of the dyads. Research from these latter two types of studies will be reviewed below under the heading of "polyadic research on families with adolescents."

2.3 Overview of Family-Based Application Efforts

What is our knowledge base about how to intervene with adolescents and their families when difficulties arise? And what do we know about preventing problems in families with adolescents? We borrow again from White and Klein's (2008) conceptual scheme of family theories to acknowledge that family-based application efforts also can take one of two basic forms. First, there are programs that serve to prevent or intervene with difficulties at a family system level. Second, there are programs that help families to prevent problems or intervene when difficulties are experienced by an individual adolescent member. In this latter case, these prevention and intervention programs have more of an "adolescent outcome" orientation. Similar to the theoretical and research efforts overviews above, in practice, many of these family-based applications represent a blend of both efforts, such that both family processes and outcomes associated with adolescent development and well-being are targeted by the program efforts.

In general, the family-based programs described in Part 4 of this book specifically serve families containing youth somewhere between the ages of 10 and 21. More explicitly, however, a prevention or intervention effort has to be intergenerational in its orientation in order to be included in this part of the book. The intergenerational criterion translates into the fact that the initiative requires the participation of *two* generations of family members (i.e. parent and adolescent) in *shared* activities. This condition rules out parenting skills programs, for instance, as well as eliminating those efforts that have parents and adolescents participating in concurrent but separate activities (Lochman, 2000). In essence, our "intergenerational nurturing" definition regarding families with adolescents is used as the basis of a litmus test in terms of which prevention and intervention programs actually "do" something that are *family*-oriented.

The first chapter of Part 4 will cover the family therapy literature that focuses on work with adolescents and their families, as well as other family-based intervention efforts that target adolescents and their families. In essence, the work reviewed in this chapter will encompass those efforts that are directed at families in need of actual treatment (i.e. those programs that provide targeted interventions, therapy, etc.) because of problems or difficulties that already have surfaced. The interventions included in this chapter involve at least two generations of family members in the activities described within the effort.

This is followed by the prevention program chapter of Part 4. In addition to an intergenerational orientation, programs reviewed in this chapter had to target positive features of family life that are applicable to universal populations of families. Hence, prevention activities are thought to be focused on the deterrence of problems, as opposed to the treatment or management of difficulties already present in the family. In acknowledgment of initiatives that target families identified as high risk, those programs invariably known as "selective prevention" efforts also will be reviewed in the prevention chapter of this book.

Part II
Theorizing About Families with Adolescents

Chapter 3
Family Development Theory

> *Call it a clan, call it a network, call it a tribe, call it a family.*
> *Whatever you call it, whoever you are, you need one.*
>
> Jane Howard, *Families*

Abstract Family development theory sensitizes users to a variety of family-oriented ideas that provide an organized approach to the pursuit of knowledge about families with adolescents. Great attention is paid to the normal and typical experiences and events contained within this family life cycle stage. The conceptual attractiveness and practical utility of this approach is evidenced in its widespread use in the family science and family therapy literatures. In the present chapter, particular consideration is given to the main theme of boundary flexibility and associated developmental tasks (or second-order changes), as well as the timing of roles and events that take place within this developmental period. Critiques of the family developmental approach are covered as well, including current limitations associated with its empirical utility, as well as questions that have been raised about its generalizability to families with adolescents living both in contemporary Western society and in other cultures.

> Jack and Mary Anderson think of themselves as typical parents who are trying to balance the needs of their teenagers – 16-year-old son Josh and 14-year-old daughter Jessica – with their own work and extended family responsibilities. The Andersons do focus a great deal of attention on Josh and Jessica. They attend all of their son's football games and track events, and are the parent leaders of the booster club for Jessica's school marching band. While Jack and Mary work full-time, both parents also spend a significant amount of time in community service efforts. Jack is a board member of the local education foundation that provides support for academic enrichment activities in the schools, and Mary spends at least ten hours a week doing volunteer work for their school district.
>
> The Andersons are excited about Josh's recent enrollment in driving school, because an extra driver in the house will relieve some of the pressure the parents

> feel about being a "taxi service" for their teenagers. At the same time, they are a little nervous about Josh fully realizing the responsibilities that come with driving, even though both parents believe Josh is a remarkably conscientious 16-year-old. More anxiety-provoking is Jessica's recent push to be allowed to date, especially in light of her desire to see someone who is in Josh's grade.
>
> And there are other things going on as well. Jack and Mary tell friends that they feel "sandwiched" between the demands of their kids and what their own parents are going through. Mary's dad died of a heart attack a while ago, but her mom lives nearby and increasingly is in need of help around the house. Both of Jack's parents are still alive but are medically fragile. They live some distance away, yet are resistant to Jack's suggestions to move them into an assisted living environment.
>
> In the midst of all of this, Jack and Mary are beginning to have conversations about what they would like to be doing when Josh and Jessica graduate from high school. Jack is in a position to take a new job within his company that will mean more income, but also will require more travel. In turn, Mary is now thinking about going back to school to get her teaching certificate.

3.1 Basic Family Development Theory Concepts

The sketch of the Anderson family given above provides us with an illustration of many of the conventional issues that would be of interest to a family developmental theorist. Most generally, family development theory concerns the description of how families make transitions across time as members enter and leave through birth and death, marriage and divorce, and otherwise deal with various normative and nonnormative life events. While there is rather substantial variation among scholars in terms of the concepts that are used to discuss family development (Rodgers & White, 1993), most theoretical applications give some attention to family life cycle stages and developmental tasks, a tradition that stems back to the inaugural work of Glick (1947) and Duvall (1957).

Through the employment of stages, family development is meant to be viewed as a linear progression of events. Hence, preceding experiences within the family are thought to directly impact what is happening in the here and now. In turn, those circumstances occurring in the present are thought to influence future family situations. Sometimes this is referred to as the "epigenetic principle," a theoretical tradition that stems back to the original work on human development conducted by Erik Erikson (1950, 1968).

The use of developmental tasks also has a rich tradition in human development theory. Havighurst (1944, 1972) and others (including Erikson) wrote about how each human life cycle stage contained its own particular challenges (tasks) that individuals had to master in order to make a successful transition to the next stage. Family development theorists have borrowed this concept and applied it to

3.1 Basic Family Development Theory Concepts

families as a whole rather than only at the level of each individual family member. Hence, there are certain challenges or tasks that must be accomplished if the family as an entity will be able to effectively move on to the next family life cycle stage.

As such, family development theory contains the notion that families with adolescents are most successful when they have mastered the developmental tasks of the "family with young children" life cycle stage (Carter & McGoldrick, 1980). The theme of this preceding stage surrounds the acceptance of new members into the family. Manifestations of this theme include the realignment of relationships not only within the marital dyad, but also with extended family, as grandparents, aunts and uncles, etc. Therefore, the successful transition to the next family life cycle stage is thought to be predicated on family members adopting new roles and obligations associated with their specific relationships to these children.

In turn, the "Families with adolescents" stage of the family life cycle (Carter & McGoldrick, 1980) is centered on the theme of increasing the flexibility of the family's boundaries in order to both facilitate greater adolescent independence, and accommodate the growing dependence of grandparents and other older family members. This theme of increased family boundary flexibility is linked to a number of key family developmental tasks (also discussed as "second-order changes" in the family literature). These developmental tasks include:

(a) The alteration of the parent-adolescent relationship in order to allow the adolescent to move more freely out of and back into the family environment
(b) A renewed focus on marital issues and parental career interests and
(c) Taking on a greater role in caregiving for older family members (Carter & McGoldrick, 1989).

In combination, these developmental tasks strongly suggest a perspective that accounts simultaneously for interacting needs and desires of three generations of family members: adolescents, parents, and grandparents (Ackerman, 1980).

Remember how Jack and Mary Anderson described themselves as feeling "sandwiched" between the needs of their teenagers and the needs of their own parents? The term "sandwich generation" in fact has been used by a variety of theorists, clinicians, and researchers to describe the caregiving responsibilities for multiple generations of family members (Loomis & Booth, 1995; Spillman & Pezzin, 2000). And it is exactly this experience of being "caught in the middle" that can be dealt with most functionally by developing and maintaining firm but flexible family boundaries. Flexible enough so that family members remain open to helping each other, but firm enough to make sure that the caregiving is both balanced between the generations and not overwhelming to the caregivers themselves.

Some of the most common issues that arise out of this multigenerational theoretical focus include issues that focus on individuality (autonomy and identity) and intimacy (dating and sexuality) concerns (Preto, 1989). As previous writings on "adolescence in contemporary families" have pointed out (Steinmetz, 1999), topics falling under these broad categories have become some of the more well-researched subject areas that are covered in the families with adolescents literature. Typically, the focus on both individuality and intimacy as expressed through family interactions seems to be balanced around the actions of the parents, who in effect become the "pivot point" for these developmental issues (Mattessich & Hill, 1987).

For instance, family developmental theorists hold that adolescents and parents are engaged in an almost constant renegotiation of issues that underscore the adolescent's autonomy claims at the very same time the parents are beginning to communicate about independent living decisions with their own parents and other older family members. Josh's recent enrollment in driving school and Jessica's push to be allowed to date are both excellent examples of how adolescents and parents must negotiate ever-changing demands for more independent functioning. And, of course, all of this is happening while Mary and Jack are being required to give greater attention to their own parent's increased dependency needs.

The failure to grant greater autonomy has been seen as one of the primary mechanisms by which families can throw off the developmental progress of adolescent members (Matjasko & Paz, 2005a). Less functional outcomes are thought to be the result of a lack of "stage environment fit" (Eccles, Midgley, Wigfield, Buchanan, Reuman, Flanagan, & MacIver, 1993),whereby a mismatch occurs between the family's inability to tolerate individuality claims at the very time the adolescents are in need of social contexts that allow for independent exploration and experimentation (Gutman & Eccles, 2007)

Family development theory balances attention paid to individuality alongside the consideration of intimacy issues. Here, adolescents are thought to be experiencing the awakening of their sexual desires while parents may be dealing with sexual issues inside of their marriage or, if the marriage has dissolved, one or both parents might find themselves reeducating themselves about sexual expectations within the current dating scene. Clearly, Jessica's desire to date brings up a whole host of issues involving both her developing sexuality and that of her brother. Just because Josh is not dating anyone presently does not mean he has no sexual interests or desires. In fact, Jack and Mary have long suspected that Josh has been accessing adult-oriented material on the Internet, something that Josh vehemently denies each time the subject is brought up.

Discussion of sexually oriented topics is not something that comes easily to Jack and Mary. Jack reports that he has had "the talk" with Josh about sex, and has supplied him with a number of books and pamphlets that focus on teen sexuality. Mary notes that she has had numerous conversations with Jessica about sex and intimacy, as well as also making written materials available. These parents, who have been married for almost 20 years, report that their own sex life has been and continues to be "comfortable." At the same time, each of them does admit that they have noticed a slow "cooling off," especially in the past couple of years. Jack and Mary also report that their more recent interactions around Jessica's dating requests have produced some friction between them as parents. Mary believes that Jessica will be able to handle herself well in a dating situation, whereas Jack would prefer that she be protected by being made to wait at least another year.

As well, Jack increasingly has become more and more uneasy around Jessica, who he describes as "14 going on 24." Jessica had her first period when she was 11 years old, and now has fully developed breasts. Whereas Jack used to hug and

3.1 Basic Family Development Theory Concepts

squeeze his daughter all of the time, he now is very uncertain about showing any sort of affection at all, making for some very awkward moments between them. In tandem, Mary reports that Josh seems to become irritated about her own attempts at affection, which she very much wants to continue. She reports that she no longer is supposed to kiss Josh in public, she has been told, and her attempts to hug him when he is leaving or returning home are received rather reluctantly.

Further, family developmental theory pays attention to parents undergoing mid-life recalibrations. Here, mothers and fathers may focus on career aspirations by seeking advancement in their current positions, and/or returning to higher educational pursuits at the very same time that their adolescents are getting ready for their first college experience. We know that Jack and Mary are discussing what life is going to be like for them after Josh and Jessica leave home. Jack is pondering a position within his company, and Mary is thinking about going back to school. Parents faced with an "emptying nest" often as not use both work and educational pursuits in order to shift the energies they had been putting into raising their adolescents to other positive activities.

Taken together, there is the clear sense that family member interactions can be "felt across generations" (Preto & Travis, 1985) as adolescents, parents, and grandparents work to resolve the developmental issues of this family life cycle stage. Of course, this description of family development theory would be incomplete if there was not some mention of the notion that future family accomplishments will be hinged on how the family meets its developmental tasks in the here and now, reflecting both continuity and change in the ways that family members interact with one another (Matjasko & Paz, 2005b).

Hence, the ability of families to make a successful transition into the "launching members and moving on" (Carter & McGoldrick, 1980) family life cycle stage will be based in large part on how well boundary flexibility is established. And this makes a great deal of sense, as the theme of this next family life cycle stage concerns the acceptance of a multitude of entries and exits by members as adult children begin to establish households of their own at the same time that members of the older generation become even more frail and eventually pass away.

It is important to note that family development theory has been discussed as being part of a larger theoretical tradition that includes the individual life course (Kohli, 2007) and family life course perspectives as well (White & Klein, 2008). As applied to the family, the life course perspective centers attention on a number of additional factors such as the timing and sequencing of roles and events (temporally, generationally, and historically) as well as the sociocultural construction of meaning surrounding these theoretical concepts (Bengston & Allen, 1993). Here, the main emphasis becomes the trajectories that families and their members follow as they move through life's transitions (Bianchi & Casper, 2005). Excellent recent examples of this type of work include life course depictions of violent behavior experienced by adolescents and their parents (Pagani, Tremblay, Nagin, Zoccolillo, Vitaro, & McDuff, 2004), for instance, as well as how later adolescents and young adults maintain contact with their parents as a function of their own life course status (Bucx, van Wel, Knijn, & Hagendoorn, 2008).

Significant attention also has been given to trajectories related to the timing of sexual activity and pregnancy in adolescent samples (Stevens, 2001). In addition to providing an exceptional summary of family life course conceptual definitions and an overview of a statistical approach (latent class analysis) that is consistent with this theoretical perspective, MacMillan and Copher (2005) offer an illustration of the use of these concepts and methods in the examination of adolescent parenthood and race. Complex differences between white, African American, and Hispanic females emerged in terms of the relationship between teenage childbearing and multiple longer-term outcomes associated with education, work, and family roles. These findings involved the delineation of a number of different pathways to adulthood (i.e., a rapid school to parenthood pathway in comparison to a school to work/work to family pathway), and included results within these pathways that the authors assert would have been "missed" by other theoretical and statistical approaches.

Hence, we might also want to view what the Andersons are experiencing through a family life course lens. This would mean gathering more information about how Jack and Mary's families of origins dealt with issues surrounding autonomy and connectedness, for instance, including whether or not certain events and the adoption of specific roles were "on time" or "off time" in comparison to what happened in previous generations. Concurrently, these same questions about the normative nature of these roles and events also would require sensitivity to the particular historical context within which the Anderson family is situated.

3.2 Reflections: Family Development Theory and Families with Adolescents

How does the reader begin to evaluate the use of family development theory in terms of understanding families with adolescents? In terms of the descriptive function of this theory, clear and consistent depictions are given of the main theme of boundary flexibility and associated developmental tasks (or second-order changes), as well as the timing of roles and events that take place within this developmental period. In terms of the sensitizing function of family development theory, we are clearly being exposed to a conceptual approach that is epigenetic in nature, one in which there are unmistakable illustrations regarding how the timing of roles and events can make a critical difference in terms of individual and family functioning.

In related fashion, it can also be said that family developmental theory "rings true" in terms of the connection between its concepts and real world experiences of families with adolescents. Discussing family developmental theory more generally, Russell (1993) notes that this perspective carries with it an "innate appeal" to family members seeking to understand the continuity and change aspects of their family relationships over time. Thus, this framework does seem to do well in terms of helping us to organize our overall thinking about these families; i.e., the integrative function of this theory.

This conceptual attractiveness also speaks to the practical utility of this framework, another hallmark of this theory's ability to create a more generalized and holistic knowledge base about families with adolescents. In addition to its widespread use in the family science (MacMillan & Copher, 2005) and family therapy literatures (Nichols & Schwartz, 2006), family development theory has been used as the foundational basis for other applied work in the social sciences. For instance, this theoretical perspective has been used to discuss parenting (Seltzer, Greenberg, Floyd, Pettee, & Hong, 2001) and career development work with families containing disabled adolescents (Burkhead & Wilson, 1995), as well as family nursing efforts targeting these families (Rankin & Weekes, 1989; St John & Flowers, 2009).

The family developmental approach is not without its criticisms, however, especially with regard to its explanatory function. In fact, in the previous decade, Rodgers and White (1993) proclaimed that family development theory was "in a state of gridlock" (p. 249), with little explanatory (or predictive) power having been generated by studies using this theoretical framework. While White and Klein (2008) were a bit more gracious in their assessment of the value of this body of empirical work, these authors also pointed out several other flaws, including the lack of appreciation for diversity and cultural variation that families display in making transitions over time.

This latter criticism speaks to the value function of this theory as well. Almost by definition, the family developmental approach asserts what the "normal and typical" experiences and events will be for families in a given life cycle stage. And the fact of the matter is that the majority of families in contemporary Western society do not experience the life cycle stages in the invariant manner as proposed by Carter and McGoldrick (1980). Another criticism has been the overemphasis on the discrete nature of the transitions regarding moving into and out of family life cycle stages (White & Klein, 2008). In point of fact, there is something intuitively appealing about the idea that these transitions are more gradual than sudden, especially in terms of families with adolescents.

In this last regard, one very interesting qualitative study conducted by Molinari, Everri, and Fruggeri (2010) may help shed some further light on the nature of transitions into and out of this developmental period. These researchers examined what they termed "microtransitions" in families with adolescents, work that emphasizes the compressed and sometimes clustered nature of transitional events that are experienced by families with adolescents.

Using the concepts of "coordination" and "oscillation," these authors identified different patterns by which families respond to change. For instance, some families were categorized as having undergone a "stormy" pattern that represented rapid and intense change. If one only studied those sorts of families, you might be drawn to the conclusion that transitions during this developmental period were very abrupt and discontinuous. In contrast, other families experienced change in a "quiet" pattern that was exemplified by stability and cooperation. If those were the sorts of families that you studied, instead you might deduce that these transitions were more gradual in nature. Hence, these findings may point the way to a "both/and" approach to transitions in families with adolescents, whereby the degree to which movement into and out of this family life cycle stage is discrete or gradual can become an additional important variable to conceptualize and measure.

In sum, family development theory clearly describes and sensitizes users to family-oriented ideas. As well, this conceptual approach provides for an organized approach to the pursuit of knowledge about families with adolescents. Future work should pay particular attention to increasing our understanding about the explanatory function of family development theory, as well as deal with some of the value function's shortcomings of this approach.

Chapter 4
Family Systems Theory

> *The overall name of these interrelated structures is system. The motorcycle is a system. A real system. ...There's so much talk about the system. And so little understanding. That's all a motorcycle is, a system of concepts worked out in steel.*
>
> Robert Pirsig, *Zen and the Art of Motorcycle Maintenance*

Abstract Family systems theory provides users with a holistic framework that centers attention on the interactive and bidirectional nature of relationships within families with adolescents. The family systems framework enjoys widespread use in the family intervention literature, as well as having been increasingly employed within the child and adolescent developmental literatures. In the present chapter, attention is paid to a number of concepts that are related to the understanding of the family as a self-organizing unit. In particular, the systems concept of the steady state is used to discuss the balance of stability and change that must be struck in families with adolescents as members negotiate the demands of this developmental period. Critiques of the family systems approach also are covered, including especially empirical limitations associated with its generating descriptive rather than explanatory abilities. Questions about its generalizability to families with adolescents in collectivist or otherwise non-Western societies are also addressed.

> Caleb Young, Evan Timberland, and Trevor Banner call themselves the three musketeers. And while these three 14-year-old best friends are indeed "one for all, and all for one," they couldn't come from more different families. These three teens most often can be found at the Timberland home, in large part because Evan's parents believe that the safest place for their son is under their watchful eyes. Mr. and Mrs. Timberland spent a great deal of time in their own homes growing up, and are quick to point out that they both "didn't do drugs and avoided all the problems other kids had growing up." Although

Evan appreciates the fact that his parents want the very best for him, at times he becomes irritated by their reluctance to let him do things for himself.

In contrast, the teens rarely if ever get together at Trevor's house. His parents are attorneys in a very successful downtown law firm. Mr. and Mrs. Banner work long hours during the week and often are called into the office on weekends as well. The result is that Trevor is left by himself quite a bit, and his parents absolutely forbid having friends over when they are not home. The Banners are glad that their son has good friends, but they also are not bothered by Trevor choosing to stay home alone once in a while as well. In fact, the Banners are quite proud of their son's ability to be so independent, and oftentimes brag that he seems more self-reliant than his 19-year-old sister, who is a sophomore in college.

When not at Evan's house, the three teens hang out at the Young home. While Mr. and Mrs. Young are very flexible in terms of allowing Caleb to visit the homes of his friends, they also make it a special point to ask their son to have his friends come over whenever they perceive that there has been an unequal amount of time spent at home versus away from home. These parents talk often with each another about how to balance their son's desire to "just be himself" with their family's need to remain connected with one another. While his parents make snacks and other treats available to his friends when they are visiting, he appreciates the fact that they largely are left alone to play videogames and listen to music in the family's basement recreational room. As a result, Caleb is quite comfortable being with friends in his own home, even though he has two younger siblings.

4.1 Basic Family Systems Theory Concepts

Perhaps the most well-known quotation in all of the writing done on systems is that "the whole is more than the sum of its parts." This statement, attributed to the ancient Greek philosopher Aristotle, is meant to imply that a system cannot be understood simply by knowing something about each of its components. Said a slightly different way, a system is not simply the adding up of what we know about each of its parts. Instead, any system (a motorcycle, a family, a corporation, an ecosystem, etc.) is best comprehended by having knowledge of both the parts and their *interaction* together. Hence, the family systems of the three teenagers described in the sketch above are thought to be best appreciated through the observation of how each set of family members behave around each other.

Most systems-oriented works in the social sciences have as their origin the General System Theory (GST) work of Ludwig von Bertalanffy (1968), whose efforts involved no less than an attempt to unify all sciences through the recognition of concepts that were common to each academic discipline. Such shared features, or isomorphic properties, were thought to exist at practically all levels of a system,

4.1 Basic Family Systems Theory Concepts

regardless of how microscopic or macroscopic your point of view. "To take a simple example, an exponential law of growth applies to certain bacterial cells, to populations of bacteria, of animals or humans, and to the progress of scientific research measured by the number of publications in genetics or science in general" (von Bertalanffy, 1968, p. 33).

Interestingly, at least one of von Bertalanffy's biographers has noted that the English language version of this author's original work in German was a mistranslation that should have read "General System *Thinking*" instead of "General System Theory" (Davidson, 1983). Hence, while the body of work that centers on a systems perspective typically is accorded the status of a theoretical framework, readers might do well to ponder the potential consequences of such a mistranslation. In particular, appreciation of this misunderstanding might go a long way toward dampening the criticism of the systems perspective as an "untestable theory" (L'Abate & Colondie, 1987).

Nevertheless, family theorists, family researchers, and family-based clinicians all have made ample use of systems concepts. The application of general systems work within the family field has emphasized the use of concepts such as:

- Hierarchy
- Boundaries
- Equifinality and multifinality
- Positive and negative feedback
- Circularity
- Organization

In combination, the concepts reflect an emphasis on understanding how family members operate as systems with properties that are of a non-summative nature (Whitechurch & Constantine, 1993). Hence, the family as a system is thought to be best understood through the recognition that family members (as the parts of the system) interact with one another in a manner such that, over time, these interactions become patterned behavior.

Although not typically discussed in such GST terms, the hallmark application of the systems perspective as applied to the study of families with adolescents surrounds the systems property of the steady state. Likened to a host of other dynamic processes (such as blood pressure, which is made up of both systolic and diastolic readings), this concept typically is used to discuss the balance of stability and change – achieving a "dynamic equilibria" (Bertalanffy, 1968) – that must be struck in families with adolescents as members negotiate the demands of this developmental period (Arnett, 2010; Koman & Stechler, 1985). The steady state is a property of open systems, or systems that have ongoing interactions with their environment. Although the steady state sometimes also is referred to as *homeostasis*, this actually is a closed system concept in the GST tradition, where the emphasis is on the lack of interaction between system and environment. Because families like all living systems are open by nature, the term steady state is preferred.

A result of this emphasis, on the steady state in the literature, on families with adolescents is the focus on distance regulation and boundary maintenance, most

Table 4.1 Family differentiation levels

	High intimacy tolerance	Low intimacy tolerance
High individuality tolerance	Highly differentiated family	Moderately differentiated family
Low individuality tolerance	Moderately differentiated family	Poorly differentiated family

often discussed in terms of differentiation levels (Bowen, 1978). Here, family differentiation is seen as the family system's ability to display both tolerance for intimacy and tolerance for individuality among its members (see Table 4.1). High tolerance for intimacy is seen in families where members experience high degrees of closeness and warmth with one another, where in contrast low intimacy tolerance is associated with family members who seem cold and distant. High tolerance for individuality is seen in families that generate the sense of being able to be oneself, whereas low individuality tolerance is related to the perception that it is not acceptable for family members to display any sense of uniqueness (Anderson & Sabatelli, 1990).

The combination of high individuality tolerance and high intimacy tolerance (termed high family differentiation), where family members are able to simultaneously experience themselves as both separate yet connected individuals, is associated with the highest levels of adolescent and family functioning. The Young family described in the vignette at the beginning of this chapter is an excellent example of a highly differentiated family. Mr. and Mrs. Young certainly seem interested in promoting their son Caleb's ability to express his own individuality, largely through the choices that he makes about who his friends are and where he spends significant amounts of time. At the same time, these parents are committed to keeping family members connected with one another, and see the openness of their home to Caleb's friends as a useful way to allow that sense of belongingness to be shared with others as well.

Conversely, low differentiation levels (where both low individuality tolerance and low intimacy tolerance are described in terms of a poorly differentiated family) have neither the experience of separateness or togetherness, and therefore are associated with the lowest functioning levels. In the middle of these polar extremes are combinations described as moderate differentiation levels that are associated with unexceptional adolescent and family functioning levels. The combination of high individuality tolerance and low intimacy tolerance is thought to reflect the sacrifice of connectedness experiences for the sake of individuality claims, while the combination of low individuality tolerance and high intimacy tolerance is the exact reverse; i.e. the sacrifice of individuality for the sake of togetherness (Gavazzi, 1993).

While the vignette at the beginning of this chapter does not contain an example of a poorly differentiated family, the Timberland and Banner families illustrate the two complementary types of moderate family differentiation levels. The Timberlands clearly care for their son Evan, and they do as much as they can to make their home both inviting and comfortable. Like the Young family, they are very open to Evan having his friends over, as they rightly recognize the need for peer companionship at this age. However, their fear of "teenage problems" tends to make them reluctant to allow Evan to make decisions by himself, even when there is little apparent cause for concern or alarm. The desire to maintain a sense of connectedness among members of the Timberland family seems to get in the way of Evan being able to express himself individually.

The Banner family seems to operate in the exact opposite fashion. Trevor has no problems whatsoever in terms of expressing his sense of separateness from his parents. In fact, he is applauded by his parents for his ability to think and act independently. Caleb's parents feel much the same way about their own son. However, Trevor has far less of a sense that he is connected to his parents and his sister Elena. This wasn't always the way things were in the Banner family, either. Mr. and Mrs. Banner both worked far less hours when their children were younger, allowing them to share many more family activities together. When Elena began to voice complaints in her junior year about how family gatherings "were just stupid," the parents started to slowly withdraw, and eventually channeled more time and energy into their work. While seeing themselves as launching their first offspring in a developmentally appropriate manner, the Banners seemed less aware of their younger adolescent's need for continued connectedness.

Other variations on the application of these distance regulation concepts exist in the systems-influenced literature on families with adolescents. For instance, Stierlin (1981) discussed the family context of the adolescent as being made up of both centripetal and centrifugal processes that alternatively push and pull family members into and out of the home environment. Another example is Hauser, Powers, and Noam (1991) work on constraining and enabling processes, whereby separateness and connectedness experiences are either restricted or facilitated through interactions between parents and adolescents. Although applied more generally to all families instead of only to families with adolescents, a review of this literature would be incomplete without mention of Broderick's (1993) bonding and buffering processes as well. Here, bonding processes are equated with the centripetal pull to remain connected with other family members, while the buffering processes are thought to be those centrifugal forces that maintain some distance between members of the family.

Family systems theory also has been used to describe the context surrounding more individual-oriented phenomena experienced by adolescents. For instance, Cook (2001a) employed a number of family systems concepts, including differentiation and triangulation, in a description of the family's influence on chemical addiction and the illegal behaviors of its adolescent members. Particularly, interesting here was the author's discussion of how the "under functioning" behaviors of the adolescent were matched by the "over functioning" behaviors of the other family members.

A second example is that of Hughes and Gullone (2008), who discuss the family systems perspective on adolescent internalizing problem behaviors (this article also stands out as an excellent review of empirical literature on this topic area). The main thrust of this article was directed toward the need for greater attention paid to the reciprocal nature of relationships within families called for by the systems concept of circularity. As well, while noting the association between the presence of an internalizing disorder and such system level concepts as lower family cohesion levels, these authors also discussed the impact of dyadic factors such as difficulties in the marital and parent-adolescent subsystems.

The reciprocal nature of parent-adolescent relationships within the family systems theoretical perspective has been extended to other forms of developmental psychopathology as well. For example, Sameroff and MacKenzie (2003) employed systems concepts such as positive and negative feedback in support of the need for transactional models that would account for the bidirectional influences of parents and adolescents. In a different realm, Corwyn and Bradley (2005) employed the systems concepts of equifinality and multifinality to describe the differential influences of economic circumstances on adolescent externalizing behaviors. Here, the authors described socioeconomic status as having an "equifinal" impact by influencing different factors in ways that produced similar outcomes, as well as observing that SES could influence numerous outcomes in more "multifinal" fashion.

4.2 Reflections: Family Systems Theory and Families with Adolescents

How does the reader begin to evaluate the use of family systems theory in terms of understanding families with adolescents? In terms of the descriptive function of this theory, there seems to be a bit of controversy in how this theoretical perspective helps scholars. On the one hand, Cox and Paley (1997) have noted that family systems concepts such as wholeness and hierarchy increasingly have been brought to bear on the child and adolescent developmental literatures as scholars have advanced their understanding of the family as a self-organizing unit. This sentiment is echoed in Masten and Shaffer's (2006) own discussion of the same literature a decade later. On the other hand, White and Klein (2006) have noted that the family systems perspective has been seen as "too abstract and global," and has been likened more to a model or a heuristic tool than a theory per se, criticisms that are echoed elsewhere (cf., Reis, Collins, & Berscheid, 2000).

Less controversial is the sensitizing function of family systems theory. Clearly, the family systems approach grounds users in a holistic framework that centers attention on the interactive and bidirectional nature of relationships within the family. Added to this is the fact that family systems theory also "rings true" for many therapists and other helping professionals in terms of the connection between its concepts and the real world experiences of families with adolescents.

Most pointedly, this conceptual framework has had a profound impact on the family therapy literature (Nichols & Schwartz, 2006). However, its influence has spread to diverse intervention areas targeting adolescents and their families such as wilderness programming (Harper & Russell, 2008), diabetes treatment (Butler, Skinner, Gelfand, Berg, & Wiebe, 2007; Wysocki, Harris, Buckloh, Mertlich, Lochrie, Taylor, Sadler, Mauras, & White, 2006), family systems nursing

(Clausson & Berg 2008), and positive youth development (Lerner, von Eye, Lerner, & Lewin-Bizan, 2009) and social justice (Lerner & Overton, 2008). Hence, the integrative function of this conceptual framework is apparent in that it does help scholars in various fields to organize their overall thinking about families with adolescents.

The family systems approach has been further criticized in terms of certain limits related to its explanatory function. For instance, Dilworth-Anderson, Burton, and Klein (2005) note that "compared with most other family theories, systems theories tend to be descriptive rather than explanatory" (p. 42). Part of the difficulty may lie in the traditional methods of research that are used in data gathering and analysis efforts. Expanding on Gottlieb and Halpern's (2002) reference to the "analysis of variance mentality" (p. 421) that permeates much of the linear thinking inherent to mainstream research, O'Brien (2005) suggested a more "holistic" approach to measurement and analysis of system-oriented phenomena. Here, use of structural equation modeling and person-centered analytic techniques – in addition to a focus on the mediating and moderating influences of family system concepts – might yield a more comprehensive set of studies that would demonstrate the actual explanatory power of this theoretical framework.

Finally, the value function of family systems theory draws attention to a worldview that emphasizes the comprehensive importance of the family context as a whole. Within this perspective, there are concepts such as family distance regulation that equate the highest functioning levels in families with greater amounts of both individuality and belongingness. It is important to note that there may be some cultural bias to this notion, however. As studies of family distance regulation in other cultures reviewed below will indicate, the relative balance of individuality and intimacy and its connection to healthy adolescent development very well may shift in more collectivist or otherwise non-Western societies. In these other cultures, there may be much more of an emphasis on the capacity for togetherness and concurrently less expectation that a sense of individuality could or should be fostered.

In sum, family systems theory does sensitize users to family-oriented ideas, but its descriptive abilities have been evaluated in a less consistent manner. This conceptual approach holds great practical utility, and as such seems to provide for a well organized approach to the pursuit of knowledge about families with adolescents. Scholars utilizing family systems theory must attend to issues surrounding the explanatory function of this approach, and must also expand the field's understanding of the cultural relevance of the values inherent to this theory.

Chapter 5
Ecological Theory

When one tugs at a single thing in nature, he finds it attached to the rest of the world.

John Muir, *My First Summer in the Sierra*

Abstract The ecological theoretical perspective most often is utilized to highlight various levels of environmental context (microsystems, mesosystems, exosystems, and macrosystems) within which families with adolescents are situated. Employed more comprehensively, this approach also can draw attention to the individual, to interactional processes among individuals, and to the impact of time. In the present chapter, ecological theory is covered in terms of its use in highlighting the interconnected nature of families with adolescents and other social contexts. While having been deemed to be one of the dominant theories utilized within this area of inquiry, the debate about its importance and usefulness is also covered, including questions about its inability to provide both conceptual and empirical assistance in describing the inner workings of families with adolescents.

> Something just didn't "add up" in the latest case that Malcolm Ward received on his probation caseload. A seasoned veteran of the juvenile court, Malcolm figured he had pretty much seen it all in his 20 years of justice system employment. The new case, however, defied most of the things he had learned to count on as conventional wisdom in his line of work. For starters, the case surrounded charges of aggravated assault with a knife, and the perpetrator was a 15-year-old female named Naomi Hendricks. Malcolm had seen plenty of these cases, but almost all of those offenses involved a male. In those cases where a female was involved, typically there was a history of conflict in the home, and often as not the charges for those females were for aggravated *domestic* violence.
>
> But this was not the situation with regard to Naomi. First of all, the charges did not involve a family member as the victim, but rather a neighbor. Also, in his initial home visit, Malcolm was greeted very warmly by Naomi's parents, who discussed her violent behavior as being out of character and not at all

connected to the way she acted at home or at school. Mr. and Mrs. Hendricks also noted that Naomi had maintained good friendships with a small number of friends over the years that the parents liked. In turn, Naomi's teachers reported she was a B+ student who pretty much kept to herself and her close circle of friends. The teachers and principal also noted that Mr. and Mrs. Hendricks were great supporters of the school, spending time in some sort of volunteer activity every couple of weeks, even though both of the parents worked full-time. The fact that Naomi is home alone for the 3 h between school dismissal and when her parents arrive home from work was the only concern that Mr. and Mrs. Hendricks expressed in terms of the likelihood of Naomi getting into trouble again.

The victim, Tiffany Little, also a 15-year-old female, lived with her mother and stepfather in an apartment complex not more than 500 yards from Naomi's house (her biological father lived in another state). Tiffany was brand-new to the school that both of the girls attended, and the court records indicated that she had felt "bullied" by Naomi and her friends in the weeks leading up to the assault. Malcolm had difficulty piecing together additional information when he attempted to talk with other teens in the neighborhood (located in an economically challenged section of town), many of whom would simply state "no snitching" and walk away when he asked questions. Eventually he was able to learn that Tiffany had started to date Mike, Naomi's ex-boyfriend, almost immediately after they had broken up. To make matters worse, some particularly steamy pictures of Tiffany and Mike began to appear on a variety of Facebook and MySpace pages.

In Malcolm's first full interview with Naomi, she stated that her reason for attacking Tiffany with a knife revolved around the pressure she felt from people in her school to "do something" about the "disrespect" that Tiffany had shown her. Naomi said that everyone thought that Tiffany had stolen Mike from her, and that the sexually oriented pictures were "just rubbing it in." "What was I supposed to do," Naomi asked, "with everybody saying that Tiffany kept fronting on me?" Naomi said she knew that her parents were disappointed with her, but she admitted that it would all be worth it if everyone at school knew that she couldn't be disrespected.

5.1 Basic Ecological Theory Concepts

Theoretical attempts to place the family system within its larger social context are indebted to the ecological approach developed by Urie Bronfenbrenner (1979). Although various aspects of human development and the individual's interaction across time with various ecological contexts are highlighted in this body of work (Bronfenbrenner, 1995), the ecological approach perhaps is most well known for its

5.1 Basic Ecological Theory Concepts

emphasis on *levels* of the ecosystem. These levels, which are conceptualized as range in size and scope from smallest to largest, are thought to include the following:

- Microsystem
- Mesosystem
- Exosystem
- Macrosystem

At the smallest level, the family is characterized as the primary "microsystem" of all human development. The family is thought to exist at this ecosystem level alongside other intimate social settings that involve ongoing face-to-face interaction. For adolescents and their families, most often, this means examining relationships within peer groups and the schools.

In turn, the next largest level is the "mesosystem." The mesosystem is meant to describe various connections between microsystems. One such example is the linkage between families and schools. Another example involves the connection between home life and the adolescent's peer group.

The next largest level is the "exosystem." The exosystem involves the influences of larger systems such as the neighborhood and community. Another important exosystem example involves the interface between parents and their work settings. This ecosystem level is especially important when variables related to time spent at work and sick leave policies impact on parents' abilities to monitor the activities of their sons and daughters as well as to care for and nurture them (Crouter, 2006).

Finally, the largest level is the "macrosystem." The macrosystem represents even larger social contexts such as nation and culture. A good deal of the ecological literature focusing on macrosystem influences are centered on media imagery that promotes or discourages certain types of behaviors (Cottrell & Monk, 2004). As well, some ecologically based writings have included a host of socioeconomic status indicators in their formulations of macrosystem features that impact adolescents and their families (Corcoran, 1999). These indicators include factors such as parent educational attainment, current occupation, income, and employment opportunities.

Malcolm Ward, the probation officer in the vignette at the beginning of this chapter, paid great attention to microsystem concerns in his assessment of Naomi's situation. Mr. Ward discovered that Naomi came from what appeared to be a well-adjusted family, she seemed to have a number of good close friends, and she was doing relatively well in school. These are microsystems that typically are not displaying such positive tendencies when a youth comes into contact with the juvenile justice system. We also have some information about the home-school mesosystem connection through the school's report that Naomi's parents regularly volunteer their time during the school day. Additionally, Mr. and Mrs. Hendricks know and like Naomi's friends, generating some evidence that there are positive exchanges occurring within the home-peer mesosystem as well.

One particular piece of information about an exosystem factor begins to help us understand something about a contributing factor to Naomi's situation. Because both of her parents are involved in the workplace, Naomi is unsupervised for extended periods of time during the week. As well, the Hendricks family lives in an impoverished neighborhood, an exosystem factor that is associated with increased risks for engaging in delinquent activities. Further, many neighbors who had contact with Mr. Ward also displayed a macrosystem factor of contemporary urban youth culture known as "no snitching," a value that oftentimes delays or prevents authorities from maintaining law and order in such environments (Rosenfeld, Jacobs, & Wright, 2003). And finally, the Facebook and YouTube postings that seemed to trigger the aggravated assault also underline the increased significance of social networking phenomena at the macrosystem level.

Peterson and Hann (1999) have asserted that there are three important elements of the ecological approach as applied to the study of families with children. First, the ecological framework maintains an emphasis on the mutually reciprocal influences between children and these social contexts. This is a departure from a more unidirectional view concerning human social development within the family. Hence, this perspective rejects the notion that youth are impacted by their parents and other environment factors, but do not have the ability to shape it. As well, this approach improves upon "child effects models" that focus on the exact reverse notion of what was described in the previous sentence; that is, examining only the effect that a youth has on their parent or parents (Ambert, 1992).

Second, Peterson and Hann (1999) assert that within the ecological approach, the influences of various social contexts are thought to be both direct and indirect. One consequence of this approach is to create an emphasis on the potential mediating and moderating effects of variables that exist at different levels of the ecosystem. For instance, while certain neighborhood characteristics may not be thought to have a direct role in shaping specific family processes, they may create conditions under which these family factors are altered; as well, their relative presence or absence may serve as an indirect "go-between" in terms of the relationship between those family processes and adolescent outcomes.

Third, and inclusive of the first two points, Peterson and Hann (1999) assert that the social contexts within this ecological approach are organized in systemic fashion. This perspective translates into the notion that no one social context can be understood in isolation from the others. Hence, in addition to seeing the family context as irreducible beyond the triad (mother–father–adolescent), the assertion that there is always "spillover" between factors at various ecosystemic levels demands that the interconnections between the family and its social context must always be taken into account (Goodnow, 2006). As such, researchers employing an ecological perspective have generated evidence underlining the primary of family factors, especially in studies that focus on adolescent outcomes associated with delinquency and violence (Bradshaw, Glaser, Calhoun, & Bates, 2006).

Applied more specifically to the social milieu of adolescence, Antonishak, Sutfin, and Reppucci (2005) have emphasized the important influences of three ecological contexts: peers, neighborhoods, and the media. Peers represent both microsystem (close friendships) and exosystem (cliques and crowds) influences, and are thought to have some of their greatest influence through sociometric status (Bagwell, Newcomb, & Bukowski, 1998), meaning the degree to which someone is liked or disliked by others. Whereas families and peers historically have been seen as opposing forces in the lives of adolescents, more recent writings have reflected a more complementary and interconnected focus regarding their mutual influences (Collins, Laursen, et al., 1997; Collins & Roisman, 2006; Updegraff, McHale, Crouter, & Kupanoff, 2001; Updegraff, McHale, Whiteman et al., 2006).

The exosystem influences of neighborhood and community, in turn, are thought to be both proximal (direct) and distal (indirect), and are dominated by the influence of socioeconomic status and other family hardship indicators (Coulton, Korbin, Su & Chow, 1995). In fact, the way that parents and families operate may be a function of the kinds of resources that are available in their exosystem and thus how they seek to utilize those sources of support (Furstenberg, Cook, et al., 1999). As with the family–peer complementarity described above, here too we see the sense that families and communities are interconnected and mutually.

Finally, the effects of the media are thought to be the most widespread across social contexts. While typically seen as part of the overall culture and therefore macrosystemic in orientation, the recent rise in social networks (MySpace, Facebook, etc.) generates evidence that these Internet-based collectives are having a more immediate microsystem impact as well. Relatedly, there is growing concern over what has been termed "compulsive internet use" (van der Aa, Overbeek, et al., 2009). Adolescents who are seen as being most at risk for this addictive behavior are those who come from less well-functioning families (van den Eijnden, Spijkerman, et al., 2009), again underlining the interconnected nature of the family microsystem and its macrosystemic environment. Also, there is evidence that greater Internet use and related social networking technologies is associated with higher amounts of substance use in adolescents (Ohannessian, 2009).

5.2 Reflections: Ecological Theory and Families with Adolescents

How does the reader begin to evaluate the use of ecological theory in terms of understanding families with adolescents? The descriptive function of this conceptual framework is a bit of a "mixed bag." On the one hand, the ecological perspective has been criticized as offering little to scholars who are interested in describing what occurs inside of families with adolescents. For instance, Granic, Dishion, and Hollenstein (2006) noted that "although the ecological framework is critical for demarcating global influences, it falls short of specifying the mechanisms by which they transform family relationships and adolescent outcomes" (pp. 60–61). These authors go on to suggest that the inclusion of "dynamic systems" concepts such as positive and negative feedback to enhance the ecological framework's ability to describe the inner workings of these families. Similar criticisms of this perspective can be found elsewhere (cf., Demo, Acquilino, & Fine, 2005).

On the other hand, the particular details of the various social contexts within which families with adolescents are embedded are very well defined by ecological theory.

In fact, this theoretical perspective is thought to have dominated the empirical literature concerning the social contexts of adolescent development, including the study of parenting and family factors (Smetana, Campione-Barr, & Metzger, 2006; Steinberg & Morris, 2001). Further, Darling (2007) has asserted that attention paid to context only is an overly simplistic representation of this conceptual framework, as the ecological approach does extend beyond the examination of system levels. A similar line of thinking is put forward by Tudge, Mokrova, Hatfield, and Karnik (2009), who argue that this emphasis on levels represents an "earlier or partial form" of the ecological perspective.

Hence, to examine the sensitizing function of ecological theory, consideration must be given to a "more mature" version of this conceptual framework. This would involve the examination of the entire Process-Person-Context-Time (PPCT) model put forth by Bronfenbrenner (2005), where "context" (representing the aforementioned levels) becomes one of the four elements that are critical to the ecological approach. In addition, "process" (or proximal processes) focuses attention on those regular interactions that occur between an individual and the people in their immediate environments, "person" refers to the idiosyncratic characteristics (e.g., age, gender, skills, motivation) that each individual brings into situations, and "time" represents the impact of being in a specific cohort or living during a certain era in history [also referred to as the "chronosystem" (Bronfenbrenner & Morris, 1998)]. Taken all together, then, there would seem to be solid support regarding the integrative function that ecological theory retains.

At the same time, it does seem to be the case that most of the evidence surrounding the practical utility of this conceptual framework addresses the context dimension. For instance, Bogenschneider (1996) advanced an ecologically based approach to the development of prevention programs and policy surrounding families with adolescents. Similarly, Stokols (1996) discussed the ecology of community health promotion, while Stormshak and Dishion (2002) addressed the use of this conceptual framework to consider the complexity of providing mental health services to adolescents and their families.

Focusing on the explanatory function of ecological theory provides us with a similar "mixed" perspective regarding this framework's ability to provide a rationale for what is being observed in families with adolescents. Certainly, the ecological perspective has been embedded in efforts to understand the impact of families and other social contexts on more individually oriented phenomena experienced by adolescents, including delinquency (Stern & Smith, 1995), internalizing and externalizing problem behaviors (Schwartz, Coatsworth, et al., 2006), teen pregnancy (Ranieri & Wiemann, 2007), smoking (Wiium & Wold, 2009), self-esteem issues (Lian & Yusooff, 2009), and school food choices (Brown & Landry-Meyer, 2007).

However, Tudge et al. (2009) noted that only 4 out of the 25 studies that they reviewed reflected or otherwise adequately addressed ecological theory in its more "advanced" form. Among other reasons surmised for this paucity of empirical work is the likelihood that some scholars are simply looking to provide general theoretical support for the examination of multiple contexts, as well as the possibility that others simply lack the conceptual clarity necessary to utilize this particular theory.

5.2 Reflections: Ecological Theory and Families with Adolescents

In addition, Tudge et al. (2009) surmise that the "final reason for scholars not treating seriously the mature form of Bronfenbrenner's theory may be that it is viewed as simply too difficult to translate effectively into research" (p. 207).

For present purposes, of those four studies that did meet the criteria set forth by Tudge et al. (2009) as representative of the more complete form of ecological theory, two were focused on some aspect of families with adolescents. In the first study, Campbell, Pungello, and Miller-Johnson (2002) utilized a PPCT model to examine academic competence and self-worth in a sample of economically disadvantaged African American adolescents. In the second study that was conducted by Riggens-Caspers, Cadoret, Knutsen, and Langbehn (2003), these researchers also incorporated a PPCT model to retrospectively explain adolescent problem behaviors in a sample of adult adoptees and their adoptive parents. Hence, it would seem to be the case that this sort of explanatory function can and has been met by scholars targeting families with adolescents.

Finally, in terms of the value function of ecological theory, some previous writings suggest that this conceptual framework is more of a "value orientation" than it is a scientific theory (White & Klein, 2006). Perhaps the most significant ideal of all within ecological theory is the notion of the reciprocal survival needs of living systems and their nonliving environment. Others have written in praise of the values underlying this perspective – including principles such as justice and freedom – which are thought to be almost "universal" in their orientation (Bulboz & Sontag, 1993).

In sum, there is some very real debate about the importance and usefulness of ecological theory in the study of families. While potential users are sensitized to a rather comprehensive set of issues, this perspective is found to be at least somewhat lacking in terms of its ability to provide assistance in describing the inner workings of families with adolescents. As is the case with many of the other theories reviewed in this book, ecological theory offers significant practical utility and a well-integrated approach to our main area of inquiry. Further, there are also some difficulties with regard to the explanatory function of this approach. Finally, the values inherent to ecological theory have made it a favorite for those wanting to highlight the interconnected nature of all things.

Chapter 6
Attachment Theory

> *Build today, then strong and sure, With a firm and ample base;*
> *And ascending and secure. Shall tomorrow find its place.*
>
> Henry Wadsworth Longfellow, *The Builders*

Abstract Attachment theory offers much substance to scholars interested in the study of families with adolescents. Developed out of a more psychological tradition, this conceptual approach all too often is given little or no mention in texts on family theories. The present chapter covers this perspective's main focus that is on internal working models (secure, ambivalent, avoidant, and disorganized) and are used to describe interactions in dyadic and larger units of analysis within the family. The ways in which these internal working models can be used to describe attachment styles that develop over time are highlighted as well. The theoretical connections between other more mainstream family science concepts are reviewed, and the well-documented empirical approach to understanding families with adolescents from an attachment perspective is discussed in detail.

> MacKenzie Williams most frequently is described as "a really well-adjusted young woman" by her teachers and other adults in her life. Not only is this 16-year-old academically successful, but she also seems to get along with everyone in her high school. She also is attractive, and recently has started to date a few of the tenth grade boys. She has kept these contacts very informal, and always has her date come to her house to meet her parents before going out. Because she has always felt a strong emotional connection to both her mother and her father, she continues to rely on them for advice and feedback about the dating process. In fact, MacKenzie is grateful that her mother was so open and honest with her about her own dating history when she had a small but significant problem with a senior who was being overly attentive at the beginning of the school year. MacKenzie notes with obvious pride that she is able to tell her parents about her feelings and experiences without her emotions being judged or her motives questioned.

> MacKenzie has had two best friends since grade school: Amanda Reynolds and Stacey Phillips. Although bright and intellectually capable, Amanda had never been a "good student," preferring instead to spend most of her waking moments fully engaged in the social life of her high school. While she has never questioned her friendship with MacKenzie due to its long-standing nature, she is decidedly anxious about her standing among many of the other girls she calls friends. As well, Amanda has dated boys since the sixth grade, and those relationships typically have been stormy and brief. She also is attractive, yet is very insecure about her looks and what the boys think and say about her. Amanda describes her relationship with her parents as "extremely hot and cold," where intensely positive periods are followed by long stretches of silence and unavailability on the part of both her mother and father. Hence, she feels that she cannot really rely on her mother or father to be there when she needs them most. As a result, more often than not, she turns to MacKenzie for advice and support.
>
> Stacey Phillips might be the most attractive of the three friends, except that she neither cares about nor attends to her looks. In fact, it almost seems as if she works to be as unappealing as possible. As a result, Stacey has never dated, much less given a boy any opening to approach her. Nor does she care much for school, always opting to do the bare minimum in order to get by. Instead, she is devoted almost single-mindedly to the poetry she writes and the photographs she takes, which for the most part are dark and brooding. Stacey's mother, who is the owner of an art gallery in a trendy downtown area, is stern and demanding but otherwise completely unavailable to her emotionally. Stacey has not seen her father since the time she was a preschooler, even though she thinks that he still lives in the area. Her mother gives little information about her ex-husband, saying only that "your father is doing you a favor in not coming around to see you." Except for her continued contact with MacKenzie (she thinks Amanda is a "boy-obsessed airhead" and wants nothing to do with her), Stacey feels very alone in her world. In fact, if MacKenzie didn't continue to insist on making plans to do things with her, Stacey probably wouldn't participate in activities with anyone at all.

6.1 Basic Attachment Theory Concepts

Attachment theory has had a long tradition as a theory in developmental psychology, going back to the pioneering work of Bowlby (1969) and Ainsworth, Blehar, Waters, and Wall (1978). Most of the early work using this perspective was focused on the developmental period surrounding infancy, where the groundwork for all subsequent attachment relationships was thought to be laid. As well, theorists and researchers using this perspective traditionally had focused on the mother–infant dyadic relationship most specifically. As we shall see, however, this perspective has

6.1 Basic Attachment Theory Concepts

expanded over time to include a more life span perspective on multiple interpersonal relationships, thus setting the stage for its use in understanding families with adolescents.

The basics of this approach surround "internal working models," which are thought to be comprised of the individual's early experiences with their primary caregiver and, as such, guide all present interactions within interpersonal relationships. The four main internal working models are thought to include the following:

- Secure
- Ambivalent
- Avoidant
- Disorganized

In turn, work on the expansion of attachment theory beyond infancy produced new labels to represent the manifestations of these internal working models later in life. Hence, secure attachment has been described as "autonomous," ambivalent attachment as "preoccupied," avoidant attachment as "dismissing," and disorganized attachment as "unresolved" (Main, Kaplan, & Cassidy, 1985).

The most well-adjusted individuals are those who are "secure," the result of having experienced consistent nurturance from the primary caregiver. Over time, secure attachment leads to an internal working model that sees relationships as trustworthy and dependable. This internal working model allows the individual to strike a relative balance between a sense of individuality and a sense of togetherness (Feeney & Nollar, 1996).

The character of MacKenzie Williams in the vignette at the beginning of this chapter provides a nice illustration of the securely attached (autonomous) adolescent. She is seen by adults as well-adjusted, she is academically successful, and she displays excellent social skills as witnessed by her ability to get along with large numbers of her classmates. Further, her continued strong emotional connections with both parents are in evidence, another hallmark of secure attachment in adolescence (Cretzmeyer, 2003; Kerns & Stevens, 1996).

Less well-adjusted individuals are represented by the three other internal working models. The ambivalent/preoccupied attached style, generated from the uneven availability of caregivers, is thought to lead to an internal working model that demands continuous monitoring of relationships due to the untrustworthy nature of relationships. In turn, the avoidant/dismissing attached style, the result of consistent rejection from the caregiver, is associated with an internal working model that thwarts others' attempts to get close. The last internal working model – the disorganized/unresolved attached style – is thought to be the product of a traumatic event associated with the sudden loss of a primary caregiver, exposure to abusive situations, or may even be the product of frightening parental behavior (Jacobvitz, Hazen, & Leon, 2006). Because the disorganization and lack of resolution surround the trauma event itself (i.e., continually experiencing the hurt associated with that loss), individuals with these experiences otherwise are thought to operate with another internal working model (Rosenstein & Horowitz, 1996).

In the vignette above, MacKenzie's friends, Amanda and Stacey are meant to represent the ambivalent/preoccupied and avoidant/dismissing attachment styles, respectively. As an ambivalently attached adolescent, Amanda constantly questions her status among friends, is very anxious and insecure about her looks and is nervous about her reputation with male peers. Amanda was raised in a household with parents she describes as "hot and cold" who only sometimes (and thus unpredictably) have been there for Amanda when she needed them to be caring and nurturing. Stacey exemplifies the avoidant attached style, as seen in her general lack of contact with male and female peers and withdrawal into her solitary world of poetry and photography. Her father has never been involved in any part of her life that she can remember, and her mother is emotionally unavailable to her. Thus, Stacey has had no real opportunities to form a meaningful attachment with a caregiver.

Liddle and Schwartz (2002) have noted that the attachment perspective is particularly well-suited for the developmental challenges faced by families with adolescents. These scholars emphasize that secure attachments during this family life cycle stage require mutually trusting relationships between adolescents and their parents as certain developmental demands are met. This is especially the case in terms of striking the appropriate balance between the adolescent's need to explore her/his social environment and the parent's need to remain connected as both a monitor and guide (Cobb, 1996), described elsewhere in the attachment literature as balancing autonomy and relatedness claims (Allen & Hauser, 1996).

There has been some important work done on the relative stability of attachment styles from infancy through adolescence and early adulthood (Waters, Weinfield, & Hamilton, 2000). In some studies, there is a consistent pattern of results indicating that attachment styles display continuity across time, at least in terms of white middle-class samples (Eiden, Teti, & Corns, 1995; Hamilton, 2000). On the other hand, the presence of family life events such as divorce (Lewis, Feiring, & Rosenthal, 2000) and other significant stressors in higher-risk samples are thought to increase the likelihood of more discontinuous attachment styles (Weinfield, Sroufe, & Egeland, 2000).

Much of the attachment literature has been based on the relationship between the youth and his or her mother. However, a number of studies have examined attachment styles to both mothers and fathers. Levy, Blatt, and Shaver (1998) reported that both parents played an important role in the development of attachment styles in later adolescents and young adults, and that ambivalence toward fathers in particular was a determinant of less secure attachment. Maio, Fincham, and Lycett (2000) found similar results in a study of attachment to mothers and fathers in a younger sample of adolescents.

Belsky (1981) and others have long maintained that the child–mother–father triad is the most appropriate unit of analysis for understanding the reciprocal influences of family members. Based on this perspective, Talbot and McHale (2003) have asserted that the internal working models offered by attachment theory can be greatly enhanced by attention to "whole-family or polyadic relationship representations." Of particular interest here is the flexibility of the internal working models (seen as a hallmark of the securely attached individual) that allow individuals to constantly integrate new information about people and relationships while preserving their emotional and cognitive balance. Such relational representations for youth are thought to be demonstrably influenced by coparenting processes, for instance.

Researchers have employed a strategy for examining multiple attachments within the family, and in so doing have uncovered both age and gender effects. For instance, Buist, Dekovic, Meeus, and van Aken (2002) reported that attachments between adolescents and their mothers, fathers, and siblings all show a significant decline as a function of age. As well, these scholars reported that the gender of both the adolescent and the attachment figure played an important role in the quality of those attachments. Here, same-sex relationships (mother–daughter, sister–sister, father–son, and brother–brother) were generally seen as retaining higher quality attachments than opposite-sex relationships (mother–son, father–daughter, and brother–sister), and attachments to females more specifically (mothers, daughters, and sisters) were of a higher quality than attachments to males (fathers, sons, and brothers).

6.2 Reflections: Attachment Theory and Families with Adolescents

How does the reader begin to evaluate the use of attachment theory in terms of understanding families with adolescents? The fact that this conceptual framework historically has been developed out of a more psychological tradition often relegates it to minor mention in texts on family theories (Bengston, Acock, et al., 2005; Boss, Doherty, et al., 1993; White & Klein, 2008). Nevertheless, attachment theory makes a solid contribution in terms of its descriptive function, both in terms of how families operate more generally when there are offspring, as well as families with adolescents most specifically.

Especially impressive is this theory's ability to depict the particular details of how dyads operate while remaining available to scholars who desire to see these aspects in a more "family systems" light (Caffery & Erdman, 2000), which affords a triadic (or greater) perspective. Of course, in terms of the sensitizing function of attachment theory, the emphasis is clearly grounded in the internal working models and related attachment styles that develop over time. At the same time, the best work with this perspective may be yet to come in terms of understanding families with adolescents. As an example, the use of systems concepts such as fusion and triangulation have been discussed as holding significant promise in expanding our understanding of parent–adolescent attachments (Benson, 2005).

Further, the ties between attachment theory and structural family therapy factors such as parental coalitions and boundary maintenance also has been recognized (Faber, Edwards, Bauer, & Wetchler, 2003), as has its ties to other approaches such as parental acceptance-rejection theory (cf., Rohner & Khaleque, 2009). This speaks well of this theory's integrative function, as the attachment perspective can be linked to other related perspectives in organizing our overall thinking about families with adolescents. This conceptual framework also has been used to incorporate information about other social contexts, including both peer and romantic relationships (Laible, Carlo, & Raffaelli, 2000; Roisman, Madsen, Hennighausen, Sroufe, & Collins, 2001).

As the amount of work linking family factors to attachment phenomena increases (Bell, 2009; Davies & Forman, 2002), there has been a corresponding rise in interest in attachment theory concepts by family therapists and others involving families in their treatment efforts (Byng-Hall, 1995; Lopez, 1995). Here, attachment theory has been used to discuss such phenomena such as therapeutic alliance with families (Johnson, Ketring, Rohacs, & Brewer, 2006), resilience (Luthar & Cicchetti, 2000), and the family-based treatment of numerous presenting problems, including eating disorders (Johnson, Maddeaux, & Blouin, 1998), depression (Sexson, Glanville, & Kaslow, 2001), and trauma exposure (Prather, 2007; Prather & Golden, 2009a, 2009b). The attachment perspective also has been used in the development of prevention programming that targets teen pregnancy and school-based issues (Allen, Philliber, Herrling, & Kuperminc, 1997).

Attachment theory has an impressive evidence base that provides clear and well-supported reasons for observations made about families with adolescents, bolstering the explanatory function served by this conceptual framework. For instance, evidence has been generated that attachment styles are related to both internalizing and externalizing problem behaviors in adolescents (Allen, Moore, Kuperminc, & Bell, 1998). Tenets of the attachment perspective also have been discussed as extending the focus on how parenting styles impact a variety of adolescent outcome variables (Pinquart & Silbereisen, 2005), as well as being associated with the adolescent's peer relationships (Schneider, Atkinson, & Tardif, 2001).

That said, Thompson and Raikes (2003) have noted that the application of attachment theory beyond the mother-infant dyad and throughout the life course has created some significant conceptual and empirical challenges that leave this conceptual framework at a "crossroads." One major point here concerns the internal working model, something that these authors consider to be "a conceptual metaphor, not a systematically defined theoretical construct" (p. 696), leaving it open to criticisms that it possibly could explain anything and everything, and hence nothing at all (also see Waters, Crowell, Elliott, Corcoran, & Treboux, 2002). Other points of concern include the theory's ability to account for multiple attachment relationships in the family and other social contexts, variability in assessment strategies, and challenges to the validity claims of studies that have examined the impact of attachment-based phenomena on longer-term outcomes associated with adolescence and early adulthood.

Finally, the value function of attachment theory draws attention to a number of principles and ideals embedded in this framework. White and Klein (2008) discussed attachment concepts as residing within both a functionalist and evolutionary framework. Here, attachment theory is thought to hold values related to adaptation and selection as a way of describing how (and thus why) relationships function best within families. Also adopting functional and evolutionary perspectives, Bell

(2009) has described the traditional viewpoint on attachment as based on "fear," where felt security to an attachment figure is equated with not being afraid. This scholar goes on to use neurobiological research to assert that there are forms of both "distressed" and "non-distressed" attachments that can be used to expand our understanding of caregiving systems.

In sum, despite the lack of coverage of this perspective in the family theory literature, there are substantial reasons for underlining the importance and usefulness of attachment theory in the study of families with adolescents. This conceptual framework offers clear and precise descriptions of relationships that sensitize users to a number of core concepts that can be used to categorize dyadic and larger units of analysis within the family. The attachment perspective displays a practical utility that is noteworthy, and thus offers up a well-integrated approach to scholars interested in families with adolescents. The explanatory function of this approach is well-documented even as others push adherents to take this empirical work to new levels. Finally, the values contained within this perspective are easily identified, and create an appeal for those scholars who are comfortable in creating accounts of "why" relationships look the way they do as a function of "how" they have come into existence for reasons related to the advancement of our species.

Chapter 7
Social Learning Theory

> By three methods we may learn wisdom: first, by reflection, which is noblest; second, by imitation, which is easiest; and third, by experience, which is the most bitter.
>
> Confucius, *Analects*

Abstract Social learning theory utilizes precise descriptions of dyadic relationships and other larger system dynamics that are present in families with adolescents. Similar to other theoretical perspectives that claim more individual psychological origins, however, this theoretical approach is not given extensive coverage in the family theory literature. The present chapter discusses how social learning theory focuses attention on the ways in which adolescent and parent behaviors are both learned and reinforced – both positively or negatively – by family members and other socializing agents. The review of empirical evidence supporting the use of this conceptual approach to families with adolescents reveals a literature that is rather well-developed, and forms the basis for a number of prevention and intervention based efforts that are based on the social learning perspective.

According to his mother, 15-year-old James Monroe had always been a "follower." Mr. Monroe used to ask James rhetorical questions such as "if all of your friends jumped off of a cliff, would you jump too?" Now, however, he was afraid that the answer would be "yes, of course." So he stopped asking. When three of his friends decided that they were going to stop playing hockey last year, James told his parents that he was going to quit as well. Horrified, his parents pleaded and begged him to reconsider, telling him that he was the star of the team. If James continued to play hockey, Mr. and Mrs. Monroe offered to buy him the Ford Mustang he always said he wanted when he turned 16. He stayed on the team through the end of the season, although he threw endless temper tantrums about the early-morning practices. Often as not, this behavior got him whatever extra privileges he had been pushing for earlier that week. After the season ended, James started to put on a good deal of weight, owing to the fact that he and his friends were currently spending a great deal of time playing video games and hanging out at the local fast food joint. Both Mr. and Mrs. Monroe were overweight, and had been so since they were teenagers themselves. They did not want their son to suffer from the same sorts of weight-related difficulties that they had experienced throughout their own lives. However, their attempts to talk with James about his recent weight gain were only met with sneers and derisive comments like "you should talk." The Monroes decided not to push the matter, hoping instead that this was "just a passing phase" for James.

Jasmine Miller wanted desperately to hang out with the most popular girls in her school. This 14-year-old had become an astute observer of the way that they dressed, and had begged her mother to allow her to shop only in those stores that carried similar clothing choices. Also, these girls all wore their hair in the latest short and layered style, so Jasmine had her beautiful shoulder length hair cut as well (much to her mother's dismay). Eventually, some of the girls she was trying so hard to be like began to befriend Jasmine and asked her to sit with them at the lunch table. One thing that Jasmine noticed right away was how much these girls liked to brag about how little effort they put into schoolwork. Who had time for schoolwork, one girl said, when there were so many boys to talk to? In a relatively short amount of time Jasmine's grades began to suffer as well. Mr. and Mrs. Miller, who both earned college degrees and were currently employed in the continuing education department of the local community college, became very angry with Jasmine over her latest report card (four C's and a D-), and demanded to know if drug use was behind this slip in grades. Jasmine became furious about the substance use accusation, asking her parents why they couldn't just be happy that she was hanging out with the popular crowd now. Mr. Miller reminded his daughter that they couldn't afford to send her to a good university without some sort of academic scholarship, something that up to this point she was in the running to receive. And Mrs. Miller noted that, while she had been flexible up to this point in terms of Jasmine's requests for more choice in clothing and hairstyle selections, she would no longer be given the same freedoms if she could not keep her grades up. In fact, Jasmine was grounded until the next interim report cards came out, and her computer and phone use was restricted as well. Five weeks later, Jasmine's interim grades all were back to acceptable levels (three A's and two B's). Mr. and Mrs. Miller eased up on the grounding, but kept the computer and phone restrictions in place pending the results of the overall marking period.

7.1 Basic Social Learning Theory Concepts

Social learning theory, another theory covered in this book that claims psychological origins, also is based as much on relationships as it is on individually oriented concepts. The underpinnings of this perspective rest in large part on the work of

Albert Bandura (1977, 1986), although it should be noted that this scholar called his own work "social cognitive learning theory" to avoid confusion with other writings also using the title of social learning theory (Woolfork 2010).

The more individually oriented components of this theory include a focus on self-efficacy and agency, which have to do with perceptions about one's own abilities to have control over their own lives (Bandura, 2001). This theoretical framework retains its more social orientation by focusing attention on how learning takes place through the observation of others' behavior, and especially those behaviors that are perceived as being incentivized in some way. Thus, imitation plays an important role in the learning process as individuals attempt to recreate the behaviors that are modeled and reinforced by the actions of others. As such, behavior is shaped by the positive reinforcement (reward) and/or negative reinforcement (removal of a punishment) that are linked as consequences to the specific actions taken by an individual (Akers, Krohn, Lanza-Kaduce, & Radosevich, 1979). These are ideas about learning that have their foundations in the much earlier psychological literature surrounding the work of Skinner (1950, 1989).

In turn, learning through reinforcement is thought to occur within three different modalities. First, there is direct reinforcement, where a behavior is praised or otherwise is situated in positive discourse with an authority figure. Second, more indirect or vicarious reinforcement can take place whereby the individual observes the rewarded behaviors of others. Third and finally, there is self-reinforcement, which as the term implies involves the individual's own self-management (or self-control) of rewarded behavior (Schunk, 2005).

In the sketch at the beginning of this chapter, the notion that James Monroe was a "follower" underscores the way this 15-year-old mimics the behaviors of his friend with regard to participation in sports and other activities. Such imitative behavior also can be seen in the way that Jasmine Miller selects her clothes and her hair, of course. And we can surmise in both cases that these adolescents are amply rewarded by their friends in terms of their approval, underscoring the power of positive reinforcement from the peer group.

At the same time, attention also can be drawn the differences in the type of reinforcement seen in terms of the parental responses from Mr. and Mrs. Monroe in comparison to the Mr. and Mrs. Miller. James' parents react to his withdrawal threats with pleas, begging, and bribery. Jasmine's parents, on the other hand, react to her slip in grades with more punitive actions, linking the eventual removal of these punishments to the more positive behavior (elevated grades) that they desire to see. Both of these situations involve negative reinforcement. However, in the Monroe family's case, it is the parents whose behavior is being shaped by the negative reinforcement; i.e. doing anything within their power to make the aversive stimuli (James' threats and temper tantrums) go away.

Attention also can be drawn to the different forms of modeling that are present in the situations of these two different sets of parents. Mr. and Mrs. Monroe were both overweight, and so in bringing up James' recent weight gain, they were communicating the message "do as I say, not as I do." Hence, there are a set of mixed verbal and nonverbal messages present within the Monroe family that weaken the impact of the overt message that these parents are trying to send to their son. On the other hand, Mr. and Mrs. Miller were asking Jasmine to follow in their footsteps by laying out a course for receiving an education from a good university. Here, contradictory messages are not an issue, and thus the impact of the messages being transmitted by the Millers to their daughter is thought to be much more powerful in their orientation.

Theorists, researchers, and intervention-based professionals have long maintained an interest in the applicability of social learning theory in efforts to understand and work with families. For instance, Crosbie-Burnett and Lewis (1993) utilized the social learning concept of "reciprocal determinism" – with its emphasis on the circular influence that occurs between the individual and her/his social context – as a way of describing the learning that is gained through family member interactions. Similarly, researchers have employed social learning theory as the basis of hypotheses that children and adolescents will learn a variety of social behaviors from their parents, and in turn will utilize those same sorts of behaviors in relationships with siblings and friends (Cui, Conger, Bryant, & Elder, 2002; Haj-Yahia & Dawud-Noursi, 1998; McHale, Crouter, & Whiteman, 2003).

Similarly, Pinquart and Silbereisen (2005) have asserted that social learning theory provides assistance in understanding how similarities among siblings are the result of shared experiences within the family environment. Siblings, peers, and parents all are seen as important socializing agents within this theoretical perspective (Ardelt & Day, 2002; De Goede, Branje, Delsing, & Meeus, 2009; McHale, Updegraff, Helms-Erikson, & Crouter, 2001), and their comparative influence has been at the center of much work in this area, especially with regard to outcome variables such as adolescent delinquency and other problem behaviors (Akers, 1998, 2000; Bank, Burraston, & Snyder, 2004; Markiewicz, Doyle, & Brengdon, 2001).

The efforts of Gerald Patterson (1982) and his colleagues at the Oregon Social Learning Center are among the most recognized bodies of work that have applied social learning theory concepts to the study of families. Focusing on the family environment as the most important context in learning antisocial behavior, Patterson's approach involved the recognition of a negative reinforcement cycle that he termed "coercive family processes." Here, parents who employ coercive tactics with their children and adolescents (such as bribing or threatening behaviors) initiate a process whereby the offspring learn how to use aggressive behaviors (flying into a rage or otherwise throwing temper tantrums) in order to avoid compliance.

Again referring back to the sketch at the beginning of this chapter, this is exactly the kind of interaction that was illustrated between James and his parents. Mr. and Mrs. Monroe use the bribe of a car in an attempt to keep James on the hockey team. As well, the temper tantrums that James threw about early-morning practices typically resulted in his parents rewarding that behavior by agreeing to give him extra privileges in an attempt to appease him. Clearly, James has learned that his threats and out-of-control behavior resulted in positive outcomes, at least with his parents.

Patterson and colleagues (Patterson, Bank, & Stoolmiller, 1990) have discussed how stresses on both parents and adolescents generate what they term "irritable exchanges" between family members. These stresses can include many different normative and non-normative transitions, including the beginning of puberty, changes in schools, changes in residence, and entrances and exits of family members (births, deaths, separation and divorce, etc.). In turn, these irritable exchanges lead to both inconsistent discipline on the part of parents, as well as a reduction in the amount of supervision and monitoring that parents do with regard to adolescent activities. Together, these factors are thought to significantly increase the probability of the youth engaging in antisocial behavior.

Over time, these behaviors are thought to generalize to other situations involving adult authority figures (i.e., schools), as well as within friendship groups (Dishion, Eddy, Haas, Li, & Spracklin, 1997). In the school context, teachers, principals, and guidance counselors all may find themselves trying alternatively to threaten and bribe a coercive adolescent into displaying better behavior at school. However, in the peer context, prosocial friends generally do not tolerate coercive behavior. Instead, well-functioning peers typically rebuff aggressive behaviors in a manner that leads to rejection (or ejection) from the peer group.

Often as not, the continued lack of contact with more positive peers contributes to a lack of development of basic social skills for these rejected youth As a consequence, such youth will begin to associate with more delinquent peer groups, whose members not only tolerate but actually reinforce various displays of antisocial behavior. In turn, a "cascade effect" (Patterson & Yoerger, 1993) is set into motion where all manner and types of problem behaviors (academic failure, substance abuse, mental health symptoms, etc.) are experienced alongside the delinquent behavior.

These patterns are thought to persist into adulthood, leading to an intergenerational cycle of antisocial behavior, unless and until certain "turning points" can be established that interrupt the modeling and reinforcement processes (Granic & Patterson, 2006; Sampson & Laub, 1997). This can include life events such as becoming romantically involved with a partner who is strongly invested in prosocial behaviors, as well as changing residences to locations that are farther away from antisocial friends and activities (Weisner, Capaldi, & Patterson, 2003).

7.2 Reflections: Social Learning Theory and Families with Adolescents

How does the reader begin to evaluate the use of social learning theory in terms of understanding families with adolescents? The descriptive function of this conceptual framework certainly helps to depict the particular details of dyadic relationship factors within the family with adolescents. However, the attempt to locate descriptions of more "whole family" characteristics within the social learning theory perspective is a bit more complicated.

The challenge of portraying family level factors may be one reason why many of the family theory texts either ignore or only superficially cover this framework. One notable exception in this regard is the work of Chibucos and Leite (2005), who assert that a variety of family development issues are compatible with the social learning approach. This text also contains an excellent chapter on the intergenerational transmission of parenting written by Chen and Kaplan (2005), which employs a variety of social learning concepts – most notably including observation, modeling, and reinforcement – in order to describe how adolescent exposure to "constructive" parenting is significantly related to their acquirement and use of those same parenting skills as adults.

Other work that employs a social learning theoretical perspective contains clear references to family level processes and characteristics. One excellent example in this regard is a study conducted by Buehler, Frank and Cook (2009), who were extending the original scholarship on a "social learning model of family process" developed by Capaldi and her colleagues at the Oregon Social Learning Center (cf., Capaldi & Stoolmiller, 1999). Focusing on family triangulation processes, Buehler et al. (2009) found that involvement in marital conflict set in motion a set of observational and participatory learning processes for adolescents that carried over behaviorally into their relationships with friends.

The sensitizing function of social learning theory spotlights the ways in which adolescent and parent behaviors are both learned and reinforced – either positively or negatively – by other family members, as well as by additional socializing agents who are outside of the family. In turn, both the straightforward use of this theory and its adaptation and use within other conceptual frameworks speaks to the integrative function of social learning theory in helping scholars to organize their work on families with adolescents. An important example in this latter regard is the incorporation of social learning theory concepts into the "social development model" developed out of the University of Washington's Social Development Research Group (Catalano, Kosterman, Hawkins, Newcomb, & Abbott, 1996; Hawkins, Catalano, Kosterman, Abbott, & Hill, 1999). In outlining the role that both risk and protective factors play in the development and maintenance of antisocial behavior, this group of researchers centered attention on the ways in which adolescents learn to act through contact with socializing agents in their families, schools, and other community contexts (Hill, Hawkins, Catalano, Abbott, & Guo, 2005; Huang, Kosterman, Catalano, Hawkins, & Abbot, 2001).

Further evidence regarding the integrative function of social learning theory resides in the significant amount of interventions that are based on this conceptual framework. One such effort involves what is known as Multidimensional Treatment Foster Care (Chamberlain & Reid, 1998), which is discussed below in the family-based application part of this book. As well, there is a rather impressive amount of literature on what collectively is now discussed as parent management training (cf., Rowe, Gomez, & Liddle, 2006), an approach to the treatment of adolescent antisocial behavior that focuses attention on the development of parenting skills such as the employment of consistent discipline strategies and monitoring of adolescent activities. This in turn has led to the development of highly effective prevention-oriented programs for parents as well (Dishion, Kavanagh, Schneiger, Nelson, & Kaufman, 2002).

The focus on how problem behaviors are maintained or extinguished through learning experiences also goes a long way toward highlighting the explanatory function served by social learning theory. For example, a very well-respected collection of studies have been conducted by Akers and colleagues around smoking (Akers & Lee, 1996) and other forms of substance use (Akers & Lee, 1999; Lee, Akers, & Borg, 2004). Many other researchers have adopted a social learning approach to the family's role in adolescent substance use and abuse (Catanzaro & Laurent, 2004), including the effects of parent alcoholism (Kuendig & Kuntsche, 2006), parent-adolescent communication about substance use (Miller-Day, 2002), and the family-peer interface (Eitle, 2005). Likewise, scholars have attended to the socializing role that religion plays within the family (Bao, Whitbeck, Hoyt, & Conger, 1999), as well as its influence on adolescent delinquent behavior (Benda & Corwyn, 1997) and substance use (Bahr, Maughan, Marcos, & Li, 1998).

The social learning perspective also has seen widespread use in areas connected to adolescent sexuality and violence. With regard to sex, this conceptual framework has been employed in scholarship surrounding the impact of the family and other social contexts on risky behaviors (Miller, Forehand, & Kotchick, 1999; Taylor-Seehafer & Rew, 2000) and the timing of first sexual intercourse for adolescents (Crockett, Bingham, Chopak, & Vicary, 1996; Goodson, Evans, & Edmunson, 1996; Hogben & Byrne, 1998).

Regarding violence, social learning theory has been utilized to examine adolescents who both witness (O'Keefe, 1997) and perpetrate violence (Mihalic & Elliott, 1997; Saner & Ellickson, 1996), especially in dating relationships (Foshee, Bauman, & Linder, 1999; Foshee, Linder, MacDougall, & Bangdiwala, 2001; Lavoie, Hebert, Tremblay, Vitaro, Vezina, & McDuff, 2002; Simons, Lin, & Gordon, 1998).

Finally, the value function of social learning theory draws attention to a number of standards and ideals that can be recognized at both the individual and social context levels. Through psychological mechanisms such as self-reflection and forethought, this perspective places a significant emphasis on the power of the individual to direct her or his life, thus placing one's sense of agency at the center of human existence. At the same time, however, the interdependent nature of individuals also is highlighted, and includes the recognition of not only the bi-directionality of relationships, but also of the way that that culture shapes the relative balance between individual and collective issues.

In sum, there are considerable reasons for underlining the value and worth of social learning theory in the study of families with adolescents, even though this perspective (like attachment theory) is not well-covered in the family theory literature. This conceptual framework offers rather precise descriptions of dyadic relationships as well as larger family system dynamics, and sensitizes users to the learning processes that are occurring within families and other social contexts within which adolescents reside. The practical utility of the social learning perspective is evidenced by its use in a number of prevention and intervention based efforts and, combined with its concepts being used within other conceptual models, seems to offer an integrated approach to the study of families with adolescents. The widespread use of this conceptual framework, especially in studies that attempt to examine the family's influence on adolescent problem behavior, underscores its explanatory worth to scholars, and the values contained within this perspective represent an important blend of individual and social context principles.

Part III
Research on Families with Adolescents

Chapter 8
Research on the Parent–Adolescent Dyad

> *Parents who are afraid to put their foot down usually have children who step on their toes.*
>
> Ancient Chinese Proverb

Abstract Historically, empirical attempts to understand families with adolescents have paid great attention to the activities of parents, especially in terms of what they are doing to socialize their offspring to become productive members of society. As a natural extension, then, the parent–adolescent dyad becomes the smallest unit of analysis that can be used in the study of families with adolescents. The seminal work of Diana Baumrind on parenting styles (authoritative, authoritarian, permissive/indulgent, and indifferent/neglectful) continues to maintain a strong influence on the most recent research that focuses attention on parent–adolescent dyadic relationships. The present chapter reviews studies that have been conducted over the last 15 years, with particular attention paid to the linkage that has been established between healthy adolescent development and an authoritative style of parenting. In addition, newer studies that have extended this work in a number of important directions are also highlighted. This includes work that examines parenting style differences between mothers and fathers, and the degree to which parenting style consistency matters. The empirical literature concerning other related parenting behaviors such as monitoring and knowledge, responsiveness, warmth, and psychological control also is reviewed, and variations that may exist as a function of race, ethnicity, and culture are discussed as well.

1. When you think about how your mother acts towards you, in general, would you say that she is very supportive, somewhat supportive, or not very supportive?

1	2	3
Very Supportive	Somewhat Supportive	Not very Supportive

2. In general, would you say that your mother is permissive or strict about making sure that you did what you were supposed to do?

    1   2
Permissive   Strict

3. When you think about how your father acts towards you, in general, would you say that he is very supportive, somewhat supportive, or not very supportive?

    1   2   3
Very Supportive   Somewhat Supportive   Not very Supportive

4. In general, would you say that your father is permissive or strict about making sure that you did what you were supposed to do?

    1   2
Permissive   Strict

The desire to understand the inner workings of families with adolescents inevitably focuses attention on the parents, who are seen as the driving force behind most matters concerning the development and well-being of family members (Bornstein, 1995). In fact, Lerner (2002) makes the statement that "*parenting* is the core function of the family" (p. 181). This sentiment certainly fits well within the "intergenerational caring" definition of family adopted by this book, as there is a great emphasis on what parents and other adult caregivers are doing in order to socialize their offspring to become productive members of society.

Historically, the literature pertaining to the impact of parents on adolescents has been based on Baumrind's (1978) original conceptualizations of authoritarian, authoritative, permissive, and indifferent parenting styles. These styles (see Fig. 10) are comprised of a two-dimensional view of parenting (Maccoby & Martin, 1983) that recognizes variation in both parent responsiveness (warmth and affection) and parent demandingness (rule-setting and discipline).

Fig.11: Parenting styles

	High Responsiveness	Low Responsiveness
High Demandingness	Authoritative	Authoritarian
Low Demandingness	Permissive/Indulgent	Indifferent/Neglectful

Although somewhat oversimplified, the items presented at the beginning of this chapter – taken from the National Longitudinal Study of Youth (Moore, McGroder, Hair, & Gunnoe, 1999) – are fairly precise representations of the two-dimensional nature of parenting styles. The response of "1" on the support-oriented question is coded as "high responsiveness," while responses of "2" or "3" are coded as "low responsiveness." In turn, a response of "1" on the permissive/strict-oriented question is coded as "low demandingness" and the response of "2" is coded as "high demandingness."

Authoritative parents, the style of parenting most often associated with positive adolescent outcomes (Collins, & Laursen, 2004; Smetana, 1995; Steinberg & Silk, 2002), represents the combination of high responsiveness and high demandingness. Because authoritative parents display high responsiveness, relationships with adolescents include a great deal of warmth, support, affection, and nurturance. At the same time, however, the high demandingness of authoritative parents translates into a great deal of structure and control being placed on the adolescent's life. Hence, there are rules that carry rewards when they are followed and meaningful consequences when they are broken or disobeyed. That said, these messages take place within a context that reads: "we are demanding this of you because we love you and know what's best for you."

While authoritarian parents also are high in demandingness, this style of parenting is characterized by low responsiveness. Hence, the expectation that rules and regulations will be adhered to occurs in a much less warm emotional environment, often with the message that you will follow directions because "I am the parent and I told you to do this." There is some research indicating that non-white parents are more likely to adopt this style of parenting (Fuligni, Hughes, & Way, 2009), and other studies have reported that authoritarian parenting can lead to positive outcomes for these minority youth (Dixon, Graber, & Brooks-Gunn, 2008).

Permissive parents (also termed indulgent) are low on demandingness but high on responsiveness. Without rules and other forms of control, permissive parents offer little in the way of expectations that are placed on their teenage sons and daughters. Instead, the emphasis is on the creation of a warm and accommodating emotional environment. In essence, the message that is transmitted in this context is one of "unconditional love," regardless of the behaviors displayed by the adolescent.

Indifferent parents (also labeled neglectful), as the label implies, are low in both demandingness and responsiveness. These parents do not place any sort of structure or control over the lives of their teenage sons and daughters, nor is there any felt sense of closeness or connection. Instead, the message is "go ahead and do whatever you please whenever you please, just please leave me out of it."

These latter two parenting styles – permissive/indulgent and indifferent/neglectful – are most representative of the types of mothers and fathers being targeted in the ancient Chinese proverb that begins this chapter. In both cases, parents are choosing not to "put their foot down," meaning that they are not placing any kinds of demands on their sons and daughters. In return, what they typically get is their own toes "stepped on," at least in terms of the parents being ineffective at curtailing the display of "out of control behaviors" by their adolescents (Conger, Patterson, & Ge, 1995).

In addition to research pertaining to parenting styles, Peterson's (2005) review of literature relevant to the influence of parents on adolescents recognizes the important contributions made regarding parental behavior on adolescent outcomes, beginning with the recognition that "the closest thing to a general law of parenting is that warm, supportive, nurturant, and accepting behavior by mothers and fathers is associated with the development of social competence by adolescents" (p. 40). Hence, research on parenting factors related to support, use of reasoning/induction, monitoring, supervision, knowledge, granting of psychological autonomy, and discipline strategies all must be recognized as additional important areas of inquiry regarding the impact of parents on adolescent development and well-being (Cox & Harter, 2003).

Crosnoe and Cavanagh (2010) recently completed the *Journal of Marriage and the Family's* decade review of articles on families with children and adolescents, which included a discussion of emerging trends in the parenting literature over the last 10 years. These scholars noted five such trends, including:

1. Greater articulation of the developmental significance of parenting behaviors
2. Greater distinction between parenting behaviors and what occurs in parent–adolescent relationships
3. Greater visibility of fathers and fatherhood issues
4. Greater sensitivity to the culturally specific meaning of parenting behaviors
5. Greater awareness of the need for more internationally diverse samples of parents

As shall be seen next, most of these trends are rather easily identified in the parenting and parent–adolescent dyadic studies selected for review. First, a representative sample of studies that focus on some of the newest approaches to this area of inquiry is reviewed, with special attention given to those research efforts that examine the relative contributions of both mothers and fathers, the gathering of information from multiple family members, and the use of data from observers outside of the family. Following this, two ongoing issues that confront researchers interested in the parent–adolescent dyad are addressed: the dimensionality of parenting behaviors, and the cultural relevance of parenting behaviors.

8.1 Selected Studies on Parenting Behaviors

Many studies that have focused on parenting styles over the past 15 years continue to underscore the long-held belief that an authoritative parenting style is associated with the most positive adolescent well-being outcomes (Weiss & Schwartz, 1996). One more recent twist on this body of findings has been a greater focus on the specific parenting styles of *both* mothers and fathers. This newer more expanded approach to parenting styles accomplishes a number of additional things, including most importantly allowing for greater specificity in terms understanding the relative importance of mothers' and fathers' contributions to adolescent development and well-being (cf., Stolz, Barber, & Olsen, 2005). In related fashion, gathering data on both mothers and fathers sets the stage for shifting the unit of analysis towards the family unit as a combination of these mother–adolescent and father–adolescent dyads.

One excellent example of how this newer approach to the study of parenting styles illuminates the particular role that fathers play in the lives of adolescents was conducted by Bronte-Tinkew, Moore, and Carrano (2006). These researchers reported that an authoritative style of parenting displayed by fathers was significantly associated with positive outcomes for adolescents (average age 15.3 years) even after a number of mother-related variables (including mother's own parenting style) were controlled. In addition, as hypothesized, these researchers found that fathers' impact was greater for male adolescents than for female adolescents.

The focus on the parenting styles of both mothers and fathers is a fortunate turn of events, especially for those scholars interested in understanding the impact of both parents on adolescent growth and development. Historically, much of this literature has been limited precisely because of its singular focus on mothers only (Phares, 1999, 2002). More recently, scholars have been uncovering differences in the amount and type of involvement that both parents have with their adolescents (Paley, Conger, & Harold, 2000; Phares, Fields, & Kamboukas, 2009; Stolz, Barber, & Olsen, 2005), as well as gender differences in terms of how adolescents relate to their mothers and fathers (Phares, Renk, et al., 2009).

In related fashion, the emphasis on obtaining information from both mothers and fathers has led to efforts to examine the uniformity of parenting styles. For instance, Fletcher, Steinberg, & Sellers (1999) reported that "interparental parent consistency" (inferred from the reports of high school students on the parenting styles of their mothers and fathers) was less important than the presence of at least one authoritative parent. Additionally, few differences in adolescent outcomes were identified between families with two authoritative parents versus those containing only one authoritative parent.

While the Fletcher et al. (1999) study helped the field to recognize the need to examine the uniformity of parental behaviors, this research was limited by the fact that adolescent perspectives only were utilized. This is a problem for a number of reasons, not the least of which is we do not have access to what the parents themselves believe they are doing behaviorally. As suggested by Sabatelli and Bartle (1995), when parental and family variables are targeted in empirical efforts, the researcher ought to let those family members speak for themselves, as well as having others comment on their activities.

Readers can ponder the relative importance of this last point. Suppose you were a researcher who was interested in learning more about parenting behaviors. Do you think it would matter if you talked to mothers but not fathers, or vice versa? And of what value would the adolescent's viewpoint be to you? It seems axiomatic to state that most people would choose to gather information from as many sources as possible. What is equally self-evident, however, is that the gathering of multiple family member perspectives is not a strategy of convenience, but rather is a challenging necessity for researchers who are invested in the notion that all points of view within the family are valuable and therefore must be sought and acquired.

An excellent example that underscores the importance of seeking multiple family member perspectives on such variables of interest comes from a study conducted by Bogenschneider, Small, and Tsay (1997), who examined the relationship between parents' perceptions of their own parenting competence and what their eighth through twelfth grade adolescents reported about their parenting behaviors. Findings indicated that higher perceived levels of competence by parents were associated with adolescent reports of greater monitoring, higher levels of parent responsiveness, and less psychologically controlling behaviors by their parents. In addition, parents who reported higher levels of competence also reported less stress in parenting their son or daughter in combination with greater perceptions of that adolescent's cooperativeness and openness to being socialized.

Said a slightly different way, it appears that parents and high school-aged adolescents tend to display agreement in their ratings of parenting behaviors. The more competent a parent feels, the more likely their son or daughter is to report higher levels of the kinds of parenting behaviors that the literature associates with constructive parenting – monitoring and responsiveness – and lower levels of questionable parenting behaviors (in this case, psychologically controlling activities). And to top it all off, mothers and fathers who engage in more competent parenting behaviors experience less stress and more cooperativeness in their relationships with their high schoolers.

A related issue involves the comparison of "insider" and "outsider" perspectives, whereby the viewpoints of family members are compared with observations made by researchers (Johnson, 2010). One great example of how to extend this type of research through use of both self-report and observational ratings (thus examining both the "insider" reports of adolescents and the "outsider" views of observers) comes from Simons and Conger (2007), who examined parenting styles of both parents with seventh grade adolescents (followed longitudinally with measures taken in the eighth and ninth grades). In addition to findings that marked notable differences between insider and outsider perspectives, these researchers reported that mothers and fathers most often were seen as sharing a common parenting style. Further, it was reported that the most positive adolescent outcomes were associated with reports indicating that both parents displayed authoritative parenting styles.

In addition to the comparison of insider and outsider perspectives, this last research article also displays the strength of having used a longitudinal design. This approach to research becomes incredibly important to scholars who are interested in tracking continuity and change throughout this developmental period. It has been noted that the increased number of large longitudinal databases made available to researchers has allowed for more focused attention on generating support for theoretically derived suppositions about how families behave over time. Further, the increased use of longitudinal designs has coincided with the development and use of more sophisticated statistical methods for handling these sorts of data (Greenstein, 2006).

8.2 The Dimensionality of Parenting Behaviors

While a number of strengths have been identified in this literature, the empirical work on parenting styles is not without its limitations and controversies, however. For instance, Barber (1997) has criticized the parenting styles literature as unnecessarily blurring the distinction between dimensions of parenting associated with connectedness, behavioral regulation, and the promotion of psychological autonomy. This assertion is backed up by studies that have purposefully kept these three dimensions

8.2 The Dimensionality of Parenting Behaviors

separate in order to compare and contrast their relative influence (Garber, Robinson, & Valentiner, 1997; Hennan, Dornbusch, Herron, & Herting, 1997; Grotevant, 1997).

Barber (1997) argues that while connectedness is represented within the more general realm of responsiveness, this dimension also can be more specifically measured as warmth, nurturance, love, cohesion, support, and attachment. Behavioral regulation also is captured by the more general realm of demandingness, yet this dimension also can be more exactly quantified as monitoring, supervision, discipline strategies, and the like. Finally, Barber (1997) discusses the promotion of psychological autonomy as a sort of "lost" dimension that has received much less identifiable attention in the literature, even though concepts such as intrusiveness, enmeshment, and (over)protectiveness are embedded in the larger parenting styles literature.

Barber's (1996) own work in this area has focused largely on parent promotion of psychological autonomy, also conceptualized as parental psychological control. In the first of three studies reported in a single article, Barber (1996) used reports from a sample of fifth, eighth, and tenth grade students in order to generate evidence that parent psychological control (as measured through a parent's use of guilt, withdrawal of love, and "excessive pressure for change") could be differentiated from parent behavioral control (in this case, as measured by monitoring of the youth's activities). In the second study, observational techniques were employed with a sample of families containing adolescents (average age: 12 years) in order to make that same claim; however, this approach yielded more mixed results. Finally, in the third study the reports of adolescents (fifth and eighth graders at the initiation of the study) over a 2-year period provided some further evidence that discriminated between psychological and behavioral control efforts undertaken by parents.

Readers might pause here to consider the relative significance of the points being made. Clearly, Barber and colleagues are emphasizing the importance of the two classic dimensions of parenting that concern the giving of warmth (responsiveness) and the provision of structure (demandingness). In addition, however, these scholars are going to great lengths to specify the differences between the behavioral control aspect of demandingness and what they have termed psychological control. While their distinctness is argued here, one might also wonder about the degree to which the utilization of psychological control is dependent on the existence of behavioral control as well. Said another way, is psychological control actually an extension of behavioral control, such that they exist on a continuum of influence that parents attempt to exert on their adolescent sons and daughters?

Yet another controversial aspect of this literature surrounds concepts related to parental monitoring and parents' supervision of their adolescent's activities, topics that more recently have come under increased scrutiny by researchers interested in parenting behaviors. For many years, consistent evidence had built up in the literature that created the sense that adolescent development and well-being was integrally tied to how much information parents had about their location and activities (Hair, Moore, Garrett, Ling, & Cleveland, 2008). The lack of such information was thought to create serious and potentially dangerous situations for adolescents (Griffin, Botvin, Scheier, Diaz, & Miller, 2000; Kim, Hetherington, & Reiss, 1999; Paschall, Ringwalt, & Flewelling, 2003).

The work of Stattin and Kerr (2000), in particular, set the stage for the need to discriminate between parental *knowledge* of adolescent whereabouts/behaviors and the specific activities undertaken by parents to track their adolescent (deemed to be actual *monitoring*). In a study using the reports of 14-year-old adolescents and parents from Sweden, these researchers documented how greater parental knowledge was most closely related to adolescent disclosure in comparison to more active monitoring attempts on the part of parents (such as parents' direct solicitation of information). A similar study using the same sample (Kerr & Stattin, 2000) replicated and extended these findings with an enhanced set of adolescent adjustment variable indicators. In essence, these findings strongly suggest that the quality of the relationship between parents and their sons and daughters may play a substantial role in determining how much information parents can gather about their adolescents' whereabouts (Smetana, 2008; Soenens, Vansteenkiste, Luyckx, & Goossens, 2006).

Hence, while parenting behaviors associated with monitoring and supervising the whereabouts and activities of adolescents has associated repeatedly with more positive outcomes, it may very well be the case that the parents who are most effective in doing this sort of supervision are precisely those mothers and fathers who have higher quality relationships with their sons and daughters in general. To wit, some of these studies suggest that because parents largely are reliant on their adolescents to provide information about their activities, they will only be supplied with such information when their adolescents are agreeable. Hence, monitoring and supervision effectiveness may be a by-product of other dynamics within the parent–adolescent dyad.

8.3 The Cultural Relevance of Parenting Behaviors

Notably, there have been a number of studies that have examined the "cultural equivalence" of parenting behaviors, including the dimensions of connectedness, behavioral regulation, and the promotion of psychological autonomy/control. For instance, Bean, Bush, McKenry, and Wilson (2003) used reports from a high-school-aged sample of African American and White adolescents regarding the parenting behaviors of both their mothers and fathers. Both similarities and differences between the two racial groups on measures of support (as the connectedness measure), behavioral control, and psychological control were reported, and the disaggregation of reports on both mothers and fathers was highlighted as a contributing factor toward the researchers' abilities to specify these comparisons.

In a second study that examined cultural equivalency, Bean, Barber, and Crane (2006) examined the reports of fifth, eighth, and tenth grade African American students on the same three measures of parenting behaviors used in the previously reviewed study. Again disaggregating the behaviors of mothers and fathers, these researchers reported findings that underscore the relative similarity of African American and White parenting behaviors and their association with adolescent outcomes, especially with regard to both parents' behavioral control efforts and fathers' support displays. At the same time, however, the lack of impact that was displayed by mothers' support displays and both parents' psychological control efforts led the researchers to call for more racially diverse studies employing these types of variables.

These two studies serve as a solid segue into another controversy within the parenting literature surrounding the "most favored status" of the authoritative style of parenting across groups who differ in terms of race, ethnicity, and culture. Some scholars have paid attention to variation in parenting styles as a function of race and economic conditions in the USA, noting that a more authoritarian style might be more functional for minority families living in dangerous neighborhoods (Steinberg, Blatt-Eisengart, & Cauffman, 2006). In essence, this viewpoint argues that the magnified sense of control that parents exert over their sons and daughters serves as an important barrier to those adolescents becoming involved in a variety of risky and problematic behaviors.

Others have argued that nonwhite parents simply express the combination of high demandingness and high responsiveness in ways that are different than their white counterparts in this country (Arcia, Reyes-Blanes, & Vasquez-Montilla, 2000; Chao, 2001; Halgunseth, Ispa, & Rudy, 2006; Smetana, Metzger, & Campione-Barr, 2004). This argument has been extended to traditional cultures outside of the USA as well (Pomerantz & Wang, 2009; Zhang & Fuligni, 2006). Hence, questions about the generalizable nature of parenting styles and their association with markers of adolescent development and well-being remain unresolved at this time in terms of potential variations that are a function of race, ethnicity, and culture.

Further research using more diverse samples undoubtedly will generate additional information about these similarities and differences in overall parenting styles and behaviors. At the same time, however, a not insignificant portion of these studies tend to use oversimplified ways of assessing parenting-oriented variables in a manner that is similar to the items presented at the beginning of this chapter. More in-depth studies of what exactly constitutes parenting styles and behaviors undoubtedly will yield more precise information about the cultural relevance of this work. On a related note, researchers typically are not asking questions about parent behaviors that surround specific situations and issues, but rather are pulling for information about more general patterns of behavior. It may well be the case that the pursuit of information about how parents behave in more particular instances also will generate data that provides a more comprehensive comparison and contrast of parenting styles and behaviors across diverse samples.

8.4 Summary of Research on the Parent–Adolescent Dyad

Baumrind's (1978) original work on parenting styles has maintained a strong influence on the most recent research that focuses on dyadic relationships in families with adolescents. The vast majority of the studies conducted over the last 15 years underscore the linkage between health adolescent development and an authoritative style of parenting. Newer studies have extended this work in a number of important directions, including work that has examined potential differences between mothers and fathers in terms of their parenting styles, as well as exploring the impact that parenting style *consistency* has within the context of families with adolescents. As well, the very definitions of parenting styles have been expanded to include variables such as monitoring and knowledge, responsiveness, warmth, and psychological control. This in turn has led to increased attention being given to further elaborations within the research literature on the parent–adolescent dyad, including variations that may exist as a function of race, ethnicity, and culture.

Chapter 9
Polyadic Research on Families with Adolescents

> *In every conceivable manner, the family is the link to our past and bridge to our future.*
>
> Alex Haley

Abstract Research efforts that have focused attention on triadic and larger (polyadic) relationships in families with adolescents largely have focused on a core number of "compelling family processes." These family processes historically have been used to describe the reciprocal and mutually causal interactions that occur between and among family members over time. The present chapter reviews studies of these family processes over the past 15 years that have included constructs such as family differentiation, triangulation, parentification, family conflict, and family decision making activities. Particular attention is paid to the increased use of multiple family member perspectives in this type of research. The increased concentration on variation in family processes as a function of race, ethnicity, gender, age and other significant demographic variables is discussed as well. Finally, empirical efforts that have focused on the impact of siblings are highlighted, as these studies are thought to represent an important and innovative advancement in the study of families with adolescents.

PLEASE INDICATE HOW OFTEN YOUR FATHER SAYS OR DOES THE FOLLOWING THINGS TO YOU. KEEP IN MIND THERE ARE NO CORRECT ANSWERS. PLEASE CIRCLE THE BEST ANSWER.

Response choices

    1 2 3 4 5 6 7
    Never   Sometimes   Always

1. My father tells me I have not been a responsible family member.
    1 2 3 4 5 6 7
2. My father criticizes the way I run my life.
    1 2 3 4 5 6 7

3. My father tells me there are certain obligations I have to the family.
1 2 3 4 5 6 7
4. My father tells me I do things a member of our family shouldn't do.
1 2 3 4 5 6 7
5. My father tells me how I should use my time and energy.
1 2 3 4 5 6 7

PLEASE INDICATE HOW OFTEN YOUR MOTHER SAYS OR DOES THE FOLLOWING THINGS TO YOU. KEEP IN MIND THERE ARE NO CORRECT ANSWERS. PLEASE CIRCLE THE BEST ANSWER.

Response choices

1 2 3 4 5 6 7
Never   Sometimes   Always

1. My mother tells me I have not been a responsible family member.
1 2 3 4 5 6 7
2. My mother criticizes the way I run my life.
1 2 3 4 5 6 7
3. My mother tells me there are certain obligations I have to the family.
1 2 3 4 5 6 7
4. My mother tells me I do things a member of our family shouldn't do.
1 2 3 4 5 6 7
5. My mother tells me how I should use my time and energy.
1 2 3 4 5 6 7

In contrast to the previous chapter on research that focuses on the parent–adolescent dyad, the present chapter focuses on empirical efforts that have viewed the families of adolescents through a systems lens. The family system is comprised of many subsystems, one of which is the parent–adolescent dyad, of course. In the more systems-oriented approach to the family with adolescents, however, the emphasis decidedly is on either the family as a totality or as the combinatorial effects of various dyads within the family.

Examine for a moment the scale presented at the beginning of this chapter. These items come from an instrument known as the Family Intrusiveness Scale (FIS: Gavazzi, Reese, & Sabatelli, 1998). The FIS was designed to measure the ways in which family members monitor and adjust the amount of closeness or distance that they experience in relationship to one another, a task that has been associated with how well the overall family with adolescents is functioning as a system. Although originally worded and thus used to gather information about the family as a totality (Gavazzi & Sabatelli, 1990), these items also have been modified in order to capture data about the mother–adolescent and father–adolescent dyadic relationships more specifically (Cohen, Vasey, & Gavazzi, 2003).

It should be noted here that researchers can and will shift the wording of items in order to best reflect the unit of analysis they are most interested in studying. The metaphor of the microscope and its core parts might fit well here. To wit, readers might think of the movement among units of analysis as the revolving of the turret in order to exchange lenses of different power. Alternatively, one might see this best illustrated through the use of the side knobs on the microscope that adjust both coarse and fine grain focus.

Whether or not a given study focuses on the family with adolescents as a totality or as the combination of multiple dyads, the empirical effort exists within a larger literature that is dominated by research on what has been termed "*family processes.*" Day, Gavazzi, Miller, and Langeveld (2009) define family processes as "the dynamics of the relationships among the multiple family members and across boundaries to those outside the system" (p. 120). As such, these family processes are meant to capture the reciprocal and mutually causal interactions that occur between and among family members over time. And as the quote from Alex Haley at the beginning of this chapter implies, these interactions or processes are thought to generate important information both about a given family's past as well as that family's prospects for the future (Moore & Lipman, 2005).

General systems theory contains a teleological argument about systems, meaning that systems like families are seen as being comprised of goal-directed activity (von Bertalanffy, 1968). For instance, recall that the FIS discussed above was thought to tap into certain "tasks" associated with family functioning. Day, Gavazzi, and Acock (2001) extend this line of reasoning by asserting that family processes are those strategies used by families to accomplish certain goals and objectives that enhance outcomes for its members.

These scholars go on to identify certain "compelling family processes" in the research literature that were thought to form the backbone of empirical work in this domain. The term "compelling" was adopted by these authors to highlight the sense that some family constructs seemed to have achieved an enduring presence over the years. In essence, theorists and researchers seemed to have conceptualized family processes in very similar ways, even though very different terms and labels were applied to these family processes.

These compelling family processes are thought to include a number of core constructs and associated areas of research. For instance, there are family processes associated with distance regulation, an area of inquiry that includes such related concepts as family differentiation, boundary maintenance, expressed emotion, and triangulation. Also, family flexibility and other concepts thought to be associated with this construct such as adaptability, problem-solving, and coping strategies make up another area of compelling family processes. Even areas of parenting covered in the previous chapter that are related more to parenting dimensions such as supervision (monitoring and behavioral control), and caring (support, affection, acceptance, and companionship) are thought to have garnered a prominent place in the family processes literature.

It should be noted that some of the research studies within these related areas of inquiry also focus attention on issues related to family structure, which largely has to do with the marital status of parents and their biological relationships with youth in the household (for an excellent review of the foundational literature on this topic, see especially Wallerstein, 1991). For instance, many studies have been conducted that examine the impact of divorce on adolescent adjustment and well-being, generally reporting on its deleterious effects (Breivik & Olweus, 2006; Cherlin, Kiernan, & Chase-Lansdale, 1995; Krohn, Hall, & Lizotte, 2009; Wallerstein & Lewis, 2009). Other researchers have focused on the disruptive impact that stepfamily formation and membership has on adolescent outcomes (Koerner, Rankin, Kenyon, & Korn, 2004; Stoll, Arnaut, Fromme, & Felker-Thayer, 2005).

In essence, these studies rather uniformly have portrayed adolescents coming from two-parent households (and especially married biological parents) as having inherent advantages in comparison to adolescents who reside in single-parent-headed households. While these sorts of studies might seemingly support the notion that there is a dominant effect of family structure, many scholars insist that any distinction made between family processes and family structure is "somewhat artificial" (Peterson, 2005; Teachman, 2000). This sentiment is perhaps best expressed by the distinguished researcher Mavis Heatherington (2006), who wrote that "happy, well adjusted children can be found in diverse types of families ... it is family process rather than family structure that is critical to the well-being of children" (p. 232).

Thus, the contention here is that any type of disturbance to the family's structure (separation, divorce, remarriage, etc.) will only impact youth well-being in a negative way if core family processes are disrupted. Such disruptions can include marked declines in father involvement (Booth, Scott, & King, 2010; Carlson, 2006; King & Sobolewski, 2006; Mitchell, Booth, & King, 2009; Scott, Booth, King, & Johnson, 2007; Stewart, 2003), alterations in the mother–adolescent relationship (Arditti, 1999; Demo & Acock, 1996; Koerner, Jacobs, & Raymond, 2000; Langenkamp & Frisco, 2008), and/or increased marital conflict levels (Buehler et al. 1998; Gagne, Drapeau, Melancon, Saint-Jacques, & Lepine, 2007; Harold & Conger, 1997).

In turn, these disrupted family processes can be further aggravated by an overall increase in cumulative risks (Cavanagh, 2008; Matjasko, Grunden, & Ernst, 2007) in other areas of family life. Especially important in this regard are economic disadvantages (Manning & Lamb, 2003) that are either in place before family disruptions occur and/or are the direct or indirect result of the disruptions themselves. As well, new relationship issues brought on through parents' dating experiences and one or both of the parents' remarriages (Halpern-Meekin & Tach, 2008; King, 2006, 2009; Yuan, Vogt, & Hayley, 2006) also are thought to hold great potential to further exacerbate disruptive family processes.

As noted in the previous research chapter, Crosnoe and Cavanagh (2010) recently completed the *Journal of Marriage and the Family's* decade review of articles on families with children and adolescents. This appraisal of empirical efforts published in the first decade of the new century utilized two primary categories to organize this literature: family status and family process. Of great interest here is the emphasis that these scholars have placed on the field's movement away from attention paid to marital status per se and towards the number and types of transitions that youth are exposed to over time. Most simply stated, the evidence strongly suggests that, when more transitions occur, poor outcomes are more likely to occur (Cavanagh & Huston, 2008; Osborne & McLanahan, 2007; Wu & Thomson, 2001).

Additionally, Crosnoe and Cavanaugh (2010) also pointed out that there was sustained growth over the last 10 years in terms of the empirical attention that has been paid to a variety of family processes. Perhaps most notably, these scholars wrote that issues such as conflict in the family "both explain and condition the negative developmental risks of parental divorce" (p. 601) and other disruptions and transitions experienced within families. This underscores the need to understand the impact of all family-based changes in light of the amount of disruption that results to the inner workings of those families.

Unfortunately the Crosnoe and Cavanaugh (2010) review did not unpack significant trends in the family process literature beyond that of the parenting behavior studies. Nonetheless, there are some important and noteworthy developments that have occurred over the last 15 years. First and foremost, a significant portion of this work falls under the general heading of family distance regulation, although the specific constructs employed in these studies (family differentiation, triangulation, and parentification) cut across a number of topic areas. These are exactly the types of "compelling family processes" that Day and colleagues have discussed in their own reviews of empirical work in this conceptual arena (Day et al., 2001, 2009), and thus a select number of studies are reviewed in order to give the reader some idea of how this type of research is conducted.

Next, an increasing number of studies have employed multiple family member perspectives in their attempts to measure family-oriented phenomena, thus moving beyond the reliance on single reporter data collection methods that had dominated the field in earlier times. As well, some of these studies utilize variables related to race, ethnicity, gender, and age in order to elucidate how families with adolescents may display certain similarities and differences as a function of those more demographically oriented variables. Because excellent examples of studies that make such comparisons and contrasts among diverse samples can be found in empirical work focusing on family conflict and family problem-solving, studies reflecting these two areas of research are reviewed in some detail as well.

Finally, there has been increased interest in an examination of how certain family processes play out in the presence of siblings. One especially interesting line of research in this regard revolves around the degree to which adolescent brothers and sisters are treated similarly or dissimilarly by their parents. Other work seeks to understand the degree to which certain processes that are contained within one part of the family system – for instance, the parent–adolescent relationship – are replicated in other dyads such as the sibling–sibling relationship. Hence, a select number of studies that focus on sibling-oriented topics also are reviewed in the closing portion of this chapter, again to help readers gain some sense of the kind of empirical work that is being conducted in this area of inquiry.

9.1 Selected Studies Regarding Family Distance Regulation

As noted above, research on family processes has been dominated by studies that have focused on distance regulation concepts. One particularly well-developed area of inquiry within the family processes literature surrounds those empirical efforts that use the family differentiation construct. As discussed in the family systems theory chapter above, family differentiation is seen as the family system's ability to display tolerance for both intimacy (closeness and warmth) and individuality (respecting the uniqueness of each family member). Well differentiated families display greater levels of both intimacy and individuality tolerance, and are thought to create environments that lead to most well-adjusted adolescents. More poorly differentiated families have lower levels of intimacy and/or individuality tolerance, which have been associated with less functional outcomes for adolescent members.

While many earlier studies of the family differentiation construct relied solely on the adolescents' perspective, the use of multiple family member perspectives in the assessment of family differentiation levels was initiated by Bartle-Haring and Gavazzi (1996). Using a family systems theoretical approach to two samples of families with adolescents (ages 11–19) and families of college students (average age 19.8 years), these researchers demonstrated how mother, father, and adolescent perspectives on family differentiation levels converged onto a latent variable that represented the family system as a single unit (i.e., the family as the unit of analysis).

The findings from this particular study indicated that the perspectives of multiple family members could be combined in meaningful ways in order to better understand a family system property. This is different than simply talking about the amount of intimacy or individuality contained within a single dyad (i.e., the mother–adolescent or father–adolescent relationship). Instead, the researchers demonstrated that multiple family perspectives could be used to describe how the overall family system has tolerance levels for both intimacy and individuality experiences that emerge from the interactions that occur amongst family members.

Furthering this line of research, Bartle-Haring, Kenny, and Gavazzi (1999) used a Social Relations Model approach to analyze data from a sample of families with college students (average age 19.6 years). Similar to the previously reviewed study, this empirical work also generated evidence that supported the operationalization of differentiation as a family system variable through the combination of multiple family member perspectives. At the same time, however, the findings of this particular study underscored the importance of understanding variation in agreement about what was happening inside of the multiple dyads of these families. For instance, it was reported that family members tended to agree most with the reports of mothers and to agree least with the reports of fathers. These results point to the fact that, while whole systems properties exist within families, these family characteristics are still comprised of dyadic relationships that can differ to greater and lesser extents.

Yet another study conducted by Cohen et al. (2003) that was referenced above (in terms of employing the FIS) used a sample of families with college-age students (average age 18.6 years) to generate support for the bidimensional structure of family differentiation (as both individuality tolerance and intimacy tolerance). In addition, the findings of this study highlighted the predictive influence of higher individuality tolerance levels on reduced adolescent internalized distress (as trait anxiety, depression, and worry). This latter result underscored the fact that family system properties as measured through multiple member perspectives have a direct and immediately measurable impact on the individual well-being of adolescents.

Family differentiation levels have also been studied cross-culturally, although regrettably, using only adolescent perspectives to date. For instance, Chun and MacDermid (1997) used a sample of Korean adolescents (average age 15.7 years) in order to examine the associations among variables related to family differentiation and adolescent individuation and self-esteem. Interesting same sex pairings resulted, including the finding that father–adolescent differentiation levels were the strongest predictors of male adolescent individuation, whereas female adolescent individuation levels were most strongly related to mother–adolescent differentiation levels. Also, adolescent individuation levels (as measured by the amount of fusion versus psychological separateness that adolescents experienced in relation to parents) were negatively associated with self-esteem, the exact opposite of what is typically found in samples from the USA.

In a second study representing international diversity, Manzi, Vignoles, Regalia, and Scabini (2006) employed two samples of older adolescents (ages 17–21) from Italy and the UK in order to examine the relationships among variables related to family differentiation [operationalized here as the combination of family cohesion and enmeshment, building off of earlier work done with these concepts by Barber and Buehler (1996)] and a host of adolescent adjustment variables. These researchers reported both the usual and typical association between greater family cohesion and positive adolescent well-being found in American samples, as well as the somewhat unusual (by U.S. standards of research) findings regarding the lack of relationship between enmeshment and adolescent adjustment in the Italian sample.

Both the Chun and MacDermid (1997), and Manzi et al. (2006) studies underscore the importance of looking beyond the findings from empirical work conducted with families residing in the USA, especially if one is interested in examining the universal nature of family processes. In essence, the findings of these two studies indicate that the associations between family processes and adolescent outcomes reported from families residing in more collectivistic societies (or in the case of Italy, those societies that place a higher value on family togetherness) will not reflect what is thought to be "commonly held wisdom" about the nature of family interactions and their impact on adolescent well-being. This follows well with a now long-standing discussion of the relative balance of separateness and connectedness experiences in families (Fuhrman & Holmbeck, 1995; Matsumoto & Takeuchi, 1996).

Another distance regulation concept that has been employed in the study of families with adolescents is the triangulation concept, whereby third family members are pulled into the conflicts that erupt between two parties within the family (Kerr & Bowen, 1988). Often as not, this family process is associated with negative effects, especially with regard to the triangulated adolescent (Bell, Bell, & Nakata, 2001). For instance, Franck and Buehler (2007) used a sample of families with sixth grade students in order to examine the relationship between triangulation, marital hostility, and adolescent outcome variables associated with problematic behavior. These findings generated evidence regarding the deleterious effects on adolescents who become "caught in the middle" of parental conflict, especially with regard to the adolescent's increased susceptibility to internalizing problem behaviors.

Similar findings using only adolescent perspectives (ages 14–19) were reported by Grych, Raynor, and Fosco (2004). These researchers also noted some interesting results regarding sibling relationships and the particularly protective role of fathers. Contrary to stated expectations, those adolescents who reported greater closeness to siblings also reported of feeling more threatened by parental conflict. Second, while closeness with both parents generally predicted better adolescent adjustment, internalizing problems reported by adolescents were uniquely predicted by the amount of attachment experienced in relation to fathers. Subsequent studies conducted by this research team have reported similar results (Fosco & Grych, 2008), including longitudinal work that supports the notion of "spillover" occurring between marital conflict and parent–adolescent relationships over time (Fosco & Grych, 2010).

This same kind of "spillover" is recognizable in other studies of triangulation and adolescent well-being. For example, Baril, Crouter, and McHale (2007) used a sample of married parents and their adolescents (where outcomes were measured at 16 and 18 years of age) in order to examine associations among variables related to marital conflict, marital love, co-parenting conflict, and adolescent well-being. These researchers reported a significant association between greater co-parenting conflict reported by parents and more risky behaviors as reported by adolescents. In addition, greater marital love was reported to have a mediating effect on the relationship between these two variables over time. Interestingly, triangulation was not strongly associated with adolescent risky behavior, although problems in the detection of this systems construct were discussed as one possible explanation of this finding.

Another concept related to triangulation is that of "parentification." This construct is defined as the assumption of a parent role by the youth in order to provide such things as emotional support to a parent. Peris, Cummings, Goeke-Morey, and Emery (2008) employed the parentification construct in a longitudinal study informed by the family systems perspective that used a sample of 14–18-year-old adolescents and their parents. Here, parentification was found to be stable over a 1-year period, and was associated both with greater marital conflict and with poor outcomes for the adolescents in terms of internalizing and externalizing problem behaviors.

Overall, the triangulation literature (including parentification) points to the deleterious effects of overburdening adolescents with developmentally unsuitable obligations within the family. When the adolescent is "triangled" into interactions between parents, including when a parent seeks emotional support from a son or daughter, this seems to set in motion a process whereby the adolescent will suffer certain consequences. This will include greater amounts of their own conflict (presumably including especially the parent against whom the adolescent has been "sided"), as well as having a greater likelihood of experiencing psychological problems and risky behaviors.

9.2 Selected Studies Regarding Family Conflict and Family Problem-Solving

In other areas of empirical inquiry regarding family processes, conflict itself has emerged as an important topic of interest in studies of families with adolescents (Adams & Laursen, 2007; David, Steele, Forehand, & Armistead, 1996; Gerard, Buehler, Franck, & Anderson, 2005; Harold & Conger, 1997; Plunkett & Henry, 1999). For instance, a widely cited study conducted by Demo and Acock (1996) reported that the most powerful predictor of adolescent adjustment across all family types is the amount of disagreement that occurs between mothers and their teenage sons and daughters. In a related vein, Buehler et al. (1998) reported findings that underscore the salience of marital conflict, generating evidence that the amount of hostility present in the marital interactions and not the amount of disagreements per se was the best predictor of adolescent well-being.

Similar to what was described earlier in terms of "spillover" effects found in the triangulation literature, these findings have been part of a growing emphasis on examining the ways that conflict-oriented interaction patterns are replicated across different family subsystems (Cui, Donnellan, & Conger, 2007; Nelson, O'Brien, Blankson, Calkins, & Keane, 2009). For example, Van Doom, Branje, and Meeus (2007) reported that the ways in which parents handled their conflicts with one another were significantly related to how those parents and their adolescents (average age 13.2 years) resolved conflict. In a similar vein, Reuter and Conger (1995) employed a longitudinal observation study of parents and adolescents (over a 4-year period from the time the youth were 12–13 years of age) and reported that more disruptive and hostile family interaction styles were significantly related to less parent–adolescent agreement over time.

The results of these studies are supported by a variety of theoretical orientations, and as such there is an almost intuitive sensibility to these findings. For instance, the family systems literature would predict similarities between marital and parent–adolescent conflict based on the concept of isomorphism, whereby processes at one system level are theorized to replicate naturally on other system levels. Social learning theory, on the other hand, would posit that the conflict tactics displayed by the parents to each other would be incorporated through an imitation process into the parent–adolescent relationship.

Beyond these more inherent aspects of family conflict, there also is some evidence that disagreements and differences expressed by family members may vary as a function of race and ethnicity. For instance, Chung, Flook, and Fuligni (2009) used a daily diary method with a sample of Hispanic, Asian American, and white adolescents in order to conduct a longitudinal examination (in the ninth and twelfth grades) of the relationships between adolescent distress and both parent–adolescent and interparental conflict. White adolescents reported the most conflict and Asian American youth reported the least conflict, and female youth reported both more conflict and greater sensitivity to that conflict across time periods. Interestingly, the relationship between interparental conflict and adolescent distress was significantly greater in immigrant families, regardless of race/ethnicity.

Family problem-solving research has also been an area of inquiry, whereby the relative influence of race/ethnicity and other demographically oriented variables (such as gender and age) has been studied. In terms of race/ethnicity and the community context of family problem-solving activities, Lamborn, Dornbusch, and Steinberg (1996) conducted a longitudinal study using a sample of ninth, tenth, and eleventh grade adolescents from four race/ethnicity backgrounds (white non-Hispanic, Hispanic American, African American, and Asian American) who resided in either predominantly white or mixed ethnicity communities (as a proxy for residing in an advantaged versus disadvantaged neighborhood). As hypothesized, adolescents who came from families displaying more joint decision making activities fared better over time in comparison to those adolescents who exerted more unilateral control in decision making.

In this same study, interesting interactions occurred between the race and community context variables. For Hispanic youth, making more unilateral decisions had more deleterious effects when their families resided in a disadvantaged neighborhood, while for African American youth the exact opposite findings were reported. Type of neighborhood did not appear to matter for the white and Asian American youth, however.

Hence, the impact of race/ethnicity may only be fully realized in combination with certain neighborhood variables, and even then may be a function of the specific cultural backgrounds of different families.

In terms of the influence of gender, Jory et al. (1996) used a sample of 17-year-old adolescents and their parents in order to study family alliances during a problem-solving task. Male adolescents were much more active in seeking alliances than females, evidenced by sons reaching out to mothers twice as often as daughters. Also, while fathers were reported to be unaffected by the gender of their adolescent, mothers of daughters sought alliances with their husbands much less often than mothers of sons.

There also is some evidence suggesting that adolescent age might also play a role in the ways in which family problem solving processes are displayed. For example, Vuchinich, Angelelli, and Gatherum (1996) conducted a 2-year longitudinal study of family problem-solving using a sample of preadolescents (average age was 9.5 years at the beginning of the study) and their parents. These researchers reported that family problem-solving abilities decreased over time as the budding adolescents became more engaged in autonomy-related activities.

Now try to envision an empirical effort focused on family processes that, within a single study, also accounts for all of the demographic variables covered within this chapter: race/ethnicity background of the family, type of neighborhood in which the family resides, age of adolescent, and the gender combinations of parent and adolescent. Among other things, we quickly begin to understand how such an effort would demand a fairly large sample in order to control for all of the different permutations, a fact that has thwarted some family processes researchers in the past. Now add additional demographic factors such as family structure while beginning to imagine a study that simultaneously examines more multiple family processes. Most probably, readers can appreciate the tremendous potential for variability and interaction effects among these demographic variables and factors associated with different family processes, and will realize why most scholars believe that such research efforts are still in a relatively early stage of development.

9.3 Selected Studies Regarding the Influence of Siblings

In terms of the trends noted at the beginning of this chapter, all of the studies reviewed up to this point are noteworthy in terms of having employed a variety of constructs that measure distinct and meaningful family processes. Also, many of these empirical efforts are significant because they employ multiple perspectives within the family in order to tap into these family system characteristics, as well as presenting information about how demographic variables help to further elaborate similarities and differences in families with adolescents. At the same time, the last area of research to be covered in detail in this chapter – research on families containing adolescent siblings – is a newer area of family process research that has made remarkable inroads into combining many of the best aspects of what makes family process research so compelling.

In this regard, variation in parenting behaviors exhibited to adolescent siblings has emerged as one fundamentally important topic within this empirical area (O'Connor, Hetherington, & Reiss, 1998; Shanahan, McHale, Crouter, & Osgood, 2008). For instance, Feinberg and Hetherington (2001) used a sample of same-sex paired sibling adolescents (between the ages of 9 and 18 years) and their parents in order to examine the impact of "differential parenting," defined in this study as the parental display of different levels of warmth and negativity to their offspring. These researchers, who were employing a family systems framework, reported on the unique, if somewhat modest, contributions of the differential parenting construct regarding its impact on adolescent well-being after parenting behaviors themselves were taken into account. Here, greater differences in terms of how parents treated siblings corresponded to more negative outcomes for the less-well-treated adolescent, even after the level of poor treatment was taken into account.

Kan, McHale, and Crouter (2008) examined a similar construct labeled "interparental incongruence" in a longitudinal study of parents and their first-born and second-born adolescents (average ages were 17.3 and 14.8 years respectively at the sixth and final year of this study). These researchers measured youth perceptions of interparental incongruence in terms of the differing levels of intimacy and conflict that were shown to the adolescent offspring. The adolescent reports of interparental incongruence at the beginning of this study were predictive of parent reports of marital quality levels (measured as the levels of intimacy and conflict shown between the parents) a full 6 years later.

These two studies might require readers to pause and reflect a bit on the findings. The first study noted that differential treatment mattered in terms of the adjustment and well-being of adolescent siblings even after the overall quality of parenting was taken into account. In some sense, it is almost as if a sibling gains some advantage simply by being treated "better" than the other sibling. In the second study, the amount of differential treatment (labeled as incongruence) among siblings had an effect over time in terms of how the parents experienced their own relationship with one another.

What might be going on in terms of these effects? A study conducted by Kowal, Krull, and Kramer (2004) might provide some partial answers. These scholars also examined differential treatment among siblings in a study of parents and adolescents between the ages of 11 and 13 years and their siblings, who were 2–4 years older. Interestingly, findings indicated that it was not the amount of difference per se that was predictive of outcomes. Instead, what was critical was whether or not the amount of difference in treatment between the siblings was perceived to be unfair. This study is particularly informative because, in the employment of multiple family member perspectives, it was determined that perceptions about the legitimacy of relationship inequalities among siblings was a more important factor than the actual amount of similarity.

The literature, regarding the impact of differential treatment of siblings, has included studies that also have examined certain "spillover" effects. For instance, Updegraff, Thayer, Whiteman, Denning, and McHale (2005) used a sample of 185 older (average age of 15.9 years) and younger (average age of 13.5 years) adolescent siblings and their parents in order to examine the connection between the quality of parent–adolescent relationships and sibling relationship quality. These researchers found that lower amounts of intimacy and greater amounts of negativity and "relational aggression" between siblings – or those actions taken to harm one another's social relationships – were significantly related to lower levels of parental warmth and father (but not mother) involvement. As well, more parental direct intervention in sibling conflict led to greater amounts of relational aggression, especially for female siblings. Differences between older and younger siblings were noted as well, including the finding that only for younger siblings was there a significant association between greater perceived differences in parental treatment of each sibling and higher levels of relational aggression.

An attempt to replicate the Updegraff, Thayer et al. (2005) findings described in the previous paragraph was undertaken by Yu and Gamble (2008). These researchers employed a sample of 433 older (average age of 14.3 years) and younger (average age of 11.6 years) adolescent siblings and their mothers, and added a measure of more overtly aggressive behaviors between siblings with the focus on sibling relational aggression. While the significant relationship between greater family cohesion levels and lower adolescent overt and relational aggression displays paralleled the findings of the Updegraff, Thayer et al. study, Yu and Gamble (2008) did not find the same differences between siblings in terms of parental differential treatment and the aggression indicators.

One other empirical effort focused on sibling relationships that deserves mention here is a study conducted by Conger, Conger, and Scaramella (1997). These scholars sought to extend commonly reported results from the parenting style literature into a more systems-oriented approach that focused on family processes. While one of the main thrusts of this 3-year longitudinal study of adolescents (mean age of 13.2 years at the initiation of the study) involved parental psychological control, these researchers also focused on the psychological control exerted by *siblings*. Therefore, this empirical work captured information pertaining both to the parent–adolescent and the adolescent–sibling dyads. Interestingly, these researchers found evidence regarding a "cumulative effect" of sibling psychological control efforts when parent psychological control was already present. Further, there seemed to have been a more pronounced impact of the sibling psychological control efforts on males in comparison to females.

9.4 Summary of Polyadic Research

Research efforts focused on polyadic relationships in families with adolescents have paid attention to a variety of "compelling family processes" that have included constructs such as family differentiation, triangulation, parentification, family conflict, and family decision making activities. Of particular note is the rising interest in the gathering of multiple family member perspectives in this type of research, as well as the increased awareness of the field's need to account for variation in family processes as a function of race, ethnicity, gender, age, and other significant demographic variables. As well, the increased attention given to siblings and the degree to which parents treat them in a *congruent* manner represents an important and innovative advancement in this empirical area.

Chapter 10
The Family's Impact on Adolescent Outcomes

> *When I was a boy of fourteen, my father was so ignorant I could hardly stand to have the old man around. But when I got to be twenty-one, I was astonished by how much he'd learned in seven years.*
>
> Mark Twain, *Old Times on the Mississippi*

Abstract Research efforts focused on both the parent–adolescent dyad and polyadic relationships inside of families with adolescents invariably are linked to attempts to understand the impact of these family-oriented variables on adolescent outcomes. The present chapter reviews the empirical literature over the last 15 years that centers attention on the linkage between family factors and various aspects of adolescent outcomes, including adolescent delinquency, mental health issues, substance use and abuse, sexual activity, education, and socially competent behaviors. Many of these studies share some important similarities, including having generated substantial evidence concerning the critical role that parenting behaviors and family processes play in adolescent adjustment and well-being. Many of these studies also underscore the corresponding impact of peers and other social contexts beyond the family, as well as highlighting the importance of sibling relationships in families with adolescents. As well, the ways in which gender, race, ethnicity and culture influence the influence of parenting and family process variables also are discussed in many of the studies reviewed in this chapter.

Below are some questions about challenges that young people sometimes face. They may or may not apply to you. Think back on how things have been for you over past 6 months to answer the questions. Please answer the questions with these responses:

0	1	2
No/Never	Yes/A couple of times	Yes/A lot

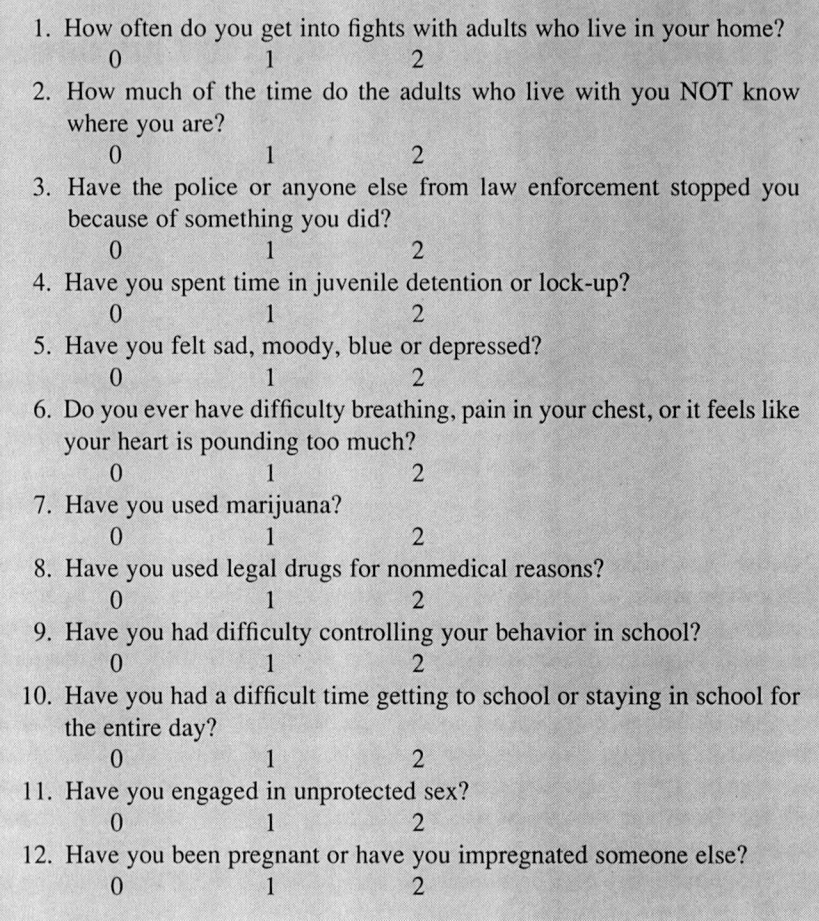

The Mark Twain quote above reflects a commonly held sentiment regarding the relationships between parents and their teenage sons and daughters. Despite overwhelming research evidence to the contrary, the general public continues to maintain the belief that these relationships almost necessarily are antagonistic by nature. For most parents with adolescents, however, this is not the norm. Although studies do indicate that there is more parent–adolescent disagreement than parent–child disagreement, these same studies indicate that, at least for most families, everyday life in no way is defined by conflict.

However, for some families this is clearly not the case. For a variety of reasons, life within these homes is more problematic. Larger amounts of conflict, problems in following rules, lack of consistent discipline, and other difficulties can and do arise in families with adolescents. In turn, the research evidence indicates that family environments characterized by these less functional family processes are significantly more likely to contain adolescents who are experiencing problems in terms of their own individual ability to function. In fact, studies often show that family factors are among the most important predictors of adolescent development and well-being.

The scale items displayed at the beginning of this chapter are from an instrument known as the Global Risk Assessment Device (GRAD: Gavazzi, Slade, et al., 2003). Originally developed for use with court-involved youth and their families, this scale more recently has been used with samples drawn from community based mental health clinics and child protective services, as well as in schools and other educationally based settings. The development of the GRAD has been built largely upon an ecological systems theoretical framework (see the discussion of this approach in the theoretical portion of this book above), which holds that a variety of individual and social context factors – including most importantly that of the family – shape the developmental pathways that can lead to either highly functional or problematic behavioral outcomes (Laub, 2002; Lochman, 2004).

Presently, the GRAD contains 11 factors that are thought to form a set of "global risks" that can significantly impact adolescent development and well-being. The scale items presented at the beginning of this chapter represent seven of these factors that are reflected in the empirical work that is reviewed here. This includes items that serve as examples of the family processes that have been used in past research examining the association between family and adolescent outcomes (items 1 and 2). As well, the outcomes-oriented variables themselves are represented through items that focus on delinquent behavior (items 3 and 4), mental health issues (items 5 and 6), substance use (items 7 and 8), educational risks (items 9 and 10), and risky sexual behaviors and consequences (items 11 and 12).

The review of research literature represented by these items will begin with studies that have examined the impact of family factors on delinquent behavior, one of the most salient outcomes within a syndrome of difficulties often categorized as "externalizing problem behaviors." These problems are external because they are directed outward toward others (aggression, criminal activity, etc.) often as not described as "acting out" behaviors. Next, associations between family processes and mental health issues are covered, expanding the review to include literature that focuses on a second syndrome of issues that typically are labeled "internalizing problem behaviors." These additional problems (depression, anxiety, etc.) are internal because they are experienced within the individual adolescent. This is followed by research that links family factors and substance use, an adolescent outcome that has been characterized as a blend of internalizing and externalizing difficulties (Steinberg, 2007). The literature review then moves to studies that have examined the impact of family processes on adolescent outcomes related to sexual activity, as well as education and other school-oriented factors. Finally, in order to provide an entry point into a more strength-based perspective, studies that have linked family factors to adolescent social competence are covered.

Readers will recall that a number of trends already have been articulated for studies of parental behaviors and family processes. Many of these trends remain relevant to the literature regarding the family's impact on adolescent outcomes. Hence, readers will notice that empirical work focusing on how parenting behaviors impact adolescent development and well-being will see examples of studies that pay attention to the developmental appropriateness of the parenting behaviors, make distinctions between those parenting behaviors and what occurs in parent–adolescent relationships, give greater visibility of to fathers as well as mothers, and attend to issues of diversity. Likewise, the empirical work focusing on the relationship between family processes and adolescent outcomes will reflect a great deal of attention paid to distance regulation concepts and other "compelling family processes," will include studies that have employed multiple family member perspectives and have attended to the impact of demographic variables like race, ethnicity, gender, and age, and will include examples of scholarly work that examine how family processes play out in the presence of siblings.

10.1 The Impact of Families on Delinquency and Conduct Disorders

The impact of parenting variables continues to dominate the literature concerning adolescent delinquency and conduct disorders (Crosswhite & Kerpelman, 2009a). As would be expected from the review of the literature covered in the research on the parent–adolescent dyad chapter, the relative effectiveness of different parenting behaviors would be significantly associated with the likelihood of an adolescent engaging in delinquent activities and other forms of externalizing problem behaviors.

One example of this approach is that of Simons, Chao, Conger, and Elder (2001), who examined the impact of parenting on adolescent self-reported delinquent behaviors in a longitudinal study of parents and their adolescents (seventh graders at the initiation of this study). The strongest associations between family factors and delinquent behavior were reported with more "inept" parenting behaviors, defined in this study as low monitoring, harsh and inconsistent discipline, and less use of inductive reasoning (these variables were discerned from the aggregated reports of parents, children, and observer ratings). However, results were also reported indicating that more functional parenting over time did serve to reduce antisocial behavior, albeit indirectly through the reduction of adolescent association with delinquent peers.

Using a combined social learning and ecological approach, Deković, Janssens, and Nicole (2003) examined a variety of parenting, marital, family, and demographic indicators in a sample of parents and three age groups of adolescents (12–13, 14–15, and 16–18 years). These researchers found that more positive parenting behaviors (more responsiveness, more involvement, less punishment, more monitoring, and greater consistency) and a more positive parent–adolescent relationship (greater attachment and less rejection and conflict) were strongly associated with less self-reported adolescent delinquent acts across these age groups. In fact, once these more "proximal" variables regarding the parent–adolescent relationship were taken into account, the impact of more "distal" factors (parent characteristics that included depression and perceived competence in parenting) and "contextual" factors (family cohesion and parent marital satisfaction) were eliminated.

There also has been sustained interest in the role that siblings play in the development of delinquent and antisocial behavior. Snyder, Bank, and Burraston (2005) conducted a 10-year longitudinal study using a social learning approach with parents, older brothers (average age 19.5 years at the end of the study) and their younger siblings (average age 16.3 years at the end of the study). Interestingly, the impact of more ineffective parenting (defined here as lack of supervision and greater parental conflict) was only related indirectly (through the older siblings' greater exposure to delinquent peers) to a set of poor adjustment indicators after various sibling variables were taken into account. Here, both greater sibling conflict and more sibling co-participation in deviant behaviors were reported to have been the main predictors of increases in the younger siblings' delinquent behavior.

Another example of sibling-focused research is that of Slomkowski, Rende, Conger, Simons, and Conger (2001), who included both brother–brother and sister–sister pairs in their 4-year longitudinal study of adolescent (ages 11–15 years at the outset of the study) delinquent behavior. Similar results were found for both brother and sister sibling pairs, such that greater older sibling delinquent behavior and more hostile and coercive sibling relationships predicted greater younger sibling delinquent behavior over time. These researchers also reported a unique finding for brothers only, whereby higher degrees of warmth and closeness were associated with greater delinquency. This latter finding was discussed in terms of the male siblings having a greater propensity to develop a "partners in crime" relationship with one another, reflecting the social learning approach adopted by the researchers.

Some other important gender-related differences have been noted in the literature connecting family factors with delinquent behavior. Emphasizing the coercion component of social learning theory, Cashwell and Vacc (1996) examined associations between family level variables and delinquent behavior as reported in a sample of sixth- through eighth-grade adolescents. These researchers reported that lower family cohesion was strongly associated with greater self-reported delinquent behavior for males only. As well, gender differences on this family adaptability indicator were reported, such that family cohesion was negatively related to delinquent behavior for females but was positively related to delinquency for males.

In addition to examining delinquency in general samples of adolescents, researchers also have employed samples of youth who have come to the attention of the juvenile court. Adopting an ecological family systems approach, Gavazzi (2006) used a sample of court-involved adolescents (average age 14.9 years) to examine the impact that "disrupted family processes" (more conflict, lack of monitoring, and inconsistent discipline) had on self-reported delinquent behavior. Results indicated a significant gender X race interaction, such that females in general and African American girls in particular reported the strongest associations between greater amounts of disrupted family processes and higher levels of delinquency. Family factors also seemed to play a pivotal role in determining the amount of prior offenses the adolescents in this sample had reported. While the males in the low family risk group engaged in more previous delinquent activities than the females, this was not the case in the high risk family group; it was almost as if the greater family risks allowed females to "catch up" to their male counterparts.

In sum, a range of poor parenting behaviors and less functional family processes have been shown to have significant associations with adolescent delinquent behavior. Interesting nuances to this work include findings that noted the intermediary influences of delinquent peer associations, the relative impact of proximal versus distal factors, the importance (and sometimes primacy effect) of sibling relationships, and the ways in which gender and race may interact around family process issues in samples of court-involved adolescents.

10.2 The Impact of Families on Adolescent Mental Health

The literature has outlined a variety of ways that family factors are associated with the mental health of adolescents (Schock-Giordano & Gavazzi, 2010). From an intergenerational perspective, parent mental health issues leave adolescents more vulnerable to suffering from psychological distress themselves (Ohannessian & Hesselbrock, 2005, 2008). As well, studies have indicated that family problems are associated with a longitudinal increase in mental health difficulties, while high quality relationships between parents and adolescents appear to function as a protective factor against the development of these mental health issues for both male and female adolescents.

Hence, family factors have been characterized as retaining both protective and risk factors in terms of mental health issues for adolescents, and especially adolescent depressive symptoms. For example, Slesnick and Waldron (1997) used a sample of depressed and nondepressed adolescents (average age 15.1 years) and their parents in a study of the association between family problem-solving and adolescent depression. Using videotaped interactions between parents and adolescents, these researchers reported that parents of depressed adolescents engaged ingreater amounts of incongruent communication than parents of nondepressed adolescents. These findings led the researchers to conclude that depressive symptoms may be an adaptive response to confusing parent behavior.

In another study employing family process variables, Herman, Ostrander, and Tucker (2007) used a sample of adolescents (ages 12–17 years) to examine the associations among variables related to family cohesion, family conflict, and adolescent depression. These researchers reported a significant interaction between adolescent race and family factors, such that African American adolescent depression was related to low family cohesion levels, while white adolescent depression was associated with high family conflict. These researchers note that the primacy of family cohesion in the lives of African American youth has been reported by others (cf., Sagrestano, Paikoff, Holmbeck, & Fendrich, 2003), whereas "reducing family conflict may be the critical leverage point in alleviating child depressive symptoms" (p. 329) for White youth.

Other researchers have sought to understand the relative influences of family structure and family processes on adolescent mental health. For instance, McKeown et al. (1997) used the reports of adolescents (seventh through ninth grades at the initiation of the study) to examine the longitudinal impact of both family structure and family processes on adolescent depression. Both the initial family cohesion levels and the changes in family cohesion 1 year later were significantly associated with adolescent depressive symptoms, whereas family structure (as the condition of living with both biological parents or not) displayed no such relationship. Race/ethnicity and gender variation also was reported, including the finding that African American females reported the lowest amounts of family cohesion and white females reported the highest cohesion levels.

Parenting behaviors also have been a focal point in this area of inquiry. For instance, a study conducted by O'Donnell, Moreau, Cardemil, and Pollastri (2010) examined the relationship between interparental conflict, parenting behaviors, and depression over time in a sample of fifth and sixth grade adolescents (average age of 10.7 years). At the outset of the study, greater amounts of both interparental conflict and poor parenting behaviors (including measures of rejection and lenient behavioral control) were associated with adolescent depressive symptoms. Using the longitudinal data, the parenting behaviors were shown to play a mediating role in terms of the relationship between interparental conflict and depression.

Other researchers have taken a more global view of adolescent mental health through an examination of both internalizing (depression, anxiety, and other emotional disorders that are experienced "inside" the adolescent) and externalizing (aggression, conduct disorders, and other psychological concerns that are "acted out" on others) problem behaviors. Forehand, Biggar, and Kotchick (1998) conducted a 6-year longitudinal study that examined the linkage between family risk factors and internalizing and externalizing difficulties in a sample of adolescents (ages 11–15 at the start of the study). This study found significant associations between family risks (more interparental conflict, lack of two parents in the home, greater parent–adolescent relationship problems, and more parent physical and mental health problems as reported by mothers) and both types of adolescent mental health concerns, such that increased numbers of these family risk factors predicted greater amounts of both short-term and long-term adolescent problem behaviors.

In general, studies tend to support the observation that females are more likely to display internalizing behaviors, while males are more likely to display externalizing behaviors. For instance, Storvoll, Wichstrom, and Pape (2003) noted that conduct problems were reported at higher levels by males, whereas suicidal behavior, symptoms of depression, and symptoms of anxiety all were reported more frequently by females. Further, Bosco, Renk, Dinger, Epstein, and Phares (2003) found a complex interaction between the gender of the parent and the gender of the youth with regard to the display of internalizing and externalizing behaviors. These researchers reported that higher levels of paternal depression and anxiety and lower levels of maternal controlled to greater internalizing problems being reported by female youth, whereas greater levels of externalizing problems reported by male youth were related to negative feelings about their mothers and lower maternal acceptance.

In another study examining both internalizing and externalizing problems, Gavazzi, Bostic, Lim, and Yarcheck (2008) used an ecological systems approach to examine the influence of adolescent gender and race on the association between disrupted family processes (more conflict, lack of monitoring, inconsistent discipline) and adolescent mental health concerns in a sample of court-involved adolescents (average age 15.2 years). Among other results, this study generated evidence that disrupted family processes mediated the impact of gender on both internalizing and externalizing problems for African American adolescents (but not the white adolescents). This is a striking contrast to the long-held notion that girls are more likely to display internalizing problems and boys are more likely to externalize their mental health issues. These researchers noted some consistency of findings when compared to other studies examining the impact that family factors have on internalizing and externalizing problem behaviors among African American youth (cf., Griffin, Botvin, Scheier, Diaz, & Miller, 2000); however, the lack of similar findings for the White youth prompted the authors to call into question the possibility that race was serving as a proxy for socioeconomic status, something that was not controlled for in this study. In other words, questions were raised about the degree to which these findings were a reflection of race/ethnicity differences or instead were a manifestation of differing family economic circumstances.

Still another set of studies has sought to examine the combined impact of both family and friends on adolescent mental health concerns. Deković, Buist, and Reitz (2004) conducted a 3-year longitudinal study of adolescent (average age 13.4 years) reports of both family and peer relationships and adolescent internalizing and externalizing problems using both a social learning and ecological approach. Parent–adolescent relationship quality (measured as greater communication quality, greater trust, and less alienation) was associated with both dimensions of adolescent mental health, whereas friendship relationship quality (also measured as greater communication quality, greater trust, and less alienation) was associated only with internalizing problems.

Within an attachment theory framework, Rubin et al. (2004) examined the associations between family, peer, and adolescent mental health variables in a sample of adolescents (average age 10.3 years), their mothers, and their best friends. More positive family (as adolescents' perceptions of greater maternal and paternal support) and more positive peer (as greater friendship quality) factors were associated with less internalizing problems. In contract, less externalizing difficulties were related only to greater maternal and paternal support. As well, a significant three-way interaction was reported for gender, friendship quality, and maternal support (but not paternal support) on the internalizing variables. For females in low or average quality friendships, greater internalizing was associated with lower maternal support, whereas only those boys in low quality relationships displayed a significant relationship between low maternal support and internalizing problems.

In sum, quite a number of family processes – including family cohesion, conflict, and communication – all have been shown to have significant associations with adolescent mental health issues and, in at least one of the studies reviewed here, the primacy of family process over family structural issues was noted. Quite a number of studies attended to the role that gender played in both internalizing and externalizing problem behaviors among adolescents. Further, the impact of race also was well attended to, including its role as a mediating variable between gender and family factors. Finally, the examination of friendship variables alongside family factors helped to further describe the presence and type of adolescent mental health issues.

10.3 The Impact of Families on Adolescent Substance Use

The family environment also is a known predictor of adolescent use of alcohol and other substances (Scheer, Borden, & Donnermeyer, 2000). Similar to mental health issues, there is an intergenerational nature to substance use, whereby parent abuse of substances increases the likelihood of adolescent difficulties (Ohannessian & Hesselbrock, 2008). Studies of family involvement across the developmental stages of substance use (initiation, escalation, maintenance, discontinuation, and renewal) have revealed that youth who experience higher quality relationships with their parents were less likely to escalate their substance use (Urberg, Goldstein, & Toro, 2005). In turn, a variety of less functional family processes also were predictive of alcohol, marijuana, and tobacco use in other studies (Vakalahi, 2002).

Clearly, family factors also can serve as both risk factors and protective elements regarding adolescent substance abuse. Brody and Ge (2001) examined the associations between parenting behaviors and adolescent (ages 11–12 years) alcohol use in a three-wave longitudinal study. Interestingly, these researchers noted that the significant association between more positive parenting (as both greater "nurturant-responsive" and less "harsh-conflicted" reports of parent behaviors by mothers, fathers, and adolescents) and less adolescent alcohol use was mediated by adolescent self-regulation, supporting the notion that parents best shield their adolescents from substance use by teaching them how to control their own behavior.

Other studies have examined the impact of parenting behaviors and parent–adolescent relationship qualities on adolescent substance use. Using a more general family socialization conceptual framework, Barnes, Reifman, Farrell, and Dintcheff (2000) conducted a six-wave longitudinal study regarding the influences of the family on the alcohol use of adolescents (average age 14.5 years at the initiation of the study). Results using adolescent reports indicated that greater parent monitoring and more support were associated both with less initial adolescent involvement with alcohol as well as predicting lower rates of misuse over time. Using both a social learning and social control theory approach, Dorius, Bahr, Hoffmann, and Harmon (2004) examined adolescent marijuana use through the reports of adolescents between the ages of 12–19 years. One interesting nuance within this study involved making the distinction between adolescent closeness to each parent, leading to the finding that greater closeness to fathers, but not mothers attenuated the relationship between more peer involvement with drugs and greater adolescent marijuana use.

As in other studies of adolescent outcomes reviewed above, there also has been increased interest in the combined impact of family and peer factors. Barnes, Hoffman, Welte, Farrell, and Dintcheff (2006) extended their earlier effort discussed in the previous paragraph by examining the impact of peer characteristics on adolescent alcohol use as well as other substances. While greater amounts of peer deviance (measured as the youth's reports of their friends' involvement in delinquent behaviors) were reported to be significantly associated with greater adolescent misuse of alcohol and other drugs, parental monitoring also was reported to have an important role in buffering these peer influences.

Studies also have sought to examine the impact of both family structure and family process variables on adolescent smoking and drinking behaviors. For instance, a study conducted by Brown and Rinelli (in press) used a social learning approach with a sample of adolescents (average age of 15.3 years) and their parents. Findings indicated that adolescents living with both biological parents were using the least amount of substances and adolescents residing with adults who were cohabiting were displaying the most substance use. Adolescents residing in single-parent-headed and stepfamily households displayed substance use rates in between these two other groups. However, the higher risk levels in part were associated with lower levels of maternal support and behavioral control, higher levels of maternal substance use (smoking and drinking), and greater economic disadvantage, thus pointing to the complex interplay of family structure and family processes.

There is also evidence suggesting that family protective factors may have less influence in higher risk social contexts. Using an ecological perspective, Cleveland, Feinberg, and Greenberg (2010) employed a sample of adolescents in the sixth, eighth, tenth, and twelfth grades from over 300 larger and smaller schools located in urban, suburban, and rural communities. Well-established factors such as greater parental supervision and more consistent discipline strategies were significantly associated with lower substance use overall, especially for adolescents in the upper grades. However, the impact of these family protective factors were more pronounced for those adolescents who were attending schools that were deemed to be more protective as compared to adolescents who were attending school in a more high-risk environment.

Another important line of research that has its parallel in other outcomes-based studies discussed above involves the effects of siblings. Rende, Slomkowski, Lloyd-Richardson, and Niaura (2005) employed a "social contagion" approach (conceptually similar to social learning theory) to the study of sibling effects on adolescent (seventh through 12th graders) smoking and drinking behaviors. The results of this study presented a strong argument that shared environment factors (including sibling contact and mutual friendships) were much stronger influences than genetic factors regarding adolescent substance use. Here, greater amounts of contact with substance-using siblings and their friends were more strongly associated with increased adolescent substance use than genetic relatedness.

In another sibling-focused empirical effort, East and Khoo (2005) conducted a 5-year longitudinal study of Latino and African American adolescents (average age of 13.8 years), their older sisters (average age of 17.0 years) and their mothers. Couched within a social learning perspective, findings were reported indicating that greater warmth/closeness in the sibling relationship and older sister's greater drug and alcohol use predicted higher levels of younger sibling drug and alcohol use in the full sample of male and female younger siblings. In addition, sibling warmth/closeness mediated the impact of family structure (single versus married mothers) on adolescent substance use (where siblings with single mothers displayed greater warmth and closeness), while mothers' monitoring behaviors were unrelated to this adolescent outcome variable.

In sum, the parallel influences of family and friends are probably most well-documented in the literature on adolescent substance use. And for good reason: family characteristics (including of course parenting behaviors) and peer relationships both play a substantial role in predicting adolescent use and misuse of alcohol, tobacco, and other drugs. Additionally, the role of siblings more specifically as part of a "contagion" effect on adolescent substance use also is highlighted in several studies.

10.4 The Impact of Families on Adolescent Sexual Activity

Parental and family factors have been linked to a variety of indicators of adolescent sexual activity (Miller, Norton, Fan, & Christopherson, 1998), and excellent reviews of this area of inquiry are available (see especially Meschke, Bartholomae, & Zentall, 2000). Similar to many of the other studies on adolescent outcomes discussed in this chapter, this empirical work tends to examine parenting behaviors such as behavioral control, monitoring/supervision/knowledge, warmth, and support, as well as parent–adolescent communication and other more family system-oriented variables.

One main component of the research regarding the impact of families on adolescent sexual activity concerns the timing or initiation of sexual activity. For example, Longmore, Manning, and Giordano (2001) used a sample of adolescents (average age of 14.8 years) to conduct a longitudinal study of dating and sexual initiation. Unexpectedly, results of the adolescent reports indicated that timing of the first date was not at all influenced by any of the parenting behaviors measured in this study, nor by family structure or family economic circumstances. In turn, monitoring was the only parenting behavior that predicted first sexual intercourse over time (whereas parental support and coercive control were not).

Other studies have found a more pronounced effect of parenting and family factors. For example, a study conducted by Regnerus and Luchies (2006) used the reports of adolescents between the ages of 15 and 19 (average age of 15.9 years) who lived with both biological parents, of particular interest because adolescents residing in these "intact" households typically are older in terms of their first sexual experiences. Results indicated that a closer relationship between female adolescents and their fathers (but not their mothers) was significantly related to first sexual experience. Closeness with either parent was not associated with sexual debut for the male adolescents in this study.

Ream and Savin-Williams (2005) employed a sample of adolescents (average age of 14.5 years) in a study of the associations between the initiation of sexual activity and the quality of mother–adolescent and father–adolescent interactions. Some well-established findings were replicated in this study, including results indicating that adolescent reports of lower amounts of closeness and shared activities and greater amounts of problem-focused interactions in parent–adolescent relationships significantly predicted earlier sexual experiences. However, evidence of a reciprocal effect also was generated in this study, in that the first sexual experience also significantly predicted subsequent increases in problem-focused interactions between parents and adolescents. Reciprocal effects regarding closeness also was found for mother–daughter and father–son dyads, as well as reciprocal efforts regarding shared activities for mother–son and father–daughter dyads.

Two studies by Roche and colleagues extended the influence of parenting and family factors in order to take into account the influence of neighborhoods. The reports of adolescents in the seventh through twelfth grades in a study conducted by Roche et al. (2005) indicated that greater parental involvement was significantly related to greater likelihood of first sexual intercourse only for adolescents living in higher socioeconomic neighborhoods. As well, parent decision-making control was significantly associated with a lower likelihood of sexual initiation for adolescents residing in lower socioeconomic neighborhoods but a higher likelihood for adolescents residing in higher socioeconomic neighborhoods. These findings were largely replicated in a second sample of adolescents between the ages of 10 and 14 and their mothers (Roche & Leventhal, 2009), along with evidence that the magnitude of relationship between lower likelihood of sexual initiation and both greater amounts of family routines and parental monitoring/knowledge was greater for those adolescents residing in lower socioeconomic neighborhoods.

Another component of the research on families and adolescent sexual activity concerns unsafe sexual practices, pregnancy, and teen parenthood. For example, Frisco (2005) employed a sample of adolescents in their first year post-high school who were unmarried and sexually active in order to examine the associations among parental behaviors and adolescent contraceptive use. Results indicated that parent involvement with their adolescent on issues surrounding education significantly increased the likelihood of contraception use in general, as well as more specifically increasing the likelihood of the adolescent using oral contraceptives and condoms.

Two recent studies conducted by Khurana and colleagues using an ecological systems perspective shed light on the connection between family factors and teen parenthood in samples of male and female adolescents coming into contact with the juvenile court. In a first sample of court-involved female adolescents between 11 and 18 years (average age of 15.0 years), those females who reported at least one pregnancy also reported greater disrupted family processes in addition to higher levels of many other risk factors (Khurana, Cooksey, & Gavazzi, in press). A second sample of court-involved male adolescents between the ages of 11 and 19 (average age of 14.9 years) indicated that having fathered a child was not at all related to disruptive family processes, but rather only to greater exposure to trauma and higher amounts of prior offenses (Khurana & Gavazzi, 2010).

Siblings also are thought to play an important role in adolescent sexual activity (East, 1996). For instance, Widmer (1997) used interview data from a sample of adolescents (average age of 15.1 years) their older siblings (average age of 17.3 years) and their parents. Results indicated that parent variables related to attitudes about sexuality were the most important predictors of the timing of the younger sibling's first sexual intercourse. However, older siblings, and especially older brothers, do have a significant influence on both the timing of sexual debut and on the use (or nonuse) of contraceptives.

In another sibling-focused study, Kowal and Blinn-Pike (2004) employed a sample of adolescents (average age of 17.7 years) in order to examine the role that siblings and parents can play with regard to discussions about safe sexual practices. These researchers reported that the combination of having conversations with parents and siblings provided a context for developing less risky attitudes about sexual behaviors and a greater likelihood of being able to communicate with potential sex partners about the need to use contraception.

In sum, parenting behaviors and family processes seem to play a complex role in issues related to adolescent sexual activity. In some studies there seems to be little if any impact at all, while in other studies the impact of parent–adolescent and sibling–sibling relationships seem paramount. There also is evidence that gender can play an important role in further delineating these associations, and the role of neighborhood context also has been shown to have a determinative effect.

10.5 The Impact of Families on Adolescent Educational Issues

A growing number of studies have documented the impact of parental and family factors on a variety of adolescent educational issues. As with studies conducted on other adolescent outcomes, this is an area of inquiry that emphasizes the relative impact of both functional and less functional family processes. In turn, this literature also reflects both competent and problematic behaviors in school in addition to variables associated with academic abilities and actual performance (Vazsonyi & Flannery, 1997).

As with many other areas of inquiry, there is a pronounced focus on the impact of parenting behaviors. For example, Melby and Conger (1996) used a social learning approach in order to conduct a four-wave longitudinal study to examine the associations between mothers' and fathers' parenting behaviors and adolescent (average age 12.6 years at the initiation of the study) academic performance. The findings of this study indicated that mother and father parenting behaviors (as greater involvement and less hostility as reported by mothers, fathers, adolescents, and trained observers) were associated both with earlier grade point average and with more positive changes in this academic performance indicator over time.

Amato and Fowler (2002) used a two-wave longitudinal design to consider the connection between parenting behaviors (as support, monitoring, and use of harsh discipline) and adolescent (12–18 years of age at the initiation of the study) school success. These researchers reported significant associations between both greater parent support and less harsh discipline in terms of greater adolescent school success, but no such relationship regarding the parental monitoring variable in the overall sample. These results did not vary as a function of race (white versus African American), but differences in family structure were detected in that parent monitoring did seem to matter more in single-parent-headed households.

Spera (2005) used a sample of adolescents (fifth through eighth grade students) to expand upon Darling and Steinberg's (1993) "contextual model" in a study of the relationship among parenting practices, parenting styles, and school achievement. Results indicated that adolescent reports of parent educational aspirations were related to parent involvement in school-related issues, which in turn was related to adolescent educational outcomes (defined here as interest in school, self-regulating academic behaviors, and pursuit of educational goals). Some interesting race and gender differences also were noted. African American adolescents reported the highest parental aspirations in comparison to white and Hispanic adolescents, and females reported greater parental aspirations in comparison to males.

Other studies have contained results indicating academic differences related to family structure alone. For example, Frisco, Muller, and Frank (2007) examined the impact of family structure changes (in terms of parental marital dissolution) on academic performance over time using a sample of parents and adolescents who were in the ninth through eleventh grades at the initiation of the study. Across a 1-year time period, significant declines in grades were displayed by those adolescents whose parents had reported the dissolution of their marriage during that time period. Although these researchers demonstrated that these results were consistent across two different types of propensity matching strategies (which can reduce the bias inherent to this type of research), there was no corresponding set of variables that could be used to examine the degree to which these results were linked to disrupted family processes.

In comparison, Demo and Acock (1996) conducted a longitudinal study of family structure and variables related to both parent–adolescent and interparental factors in a sample containing reports of adolescents (ages 12–18) and their mothers. These researchers reported that adolescents residing with never-divorced parents fared best in terms of mother reports of academic performance. However, less mother–adolescent disagreement itself was the strongest overall predictor of better grades, pointing to the complex interplay of family structure and family processes that has been noted in many other studies reviewed throughout this book.

Conflict within the parent–adolescent relationship also has been linked to academic performance. Dotterer, Hoffman, Crouter, and McHale (2008) reported on findings from a 2-year longitudinal study of adolescents (average age 14.9 years) and their mothers and fathers undertaken within an ecological approach. A number of interesting bidirectional associations were discussed, including how greater parent–adolescent conflict as reported by both parents predicted lower grades (from student report cards) at the end of the study, as well as how lower grades in math at the onset of the study predicted greater parent–adolescent conflict 2 years later.

A study conducted by Ghazarian and Buehler (2010) to test a risk and resiliency model used a sample of adolescents (average age of 11.9 years) in order to examine the impact of interparental conflict and parenting behaviors on adolescent academic performance. These researchers reported that, as expected, higher levels of interparental conflict were significantly associated with lower grades. In addition, adolescent self-blame significantly mediated this relationship, and greater amounts of maternal acceptance and monitoring behaviors were reported to have buffered the relationship between the self-blame variable and interparental conflict.

Other studies have generated more detailed information about the subject matter of these disagreements and whether or not potential gender differences exist. For example, Allison and Schultz (2004) compared the reports of adolescents (sixth through eighth graders) regarding the amounts and types of conflict they experienced with their parents. Homework and school performance were among the most frequent domains of conflict endorsed by adolescents. These researchers reported that these topic areas were especially important in parent–son relationships. Also, while the amount of conflict was a frequent occurrence as reported by the adolescents, the intensity level of these parent–adolescent disagreements was relatively moderate.

Possible linkages between family factors and relationships outside of the home also have been highlighted within this area of inquiry. Using a life course theoretical perspective, Crosnoe and Elder (2004) conducted a longitudinal study of adolescents (average age 16.0 years at the initiation of the study) and their parents. Results indicated that greater parent–adolescent emotional distance as reported by parents was associated with more academic difficulties (being held back, suspended/expelled, skipping classes, homework trouble, and low grades). Although variables related to friendship (lower numbers of friends and less peer support) and lower levels of teacher–adolescent bonding also predicted greater academic difficulties, these variables generally were not shown to buffer the effects of the parent–adolescent relationship.

Using a similar sample from the same database, Crosnoe (2004) examined the impact of indicators of both family social capital (measured as emotional distance between parents and adolescents) and school social capital (student–teacher bonding, parent educational attainment, and parent educational aspirations for their adolescents) on self-reported adolescent grades. In addition to the replicated findings regarding the main effects for the family and school factors employed in the previously discussed research effort, this study also generated evidence of "mesolevel interactions" indicating that those students with the most social capital at home were more likely both to have greater social capital at school and to take advantage of those resources.

Perhaps most notable is the exponential growth of studies that have used racially and culturally diverse samples in order to refine work in this area. For instance, Heard (2007) used a longitudinal database containing reports from white, African American, and Latino adolescents (average age 14.9 years at the initiation of the study) and their parents to examine the impact of both the duration of time spent in various family structural situations and the total number of family constellation changes on grade point average. Interpreted from a life course theoretical perspective, African American adolescents were reported to have been less negatively impacted by exposure to single parenthood and Hispanic adolescents less negatively impacted by time lived with nonparents; however, these race/ethnicity differences in grades were due to variables related to social support, stress levels, and school-related difficulties.

Using a social learning framework, Aldous (2006) employed a sample of adolescents and their parents who had emigrated to the USA from Asian, Hispanic (Central America and South America), or European countries in order to examine the potential impact of family factors on educational achievement. While students emigrating from Asian countries did best academically and those students from Hispanic countries did least well, parental educational aspirations for their offspring and the adolescent's own aspirations were significantly associated with educational achievement regardless of country of origin.

A study conducted by Alfaro, Umaña-Taylor, and Bámaca (2006) within an ecological approach used the reports of Hispanic adolescents between the ages of 14 and 17 (average age of 15.3 years) in order to examine the influence of mothers, fathers, teachers, and peers on adolescent academic motivation. Female adolescent motivation was most significantly affected by the academic support given by mothers and teachers, whereas the academic support provided by fathers and teachers were most salient for the male adolescents. Interestingly, neither "generational status" (whether or not the parents were born in the USA) nor parent educational attainment was a significant predictor of adolescent academic motivation in this study.

Dumka, Gonzales, Bonds, and Millsap (2009) examined the impact of parenting behaviors on academic success using a sample of Hispanic adolescents of Mexican origin between the ages of 11 and 14 (average age of 12.3 years) and their mothers, fathers, and teachers. Interpreted within a developmental contextual perspective, findings indicated that greater harshness used by both mothers and fathers was related to more problematic classroom behavior for male adolescents, while greater father harshness was related to more involvement with problematic peers for the sons. As well, greater mother harshness was associated with more problem peer involvement yet *higher* grade point averages for the daughters.

Two studies conducted by Eng and colleagues using an ecological approach have generated important information about the families of adolescents from Asian backgrounds. In the first study, school achievement (as grade point average) in a sample of Chinese American and Filipino American adolescents (average age of 16.5 years) was found to be significantly related to parent–adolescent attachment levels but not parent involvement in school work (Eng et al., 2008). In the second study, a sample of Cambodian adolescents between the ages of 13 and 22 (average age of 17.0 years) and their parents revealed that higher adolescent grades were significantly related to being female, greater amounts of study time, higher levels of father education, and less parental exposure to traumatic events (Eng, Mulsow, Cleveland, & Hart, 2009).

Building on previous research (Gavazzi, Yarcheck, Sullivan, Jones, & Khurana, 2008) that noted the primacy of educational risks in predicting delinquent behavior, Gavazzi, Russell, and Khurana (2009) used an ecological systems perspective to examine a sample of court-involved African American adolescents (15.1 years) regarding the association between educational risks and a variety of "nonacademic barriers to learning." Results indicated that there were three main forms of educational risks – disruptive classroom behavior, learning difficulties, and threats to academic progress – that were significantly predicted by disrupted family processes, delinquent peer associations, and mental health issues.

In sum, the impact of both parenting behaviors and family processes on a wide variety of educational outcome indicators – including grade point average and other forms of academic performance and school success, as well as academic motivation and interest in school – has been well-documented. Quite a number of studies have attended to the role that race, ethnicity, and culture play in shaping similarities and differences regarding the relative associations among family variables and educational outcomes. Further, more ecologically oriented variables outside of the home (including friendships and relationships with teachers) also have been shown to have an important impact on these educational outcomes.

10.6 The Impact of Families on Adolescent Social Competence

There has been increased interest in documenting the role that family factors play in the development of adolescent social competence. Alongside the examination of educational outcomes reviewed above, research on adolescent social competence – those behaviors associated with positive outcomes in the lives of youth – are thought to serve as an important counterbalance to the widespread examination of adolescent problem behaviors that have been reported throughout this chapter.

Socially competent behaviors have been measured in a variety of ways in studies that have focused on the impact of parenting and family factors. Using an ecological perspective, Henry, Sager, and Plunkett (1996) conducted a study on adolescent (average age 14.7 years) perspectives regarding parent and family factors and how they were linked to adolescent social competence as measured by both emotional and cognitive dimensions of empathy. Results were reported indicating that greater adolescent emotional empathy was associated with more family cohesion and higher levels of parental support, while greater amounts of the cognitive dimension of adolescent empathy was related to more parental inductive behaviors.

A study conducted by Hardy, Carlo, and Roesch (2010) used the reports of adolescents (average age of 16.8 years) and their parents and teachers in order to examine the relationship between adolescent prosocial behavior and their expectations about parental behaviors. The findings of this study included reports of a significant association between adolescent perceptions of the degree to which their parents would respond "appropriately" to their behaviors (both prosocial and antisocial) and the parent and teacher reports of the adolescent's tendency to engage in prosocial behavior.

Padilla-Walker (2007) used reports from mother–adolescent (average age of 16.3 years) dyads in order to examine the relationship between prosocial behaviors and family member values related to honesty and kindness. Female adolescents reported significantly higher values than their male counterparts, and significant disparities existed between the reports of mothers and adolescents on each other's values. At the same time, however, greater prosocial behavior was related to both greater congruence between mother and adolescent perceptions and when adolescents largely had adopted their mother's values.

Other studies have examined the reciprocal influences of family factors and adolescent social competence. O'Connor, Hetherington, and Clingepeel (1997) reported on a study of adolescents (average age 11.4 years) that used the combined reports of adolescents, both parents, teachers, and trained observers on various measures of social competence. Using a family systems approach, these researchers reported strong support for the bidirectional influence of variables that tapped into parent-to-adolescent and adolescent-to-parent behaviors, whereby greater "positivity" (as reflected in family member enjoyment of the relationship, affection displayed, and positive communication) was related to indicators such as social competence, cognitive competence, physical competence, prosocial behavior, and global self-worth. Some gender differences also have been reported as well.

Using a more general social interaction approach, Schoenrock, Bell, Sun, and Avery (1999) collected data from male and female adolescents (ages 17–19) in order to examine the impact that parent and family factors had on a global measure of social competence. For male adolescents, greater social competence was associated with higher levels of family support and family autonomy. For females, greater adolescent social competence was related to higher levels of family support only.

Potential differences in the relationships between family factors and adolescent social competence have been studied in terms of race/ethnicity and cultural variation, as well as the potential intermediary nature of these variables. Prelow, Loukas, and Jordan-Green (2007) conducted a longitudinal study of Latino adolescents (average age 11.9 years at the initiation of the study) and their mothers within a family economic stress model. These researchers reported that both family routines (measured as the regularity of family events in the home) and adolescent social competence mediated the impact of socioenvironmental risk (operationalized as the accumulation of risks associated with family financial strain, neighborhood problems, and maternal psychological distress and parenting stress) on adolescent externalizing problems.

Garcia and Gracia (2009) used an ecological approach in order to examine the reports of adolescents (average age 14.9 years) from Spain in a study of parenting styles and self-perceptions of social competence. Results indicated that authoritative and permissive/indulgent styles of parenting both were associated with the highest levels of social competence. Interestingly, these researchers concluded that adolescents from Spain experienced the most optimal family environment from parents employing the permissive/indulgent style, as their scores on all of the outcomes measures were either the same or better than adolescents with authoritative parents.

Carson, Chowdhury, Perry, and Pati (1999) used the reports of adolescents (average age 13.7 years) from India along with their fathers and teachers in order to examine the associations between a number of parent and family variables and adolescent social competence in school. Findings revealed that the most socially competent adolescents come from families that display lower enmeshment styles in terms of family cohesion, employ more democratic family styles, and score lower on a measure of external locus of control within the family.

In sum, while there is some variability in how social competence is defined and measured, there is a growing body of evidence that documents how parenting behaviors and family processes play an important role in the development of prosocial behaviors. Of particular note here is the wide-ranging nature of studies that have been conducted on racially and internationally diverse samples. These findings seem to indicate that there are both similarities and differences across samples that warrant further exploration in future studies.

10.7 Summary of Research Regarding Family Influences on Adolescent Outcomes

The research literature regarding the linkage between family factors and various aspects of adolescent outcomes share some very important similarities. First and foremost, these studies uniformly underscore the critical role that parenting behaviors and family processes play in adolescent adjustment and well-being. Quite simply put, whether the particular empirical focus is delinquency, mental health, substance use, sexual activity, education, or social competency, parent and family factors matter a great deal.

Other similarities include the parallel influence of peers and other social contexts, the importance of sibling relationships, and the ways in which gender, race, ethnicity and culture all may have an impact on findings related to the adolescent outcome variables in question.

Part IV
Application Topics Concerning Families with Adolescents

Chapter 11
Family Therapy and Other Family Intervention-Based Efforts

> *Healing is a matter of time, but it is sometimes also a matter of opportunity.*
>
> Hippocrates, *Precepts*

Abstract In many ways, the history of family therapy is the history of interventions that target families with adolescents, as many early family therapists were focused on adolescent-oriented issues that were being seen for the first time within the context of the family. The present chapter covers a number of interventions targeting families with adolescents that have received sizable empirical attention over the past 15 years, including: Brief Strategic Family Therapy, Functional Family Therapy, Multidimensional Family Therapy, and Multisystemic Therapy. A brief summary of each approach is given, including information regarding its theoretical foundations, and is followed by an overview of the empirical attention that each of these models have been given to date.

In addition to these major modalities of family therapy, attention is paid to a number of other forms of family-based interventions that also have received empirical attention during this same time period, including Multidimensional Treatment Foster Care, Attachment-Based Family Therapy, and Ecologically Based Family Therapy.

> John, a 17-year-old white adolescent, and Jane Downs, his mother, were referred for family therapy services after John had been released to parole following a year-long commitment at a state juvenile training school. During an initial phone conversation, Mrs. Downs told the clinician that the family had "lots of problems," and that she was interested in anything that could assist her in working with her son to prevent his future parole revocation. In their first session, John and his mother reported a number of significant risk and protective factors. Risks included an intergenerational family history of alcoholism, significant anger management problems for many family members (including John and his biological father), and conflict around

rules in the home. Protective factors included reports that John and his mother felt that they were emotionally available to each other, as well as John being willing to get a job and finish his GED.

In the second therapy session, John and his mother began to discuss how nearly every illegal act John took part in involved some form of substance abuse. In fact, John had an upcoming court date for an illegal activity related to substance abuse issues for which he was arrested (driving while under the influence), the result of which could seriously jeopardize his parole status. John's parole officer made it clear that, though he would advocate for John because of his positive efforts made to date, he would also recommend and support the court's mandating intensive substance abuse treatment for John, including the possibility of using residential treatment, in addition to John and his mother participating in family therapy.

In addition to monitoring the ongoing need for counseling related to alcohol and drug use, the family therapy sessions began to focus on how to repair the harm that had been done by John's offenses, including the most recent DUI charge. Fortunately, John's DUI did not result in a direct victim (e.g., someone hit by his vehicle), and John was quick to identify himself as the person who needed to take full responsibility for his actions. John also determined that the harm done to himself by his actions was putting his parole (and his future as a productive member of society) at risk. Additionally, he identified his immediate family and his good friends as having been harmed by this incident because of their loss of trust in his previous vow to "turn his life around."

John and his mother were able to identify a number of things that John had already done to repair the harm done by this offense. Since the incident, John had chosen to walk whenever he could to work, school and social activities, he had ceased drinking alcohol (though admittedly still smoking marijuana once in a while, as evidenced by two failed urine screens), and he had prepared himself for his upcoming court date by, among other things, consistently attending and participating in the family therapy sessions. At home, John had put more energy into doing household chores and "getting along" with other family members. Mrs. Downs explained to John that his cooperation and help at home had allowed her to focus more of her energy on dealing with other family members, thereby lessening the amount of conflict in the home, and in turn affording her more time to assist him with his new circumstances with the court.

What do we know about intervening when problems arise in families with adolescents? This chapter covers family therapy methods and other family-based intervention efforts that target the many types of difficulties and issues experienced by adolescents and their families. As noted above, interventions included in this portion of the book involve at least two generations of family members in the efforts undertaken within the family-based effort.

11 Family Therapy and Other Family Intervention-Based Efforts

The mother of the Downs family in the vignette that begins this section was referred for family therapy services because of her son's delinquent behavior. However, she reported to her clinician that members also were attempting to deal with a number of other problems in the family as well, including interpersonal conflict and an intergenerational history of alcoholism. Hence, the family-based services being requested would necessarily need to involve activities that both prevented future illegal activity and helped to alleviate present difficulties that were being experienced by all members of the Downs family. The need to focus on such a diverse range of goals and objectives within a single family, taken from writing that examines the interplay of prevention and intervention efforts (Gavazzi & Law, 1997), is an all-too-typical scenario faced by clinicians whose work primarily involves families with adolescents.

The history of family therapy in various ways is the history of interventions that target families with adolescents. Many of the early family therapy pioneers were focused in whole or in part on adolescent-oriented issues that were being seen within the context of the family for the first time. One example is the structural family therapy approach developed by Salvador Minuchin, who had based much of his earliest work on understanding and treating adolescent anorexia in a family context (Minuchin, Rosman, & Baker, 1978). A second example is the work of Nathan Ackerman (1966), whose family-based work included the notion that adolescent individuation occurred as a result of repetitively pulling away from mother by becoming closer with father, and then pulling away from father by becoming closer to mother. Other examples come from work that surrounded schizophrenia, whereby several foundational family therapy models paid great attention to the families of adolescents and young adults who were suffering from this mental disorder (Nichols & Schwartz, 2006).

The family therapy movement was as much about family-based research as it was about family-centered practice, at least in the early years of the 1940s and 1950s. Mental health professionals who were experimenting with family-based work often as not were working within research programs. However, for some amount of time (especially in the 1960s and 1970s) a "split" of sorts seemed to occur between the practice of family therapy and the conduct of family research. This divisiveness seemed to take the form of an opposing set of value systems, where the researcher was seen as wanting to explain "complex variables" and the therapist was after "simple ideas" that worked to meet therapeutic goals (Haley, 1978).

This viscerally appealing yet factually erroneous dichotomy set up between research and therapy took on a life of its own, and unfortunately was perpetuated for many years. This may have had more to do with solidifying the distinct identity of family therapy as a profession (Shields, Wynne, McDaniel, & Gawinski, 1994) and less to do with any inherent contradiction between conducting therapy and carrying out research with families.

Perhaps as early as the 1980s (Wynne, 1983), but most certainly by the 1990s, there was a rapprochement between family therapists and family researchers. As evidenced in 1995, a series of review articles regarding studies of family therapy were published by the *Journal of Marital and Family Therapy*. These reviews included studies of family-based treatment for adolescents and their families, most notably in the areas of conduct disorders/delinquency (Chamberlain & Rosicky, 1995) and substance use (Liddle & Dakof, 1995).

Pinsof and Wynne (1995a, 1995b), the guest editors of that special issue of the journal, concluded from these reviews that family therapy had significantly greater effects on both adolescent conduct disorders and substance use in comparison to therapies that did not involve family members. In addition, family therapy was seen as superior to no treatment at all for early adolescent anorexia and obesity. However, these authors also made it clear that family involvement was a *necessary but not sufficient* part of treatment for these difficulties. "An emerging hypothesis from these data is that multicomponent, integrative, and problem-focused treatments may be necessary to treat severe behavioral disorders effectively in adults, adolescents, and children" (Pinsof and Wynne, 1995b, p. 605).

In the past 15 years since this special issue was published (and conveniently throughout the time period covered in the present book), the family therapy field has witnessed a great deal of effort put into the development of interventions that are evidence-based examples of "multi-component," "integrative," and "problem-focused" forms of family treatment. This section focuses on a number of those forms of therapy that have received sizable empirical attention, including: Brief Strategic Family Therapy (Szapocznik, Hervis, & Schwartz, 2003), Functional Family Therapy (Alexander & Parsons, 1982), Multidimensional Family Therapy (Liddle, Dakof, & Diamond, 1991), and Multisystemic Therapy (Henggeler & Borduin, 1990).

11.1 Specific Family Intervention Models

Each of the family intervention models will be discussed in alphabetical order below. A brief summary of each approach will be given, including information that is available on its theoretical foundations, as this type of information oftentimes is not easily discerned in the family therapy literature (Hawley & Geske, 2000). This will be followed by an overview of the empirical attention that each of these models have been given to date.

11.1.1 Brief Strategic Family Therapy

Brief strategic family therapy (BSFT: Szapocznik et al., 2003) is a family-based treatment that was developed out of both applied and basic research efforts conducted through the Center for Family Studies at the University of Miami (Santisteban, Suarez-Morales, Robbins, & Szapocznik, 2006). This approach largely targets substance use and delinquent behaviors presented by Hispanic (and to a lesser extent African American) youth (Szapocznik & Williams, 2000). The BSFT model is closely related to other family interventions found in the literature that are culturally informed (Santisteban & Mena, 2009), and shares a common heritage with family engagement activities (Szapocznik et al., 1988; Santisteban et al., 1996) and prevention efforts (Szapocznik et al. 1989).

In practice, the BSFT model reflects a combination of concepts borrowed from the structural and strategic schools of family therapy, both of which claim a systems theory heritage. According to Santisteban et al. (1997), there are three basic parts to this approach. First, there is a great deal of consideration given to *joining* activities, or those attempts to create a working partnership with family members. Second, there are activities related to *family pattern diagnosis* that involve attention being paid to the ways in which habituated family interactions are linked to the problems being experienced by the adolescent. Third, *restructuring* activities are then employed to disrupt and change those family interactions in ways that help to reduce or eliminate the adolescent problem behaviors.

The empirical evidence provides solid support for the use of the BSFT model. A study conducted by Santisteban et al. (1997) of 122 families containing adolescents (85% Hispanic and 15% African American) between the ages of 12 and 14 years reported that the BSFT approach was able to significantly reduce problem behaviors and improve family functioning level. Also, significant reductions in substance use also were reported in a subsample of youth who already had initiated use.

Santisteban et al. (2003) compared BSFT to group treatment in a sample of 126 families of Hispanic adolescents between the ages of 12 and 18 (average age of 15.6 years). Reports of parents from families receiving BSFT indicated significantly lower conduct disorder difficulties, delinquent behaviors, and marijuana use in comparison to those parents from the control group. As well, both observer and parent ratings of family functioning were significantly greater for the families receiving BSFT.

There also are indications that the BSFT model is effective at improving therapeutically important factors such as engagement and retention. Coatsworth, Santisteban, McBride, and Szapocznik (2001) used a sample of 104 families containing adolescents (75% Hispanic and 25% African American) between the ages of 12 and 14 years who were randomly assigned to receive BSFT or individual and family therapy "treatment as usual" within a community setting. This study reported significantly greater family engagement and retention versus the comparison group, although treatment effects were similar between the two groups.

11.1.2 Functional Family Therapy

Functional Family Therapy (FFT: Alexander & Parsons, 1982) is among the oldest of all family-based approaches discussed in this section, having been developed at the University of Utah in the early 1970s (Alexander & Parsons, 1973). This approach targets delinquency and other associated adolescent problem behaviors (Sexton & Alexander, 2002), and has been identified as one of the few family-based intervention models that combines qualities related to a rigorous research design, a body of evidence regarding significant treatment impact, multi-site replication, and evidence of treatment sustainability (Mihalic, Fagan, Irwin, Ballard, & Elliott, 2004).

This model uses concepts from the family systems framework as well as adopting a more behavioral and social learning inspired approach in order to disrupt and reduce negative family interactions that contribute to adolescent problem behavior (Robbins, Alexander, & Turner, 2000). As well, attention to the establishment and maintenance of a therapeutic alliance with family members is thought to be a key ingredient in the success of the FFT approach (Alexander, Barton, Schiavo, & Parsons, 1976; Robbins, Turner, Alexander, & Perez, 2003), as is the use of therapeutic reframes and other non-blaming restatements of client situations and experiences (Robbins, Alexander, Newell, & Turner, 1996). There is stage-like method employed in the FFT model, whereby family engagement (phase 1) is followed by a focus on changing family interactions (phase 2) that, in turn, is generalized into the larger community context (phase 3) in which the adolescent and family resides (Henggeler & Sheidow, 2003).

In order to examine the bulk of empirical evidence published in refereed journal articles that provides support for the use of the FFT model (a sizable number of studies have been conducted more recently but have been published in books and book chapters), our review must extend back to a prior set of studies that were conducted in the 1970s and 1980s. The earliest empirical work was conducted by Alexander and Parsons (1973), who used a sample of 86 families containing delinquent adolescents who were 13–16 years of age. Those families that were randomly assigned to the FFT approach experienced significantly greater gains on family functioning measures and witnessed significantly less recidivistic activity with their adolescents in comparison to no treatment at all and a different family therapy treatment.

Klein, Alexander and Parsons (1977) conducted a study of the FFT model's impact on primary, secondary, and tertiary prevention indicators using a sample of 86 families containing delinquent adolescents who were 13–16 years of age. Families randomly assigned to the FFT approach experienced significantly greater gains on family process measures (the tertiary effect), witnessed significantly less recidivistic activity (the secondary effect), and significantly less younger sibling referrals to court (the primary prevention effect) in comparison to no treatment at all and a different family therapy treatment.

The generalizability of FFT was demonstrated in a series of three studies reported by Barton, Alexander, Waldron, Turner, and Warburton (1985). In the first study, 27 families of adolescents referred for therapy by juvenile court workers displayed a 50% reduction in adolescent recidivism rates compared to the general population of adolescent offenders. In the second study, FFT as implemented with 109 families with adolescents coming into contact with child welfare professionals generated a 37% reduction in foster care utilization as compared to 206 families also referred to the child welfare system during the time of this study. In the third study, 30 families of incarcerated adolescents who received FFT displayed a 33% reduction in adolescent recidivism rates as compared to 43 families of youth who were randomly selected as a comparison group.

Gordon, Arbuthnot, Gustafson, and McGreen (1988) employed a sample of 54 families of adolescents (average age of 15.6 years) who were placed on probation for a variety of criminal offenses. Approximately, 30 months following the end of treatment, adolescents from families who received FFT had a recidivism rate of 11% in comparison to a recidivism rate of 67% in the no-treatment control group. While treatment assignment was nonrandom, these authors argued that these results were all the more impressive due to the fact that court staff assigned the "highest risk cases" to the FFT approach.

11.1.3 Multidimensional Family Therapy

Multidimensional Family Therapy (MDFT: Liddle et al., 1991) is a family-based treatment that initially was developed through Howard Liddle's work at the Philadelphia Child Guidance Clinic, the University of California at San Francisco, the Institute for Juvenile Research in Chicago, and the Mental Research Institute in Palo Alto, California (H.A. Liddle, May 16, 2010, personal communication). Eventually, what has become known as MDFT was refined both at Temple University's Center for Research on Adolescent Drug Abuse and then at the University of Miami's Center for Treatment Research on Adolescent Drug Abuse. For all intents and purposes, the MDFT model targets adolescent substance use and antisocial behavior, although associated behaviors such as increased HIV/AIDS risk factors also have been the focus of more recent efforts (Marvel, Rowe, Colon-Perez, DiClemente, & Liddle, 2009). Like many of the other models in this section, there is a strong research to practice link (Liddle, 2004). However, the MDFT approach seems to be as much about reshaping the field of family therapy itself – at least in terms of asserting a strong research component that is translatable into clinical practice – as it is about creating effective family-based treatments for adolescent problem behaviors (Liddle, 1991).

The "multidimensionality" of this model points to its use of a variety of theoretical frameworks and concepts. Perhaps most prominent is the use of a developmental framework to understand both family and individual growth and development (Liddle et al., 2000), although attachment theory is used recurrently to conceptualize strengths and limitations inherent to the parent–adolescent relationship (Liddle & Schwartz, 2002). There is a heavy emphasis on assessing and changing parenting practices and involvement levels (Schmidt, Liddle, & Dakof, 1996; Henderson, Rowe, Dakof, Hawes, & Liddle, 2009), activities that in turn are translated into more family systems-oriented efforts to alter the parent–adolescent relationship (Liddle, Rowe, Dakof, & Lyke, 1998), the individual functioning of the teen and the parent, as well as the family members' interactions with extrafamilial influences such as schools and the juvenile justice system. Attention also has been paid to culturally specific elements within this approach (Liddle, Jackson-Gilfort, & Marvel, 2006).

There is a rich and detailed set of studies published as refereed journal articles that has generated support for the use of the MDFT model. For example, Liddle et al. (2001) used a sample of 182 families of adolescents (51% white and 49% minority youth that were predominantly African American or Hispanic) between the ages of 13 and 18 (average age of 15.9 years) who were actively using illegal substances at the time of entry into the study. These families were randomly assigned to the MDFT approach or two other conditions: adolescent group therapy or a multifamily educational intervention. Although all three groups displayed gains following treatment in terms of decreased adolescent substance use and increased family competence, families assigned to the MDFT condition displayed the most improvement. As well, MDFT youth experienced greater amounts of clinically significant change in substance use and more improved grade point averages at the 1-year follow-up in comparison to youth exposed to the two other conditions.

Liddle, Dakof, Turner, Henderson, and Greenbaum (2008) conducted a study comparing MDFT with cognitive behavioral therapy using a sample of 224 families containing adolescents (73% African American, 17% white, and 10% Hispanic) between the ages of 12 and 17 (average age of 15.3 years) who were actively using substances at the time of enrollment in the study. Adolescents from families exposed to both conditions displayed significant decreases in marijuana and alcohol use at the end of treatment. However, adolescents from families enrolled in MDFT displayed greater substance use reduction at the 1-year follow-up in comparison to those adolescents from families enrolled in the cognitive behavioral therapy condition.

A study conducted by Liddle, Rowe, Dakof, Henderson, and Greenbaum (2009) used a sample of 83 families containing adolescents (predominantly Hispanic or African American) between the ages of 11 and 15 (average age of 13.7 years) who were referred for outpatient substance abuse treatment in order to compare the impact of MDFT with adolescent group therapy. Although adolescents in both conditions experienced treatment gains, adolescents from families exposed to the MDFT approach displayed significantly reduced substance use difficulties, as well as demonstrating lower risk levels in family, peer, and school contexts as compared to adolescents from families exposed to the control condition.

Liddle, Dakof, Henderson, and Rowe (in press) employed a sample of families containing substance-abusing adolescents (predominantly Hispanic or African American) between the ages of 13 and 17 (average age of 15.5 years) who were incarcerated in a juvenile justice facility in order to compare MDFT to "enhanced services as usual" (ESAU). Parents and adolescents enrolled in MDFT reported significantly more satisfaction with services, were significantly more likely to remain in treatment, and received significantly more services in comparison to the control group. In addition, data collected only on MDFT cases indicated that higher levels of collaboration among professionals working on a given case (a stated goal of the MDFT approach in this study) were significantly related to lower levels of adolescent substance use following discharge.

11.1.4 Multisystemic Therapy

Multisystemic Therapy (MST: Henggeler & Borduin, 1990) is a family-based treatment that was developed through a partnership between Scott Henggeler at the University of South Carolina and Charles Borduin at the University of Missouri. While the major focus of MST surrounds the treatment of issues for families of delinquent youth (Henggeler, Schoenwald, Borduin, Rowland, & Cunningham, 1998), including substance use (Henggeler, Pickrel, Brondino, & Crouch, 1996) and juvenile sex offenses (Borduin, Henggeler, Blaske, & Stein, 1990), this approach also has been applied to other areas, including most notably youth in psychiatric crisis (Henggeler, Rowland, Randall, & Ward, 1999) and the ancillary treatment of adolescent diabetes (Ellis et al., 2005; Ellis, Naar-King, Frey, Rowland, & Greger, 2003).

Liddle (1996) has noted that the attention given to myriad social context factors that contribute to adolescent problem behavior demarcate the ecological underpinnings of the MST approach. Therapy is conducted by teams of professionals in a home-based service delivery model, and targets individual attitudes, parenting behaviors, peer influences, academic performance, and social support factors (Henggeler, Pickrel, & Brondino, 1999). That said, this model also contains concepts from both the structural and strategic schools of family therapy, as well as elements of cognitive therapy and parent training (Henggeler & Sheidow, 2003).

The available empirical evidence provides substantial support for the use of the MST model. For example, Henggeler et al. (1999) used a sample of 116 families of adolescents between the ages of 10 and 17 years who had been referred for emergency psychiatric hospitalization. Families enrolled in MST displayed significantly lower adolescent externalizing problems, greater family functioning, better school attendance, and more satisfaction in services as compared to those families whose adolescents experienced the control condition of inpatient hospitalization. Interestingly, the adolescents in the control condition experienced more significant improvement in self-esteem as compared to the adolescents in the MST condition.

Henggeler, Clingempeel, Brondino, and Pickrel (2002) used a sample of 118 families containing adolescents (average age of 15.7 years) who were using substances and involved in the juvenile courts (evenly split between African American and white youth) in order to examine the longer-term impact of MST. At a 4-year follow-up, adolescents from families enrolled in MST displayed significantly fewer aggressive criminal behaviors and significantly less marijuana use in comparison to adolescents placed in the "usual community services" condition. Further analyses revealed that these treatment results did not vary as a function of age, race, or gender, nor did the impact of treatment differ because of the level of psychological difficulties or types of criminal behavior displayed by adolescents at the outset of the study.

In a study conducted by Henggeler et al. (2006), 161 families contained adolescents between the ages of 12 and 17 (average age of 15.2 years) who were using substances and involved in the juvenile courts (two-thirds African American and one-third white youth) in order to examine juvenile drug court outcomes. Cases were assigned to one of four conditions: Family Court (FC), Drug Court (DC), Drug Court with MST (DC/MST), or Drug Court with MST and Contingency Management (DC/MST/CM), a second evidence-based practice that has been used to effectively treat substance abuse (Budney & Higgins, 1998). Significantly reduced alcohol use was displayed only by the DC/MST/CM group, while all three Drug Court groups displayed significantly reduced marijuana use, polydrug use, and status offenses. Additionally, within group analyses regarding the three Drug Court conditions indicated that MST served to significantly reduce positive drug screens and significantly increase program graduate rates in comparison to the non-MST condition.

Borduin, Schaeffer, and Heiblum (2009) compared MST to "usual community services" with a sample of 48 families containing adolescents (average age of 14.0 years) who had been arrested on a serious sex offense charge (approximately 75% white and 25% African American). Families placed in the MST condition experienced significantly reduced adolescent psychiatric symptoms, significantly increased family cohesion and adaptability, significantly improved peer relationships, and significantly increased grades in comparison to families placed in the control condition. As well, follow-up for almost 9 years after treatment ended, indicating that adolescents from families placed in the MST condition were significantly less likely to have been arrested for both sex-related and non-sex-related crimes.

11.2 Other Family-Based Intervention Efforts

In addition to the modalities of family therapy covered above, Rowe, Gomez, and Liddle's (2006) review of the family therapy research literature covered a number of other forms of family-based interventions that also have received empirical attention. These interventions tend to be targeted directly toward the amelioration of a specific problem or issue being faced by the adolescent.

For instance, the Multidimensional Treatment Foster Care (Chamberlain & Reid, 1998) approach is used as an alternative to more intensive residential placements for delinquent and antisocial youth. This model, which centers on the use of trained foster care parents to provide structure and consistency in the lives of troubled youth, has been shown to be very promising in reducing adolescent problem behavior (Eddy, & Chamberlain, 2000; Kerr, Leve, & Chamberlain, 2009). Developed at the Oregon Social Learning Center, this initiative exists alongside other more parent-centered intervention efforts that have adopted a social learning approach to reducing antisocial behavior (Connell, Dishion, Yasui, & Kavanagh, 2007; Dishion, Nelson, & Kavanagh, 2003; Gardner et al., 2009).

More emotionally based problems such as depression and anxiety also have been treated successfully by family-based interventions. For instance, a close cousin to MDFT known as Attachment-Based Family Therapy (Diamond, Reis, Diamond,

Siqueland, Isaacs, 2002; Diamond, Siqueland, & Diamond, 2003) has been used effectively with families of depressed adolescents, including its use in reducing suicidal ideation (Diamond et al., 2010). Depression and other mood disorders also have been treated successfully with family psychoeducation programs in work with families of both preteens (Fristad, Gavazzi, & Mackinaw-Koons, 2003; Fristad, Goldberg-Arnold, & Gavazzi, 2002) and adolescents (Miklowitz, George, Axelson, Kim, Birmaher et al., 2004; Miklowitz et al., 2000).

A number of family-based interventions exist for the treatment of adolescent eating disorders as well. There are efforts using structural family therapy concepts (Lemmon & Josephson, 2001) that are logical extensions of the original family-based work conducted by Minuchin et al. (1978). As well, there are other efforts extending the structural family therapy work to also include elements of the strategic and Bowenian schools of family therapy (Krautter & Lock, 2004), and family psychoeducational efforts also have been employed with some success (Geist, Heinmaa, Stephens, Davis, & Katzman, 2000).

Finally, newer forms of family-based interventions are being developed for harder to reach adolescents and families. For instance, an Ecologically Based Family Therapy (Slesnick & Prestopnik, 2005) has been developed in order to treat the families of runaway adolescents. This approach was shown to have a similar impact on reducing substance use as FFT, and was superior to a control condition of treatment as usual (Slesnick & Prestopnik, 2009). As well, Slesnick, Erdem, Collins, Bantchevska, and Katafiasz (in press) have reported that this model has a superior impact in terms of higher engagement into treatment in comparison to two other forms of treatment that have been used in previous work with the families of runaway youth: the Community Reinforcement Approach (Meyers & Smith, 1995) and Motivational Enhancement Therapy (Miller & Rollnick, 2002).

11.3 Summary of the Family Intervention Literature

The chronology of the overall family therapy movement in many ways is intertwined with the history of interventions that target families with adolescents. The empirical evidence generated by scholars working in this portion of the clinically based literature is substantial, and in many ways leads the rest of the field in its breadth and depth. As well, this set of studies provides many excellent examples of how to include specific family theory frameworks in these sophisticated research and application activities conducted on behalf of families with adolescent members.

Chapter 12
Family Prevention Programs

It is easier to prevent bad habits than to break them.

Benjamin Franklin

Abstract A variety of approaches and labels currently exist with regard to the development and implementation of prevention efforts targeting families with adolescents. This chapter first covers a number of principles that are thought to characterize effective family-focused prevention efforts. Next, the present chapter goes on to review those prevention efforts that have received empirical attention over the past 15 years, with special emphasis given to those initiatives that require the participation of two generations of family members in shared program activities. Programs are described in according to their main objectives, their theoretical orientation is discussed, and the empirical evidence that has been generated through implementation and evaluation efforts is covered as well. Finally, a number of web-based resources are offered in order to assist readers in finding continuously updated information on these and other family-based prevention programs.

> The Green family consisted of 15-year-old Jennifer, her mother Kate and her father John, who chose to participate in the Growing Up FAST program after another family in their neighborhood had participated earlier in the year. After introductions were made, the program facilitator (PF) reviewed the goals of the program. The session then began with the PF explaining that the Green family was going to be left on their own for 5 min in order to create a definition of what it meant to be a successful adult. While encouraging the family to come up with as many ideas as they could in the brief time that they had, the PF stated that all three family members needed to be in agreement with all components of this definition that they would use for the remainder of the session. The Green family also was instructed to choose a "scribe" in order to record those parts of the definition that they agreed on. The Greens

were asked if they had any questions about the exercise. Having none, the PF then left a clipboard with paper and pen on the floor (for use by the scribe) and exited the program room.

After the 5-min period elapsed, the PF reentered the room. Jennifer stated that she had agreed to be the family scribe and had just finished writing the last part of their definition. Jennifer was asked to read her family's definition. There were six components, including: "to be financially independent," "to get a college education," "to be involved in the community," "to be trusting and honest," "to be able to manage your finances," and "to be an active family member." After recording the family's definition on a program worksheet, the PF then read a series of prompts to the family that could be used to expand their definition if desired. The Greens agreed that the prompt related to "effective problem-solving and decision-making skills" was something that should be placed inside their family's definition, and chose to add "to be a good problem solver" as another component.

The family members agreed that they were ready to move on with the rest of the program. First, however, the PF explained that the program is most effective when only four or five components are made the focus of the remaining tasks. It was explained that too many components could make each part of the program seem unduly long, and hence there was the risk that their family could lose focus and stamina. After a brief discussion, the Greens decided to drop three of their components – involvement in the community, managing your own finances, and being an active family member – for the purpose of moving on through the rest of the program. They explained to the PF that the components that had been dropped were less important to focus on in terms of Jennifer becoming a successful adult. At that point, and with the Green family's definition comprising a total of four components, the PF stated that they were ready to work on to the next session goal.

What is our knowledge base about how to prevent problems in families with adolescents? This chapter deals with prevention programs serving families with adolescents that are intergenerational in orientation and that are applicable either to universal or selective populations of families. The vignette that begins this section briefly discusses the Green family's participation in the Growing Up FAST program (reviewed more extensively below). We witness the program facilitator setting up an opportunity for Mr. and Mrs. Green to work with their daughter Jennifer in building a definition of what it means to be a successful adult in their family. As with many of the programs that will be covered in this section, the approach is designed to prevent any number of adolescent problem behaviors by building up certain protective factors in the family; in this case, the family's ability to create a strength-based identity regarding behaviors associated with the successful transition into adulthood status in their family.

A variety of approaches and labels currently exist with regard to the development and implementation of family-based prevention efforts, and in fact the focus on families seems to have grown significantly over the years (Bloom, 2000). Some of these initiatives are explicitly discussed as "family strengthening" programs; other descriptors include "family enrichment," "family life education," "family skills training," "family wellness," and "family support" programs. At least one comprehensive review of these family-based prevention programs has been conducted previously (Gavazzi, 2003). As such, the present chapter incorporates this earlier effort to compile information about these types of programs and the characteristics of these initiatives. At the same time, a number of new initiatives have made their way into the literature since this review was published. Hence, the present section augments this original anthology with information about these newly developed programs. As well, this section incorporates additional evidence from evaluation efforts of programs that already were in existence at the time of the Gavazzi (1993) review.

12.1 Characteristics of Effective Family Programs

Kumpfer and Alvarado (1998) provided a slightly more restrictive review of family-based programs that specifically targeted the reduction of adolescent involvement in delinquency and substance abuse. Borrowing from guidelines developed through the National Institute on Drug Abuse (NIDA), these reviewers called attention to a set of principles that they believed seemed to characterize effective family-focused interventions. These principles included the following:

- Allowance of family members to remain involved in programming for a sufficient length of time and intensity level that would permit them to solidify changes in family dynamics
- Use of post-program booster sessions to counter the degradation of program gains
- Comprehensive attention given to skill development in areas such as family cohesiveness, interpersonal communication, and parental monitoring
- Attention paid to culturally-specific issues in both program content and recruitment/retention efforts
- Program material being developmentally appropriate to adolescents and starting as early as possible in this developmental period
- Use of audiovisual instructional material for skill-building components of the program
- Attention given to advanced training opportunities for program facilitators.

Parenthetically, these same NIDA guidelines have been applied to the prevention of substance use in other realms that also touch on families, including most notably school–community–home collaborations (Adelman & Taylor, 2003).

The first issue that Kumpfer and Alvarado (1998) target – program time and intensity level – concerns what might best be called "dosage." In essence, time and intensity surround the central question of how much programming is enough to make a difference in family functioning levels. However, rather than making the assertion that there is some minimum number of contacts with families that will make a given program effective, it is asserted here that it is more useful to adopt the general principle that more sessions are needed for families that are at lower levels of functioning and/or higher risk for the development of problems. The dosage issue overlaps with the second principle regarding program booster sessions or other methods of "follow up." Here, programs that have more built-in contacts with families are thought to be better able to retain program gains in comparison to programs that do not offer such booster sessions.

Whether the focus is dosage or follow-up, it is important to acknowledge that lower functioning families may be more challenged to access greater amounts of program resources. In turn, it almost certainly is the case that higher functioning families are more able to choose nonparticipation without negative repercussions. Hence, this leaves families functioning at some "mid-range" level that are the ones who are most likely to take full advantage of programs that offer the most contact points.

The third issue covered by Kumpfer and Alvarado (1998) – attention to skill development – concerns specific areas of family dynamics that are directed targeted by family-based prevention programs, such as family cohesiveness, interpersonal communication, and parental monitoring. At the same time, these programs also are thought to impact other important areas of family life, even if, only indirectly. Such family-oriented areas include adaptability, family problem-solving and decision-making skills, conflict management in the family, and the interplay of family and larger social systems (including most notably the school setting).

The fourth issue – being culturally-specific – has been discussed in the general social sciences literature as being one of the most important yet underutilized factors related to the successful transition into adulthood in past discussions of program focus. More recently, however, attention to racial/ethnic background and the geographical location of the families have become two of the more salient issues that have begun to permeate program efforts (Turner, 2000).

In turn, the issue of cultural specificity can be linked to the fifth effective programming principle concerning the developmental appropriateness of program content. In essence, both of these issues involve attention paid to the fit between the idiosyncratic needs of the targeted population and what the programs actually provide. Currently, while family-based prevention programs have targeted youth of all ages, the majority of these programs tend to target the lower bounds of the adolescent period.

The last two principles of effective program covered by Kumpfer and Alvarado (1998) include the use of audiovisual instructional material and advanced training opportunities for program facilitators. Having audiovisual material available for use by family members is thought to better facilitate the transfer of learning of skills covered by program facilitators in family sessions, something found in parenting skills programs as well (Gordon, 2000). In turn, the use of lecture-based formats (Tobler & Stratton, 1997) and other information-only modalities of program implementation (Norman & Turner, 1993) largely have failed to generate much in the way of empirical support. Advanced training opportunities hold the promise of increased program effectiveness and fidelity to the family-based model being offered by a given program. That being said, little documentation of this issue currently exists in the family-based prevention literature.

Small and Huser (in press), following the model advanced by Small, Cooney and O'Connor (2009), expanded on the work of Kumpfer and Alvarado (1998) by asserting a total of 11 principles of effective programs that are classified into four categories. These principles included:

- Program Design and Content
    - Being theory-driven
    - Use of sufficient levels of dosage and intensity
    - Program comprehensiveness
    - Use of active learning techniques
- Program Relevance
    - Being developmentally appropriate
    - Reaching participants at the point they are ready to change
    - Remaining socioculturally relevant
- Program Delivery and Implementation
    - Fostering good relationships
    - Delivery by staff who are well-trained
    - Implementation with fidelity
- Program Assessment and Quality Assurance
    - Thorough documentation of effectiveness evidence
    - Continuous refinement and evaluation of program efforts

Due to the overlapping nature of these principles with the prior work of Kumpfer and Alvarado (1998) reviewed above (common characteristics also can be found in other articles that provide overviews of the prevention literature as well, including Dusenbury, 2000), two particular principles – the theory-driven nature of the program and the thorough documentation of program effectiveness – are selected for further discussion here.

The theoretical underpinnings of family-based prevention programs found in the literature are quite different. For instance, some programs were developed by professionals who were interested in outcomes related to delinquency and related antisocial behavior, and thus based their work on principles that came out of social learning theory and/or the social development model. Other professionals were influenced by theories coming more directly from the family therapy movement. In another realm, family life education programs largely were created by family scientists who utilized family development theory to guide their work. Different still are those family support programs that largely came out of an ecological systems framework.

Just as there is great variety in terms of the theoretical backgrounds represented in the literature concerning family-based prevention programs, so too is there a rather wide range of efforts undertaken in order to conduct an empirical evaluation of the implementation of these programs. First of all, it should be said that there are many more family prevention programs currently being implemented than are contained in the literature that has been reviewed. Most simply put, many of the programs that are absent from this literature have lacked the empirical testing required for acceptance into many refereed journals. Those programs that have undergone such rigorous examination are oftentimes given the label "best practice." At the same time, the gathering of summative evaluation data is not an appropriate task for those developers whose programs are at the more beginning stages of development. Hence, there are some programs that have made it into the literature with formative evaluation data, often with the label "promising approach." These latter efforts may be guided by any number of continuous quality improvement activities (cf., Wandersman et al., 1998).

12.2 Examples of Specific Family-Based Prevention Programs

Programs are reviewed in alphabetical order, and are described in summary fashion according to their main objectives. Where possible, their theoretical framework and the empirical evidence that has been generated through implementation and evaluation efforts are covered as well.

The Bridges to High School Program (Bridges/Puentes) (Gonzales, Dumka, Deardorff, JacobsCarter, & McCray, 2004) is a 10-week prevention initiative that targets the families of adolescents (predominantly focusing on Mexican Americans) who are entering middle school (junior high school), with particular attention paid to mental health issues and school retention. Program activities include: adolescent skills for dealing with stress; parenting skills related to discipline, monitoring, and support; a combined parent–adolescent family strengthening task that is designed to increase family cohesion levels; and a home–school linkage component.

Based on focus groups and other initial qualitative data gathered during the planning phase (Dumka, Gonzales, Woods, & Formoso, 1998; Lengua et al., 1992), this program is based on a "small theory" approach that positive changes in the adolescent, parent, and family factors noted above would significantly decrease the likelihood of mental health issues and school drop-out. Initial results of one quantitative study included both adolescent reports of significantly increased coping skills and maternal reports of significant decreases in inconsistent discipline, significant increased in parental support, and significant decreases in adolescent behavioral difficulties (Gonzales et al., 2004).

The Chicago HIV Prevention and Adolescent Mental Health Project (CHAMP) (Madison, McKay, Paikoff, & Bell, 2000; McKay et al., 2004; Paikoff, Parfenoff, Williams, & McCormick, 1997) is a 12-week family strengthening program that is designed to help urban families of early adolescents (aged 10–12 years of age) deal with sexual activity and related behaviors that increase HIV exposure risk. Program activities include: family communication skill building; discussion of the impact of neighborhood and peer environments; the role of parental monitoring and discipline; and education about issues concerning adolescent sexuality and HIV/AIDS transmission.

The program utilizes a generic set of theoretical assumptions stemming from the adolescent developmental literature that includes the impact of biological, cognitive/psychological, and social context factors on risk-taking behaviors. Data have been reported on relatively successful recruitment and retention rates, as well as preliminary outcomes that suggest programmatic impact on variables related to knowledge gain and increased parental functioning.

Familias Unidas (United Families) (Coatsworth, Pantin, & Szapocznik, 2002) is a family-based program targeting recently immigrated Hispanic families with adolescents that is meant to be carried out on a weekly basis throughout the school year. The program centers on factors that provide protection against the development of adolescent problem behaviors, including parental involvement and adolescent abilities related to self-regulation, social competence, and academic achievement.

The program adopts what the authors term an "ecodevelopmental" theoretical perspective, whereby the ecological perspective is combined both with elements of developmental theory as well as attention to social interactions (largely influenced by the structural family therapy perspective). Predated by earlier work known as the Family Effectiveness Training Program (Szapocznik et al., 1989), this program has a solid history of generating both program efficacy data and the effectiveness of family engagement strategies. One interesting recent study also documented the "value-added" nature of Familias Unidas when combined with other selective prevention efforts (Prado et al., 2007).

The Families and Schools Together Program (Kratochwill, McDonald, Levin, Bear-Tibbetts, & Demaray, 2004; McDonald & Frey, 1999) is an initial 8–10 session family strengthening program (followed by 2 years of monthly booster sessions) that is designed to assist families of youth (up to the age of 14 years) to prevent school failure and substance use while concurrently increasing family functioning levels. Program activities include quite a variety of experiential activities (singing, game-playing, eating, and drawing) that are linked to programmatic objectives.

The theoretical frameworks of this program include a number of therapy literatures (psychiatry, psychology, play therapy, and family therapy), as well as more generic parent, family, and communication literatures. Interestingly, this program is strongly connected to the school system as a source of referrals, a site for program implementation, and a connection point for family member involvement in community-oriented activities. This program has been evaluated through a number of studies that have gathered follow-up data from program participants, and analyses have indicated programmatic impact in terms of decreased externalizing problem behaviors and increased family functioning. Additionally, the results of one unpublished experimental design study are reported to show significant improvement in participating youth versus controls.

The Families in Action Program (Abbey, Pilgrim, Hendrickson, & Buresh, 2000; Pilgrim, Abbey, Hendrickson, & Lorenz, 1998) is a six-session family strengthening program that is designed to assist rural families of adolescents (entering junior high or middle school) increase protective factors and decrease risk factors associated with alcohol, tobacco, and other substance use. Program activities include communication skill building, focusing on positive thinking, school success, and substance use avoidance strategies.

Theoretically, this program is based on the social development model. Formative data has focused on curriculum adherence and group discussion facilitation. Additionally, the results of one quasi-experimental design study have indicated that participating adolescents were more receptive to the use of social services than were adolescent controls, while male adolescents (but not females) reported greater attachment to school and peers and more functional attitudes toward substance use. In turn, participating parents reported increased family functioning and more functional attitudes towards substance use than did parent controls.

The Growing Up FAST: Families with Adolescents Surviving and Thriving Program (Gavazzi, 1995; Law & Gavazzi, 1999) is a two-session family strengthening program that is designed to assist families of adolescents (aged 12–18 years) in meeting a variety of developmental demands through identification of family strengths and capabilities. Program activities include: the creation of a definition of what successful adulthood means to family members; identification of those behaviors family members are engaged in presently or could become engaged in that support achievement of successful adulthood status; development of needs assessment and decision-making skills; and the utilization of community resources.

The theoretical framework of this program includes a blend of literatures concerning rites of passage, multicultural studies, and the solution-focused perspective. To date, empirical evidence is primarily formative. This information includes the actual use of this program to generate outputs that are consistent with its stated objectives (i.e., creating definitions of successful adulthood), as well as family member perceptions of program effectiveness. More comprehensive juvenile justice diversion (Gavazzi, Wasserman, Partridge, & Sheridan, 2000) and parole (Gavazzi, Yarcheck, Rhine, & Partridge, 2003) versions of this program also have been developed for use with more selective populations of families with adolescents.

The Home and On Your Own Program (Colan, Mague, Cohen, & Schneider, 1994) is a six-session family strengthening program designed to increase safety in homes where adolescents are alone for periods of time after school (although no age range is specified by the program developers, this program was included in the present chapter due to the program's general applicability to 12–18-year-old students). Program activities include: family communication and decision-making skill building; education about safety issues in the home and neighborhood environments; and issues involving risk-taking behaviors, including substance use.

The self-care literature is the primary theoretical underpinning of this program. Interestingly, this program utilizes a recruitment strategy that involves employee assistance programs. Reported evaluative data is formative, and involves participant perceptions of the program's effectiveness. Additionally, relatively high rates of retention are reported.

12.2 Examples of Specific Family-Based Prevention Programs

The Preparing for the Drug Free Years Program (Haggerty, Kosterman, Catalano, & Hawkins, 1999; Park et al., 2000) is a five-session family strengthening program designed to assist families of adolescents (up to 14 years of age) in reducing risk factors and increasing protective factors related to substance use and related problem behaviors. Many of the program activities are attended by parents only, and include family conflict management, education on the extent of substance use and its connection to family and peer factors, and parent communication skill building. There also is a session attended by parents and adolescents together that focuses on the development of substance use refusal skills.

This program is grounded in the social development model (the program developers include some of the original theorists who created this model). Evaluation of this program has included both formative and summative data collection efforts. Formative data collected on program dissemination indicated that the program reaches its intended audience and that parents perceive their participation to have been helpful in reaching the program's stated objectives. The results of one experimental design study indicated improvement in participating adults' parenting and communication skills versus controls, as well as decreases in adolescent substance use.

The Strengthening Families Program (Kumpfer, Alvarado, Smith, & Bellamy, 2002; Kumpfer & Tait, 2000) is a 14-week family strengthening program that is designed to assist families of adolescents (up to 14 years of age) in the deterrence of substance use and the improvement of parent–adolescent relationships. Program activities include a combination of parent skill development (anger and stress management, discipline, use of rewards, and communication), adolescent skill development (social skills, coping, and communication), and family skill development (problem-solving, practicing communication skills, and use of family meeting times).

The theoretical framework of this program is a combination of the VASC and Social Ecology models of substance abuse. This program has been rigorously examined in at least 12 summative evaluation studies conducted by independent program evaluators. Reports of results include significant decreases in adolescent substance use and increased family functioning. A number of culturally specific variations of this program concurrently have been developed (Aktan, 1999; Marek, Brock, & Sullivan, 2006), and include initiatives that target African American, Hawaiian Asian/Pacific Islander, Hispanic, American Indian, and Appalachian families. Of these, the program seemingly with the greatest amount of work put into its cultural adaptation has led to its own relabeling as "The Strong African American Families Program" (Brody, Kogan, Chen, & Murry, 2008; Brody et al., 2006).

The Strengthening Families Program: For Parents and Youth 10–14 (Molgaard, & Spoth, 2001; Molgaard, Spoth, & Redmond, 2000) is a 7-week family strengthening program (with four additional booster sessions) that resulted from a significant modification of the original Strengthening Families Program (SFP) described above. In essence, the program was altered in order to better fit the universal needs of rural families with adolescents (aged 10–14 years of age) such that intermediate outcomes related to improved family skills would serve the more long-term outcome of decreased adolescent problem behaviors. Each program session consists of one hour of separate parent and adolescent activities that cover a spectrum of skills, and a second hour that unites the family members in order to put into practice the skills just learned.

While there is theoretical kinship to the original SFP initiative, conceptual linkages to a biopsychosocial vulnerability model, the resiliency literature, and attention to family processes also are emphasized. At least one study incorporating an experimental design has been conducted to date, and results are reported that indicate increases in functional parenting skills, as well as decreases in a variety of adolescent problem behaviors. Interestingly, researchers were able to document the direct and indirect effects of this program on certain parenting variables as part of this study. Finally, more recent efforts that have been undertaken to develop a videotape-based curriculum are particularly noteworthy.

12.3   Web-Based Resources on Family Programs

In order to find continuously updated information on family-based prevention programs, as well as to examine other programs that are not focused exclusively on working with families, Small and Huser (in press) offered up a number of reputable registries of programs that can be accessed through the Internet, including:

- Blueprints for Violence Prevention
    - http://www.colorado.edu/cspv/blueprints/index.html
- California Evidence-Based Clearinghouse for Child Welfare
    - http://www.cebc4cw.org/
- Office of Juvenile Justice and Delinquency Prevention Model Programs Guide
    - http://www2.dsgonline.com/mpg/
- Promising Practices Network on Children, Families and Communities
    - http://www.promisingpractices.net/programs.asp
- Strengthening America's Families: Effective Family Programs for Prevention of Delinquency
    - http://www.strengtheningfamilies.org/
- Substance Abuse and Mental Health Services Administration (SAMHSA) National Registry of Evidence-based Programs and Practices
    - http://www.nrepp.samhsa.gov/

- What Works Wisconsin: Evidence-based Parenting Program Directory
  - http://whatworks.uwex.edu/Pages/2parentsinprogrameb.html
- Youth Violence: A Report of the Surgeon General
  - http://www.surgeongeneral.gov/library/youthviolence/chapter5/sec3.html

12.4 Summary of the Family Prevention Literature

There is a considerable literature that informs the practice of preventing problems in families with adolescents. This chapter reviewed a number of principles thought to be reflective of effective family-focused prevention efforts, and then covered a variety of evidence-based approaches to this type of work. Special emphasis was given to those initiatives that require the participation of two generations of family members in shared program activities, in many ways the main litmus test for determining what comprised a family-based prevention program. Many of the programs covered in this chapter not only displayed empirical sophistication, but also contained clear and useful linkages to family theory frameworks.

Part V
Summary and Future Directions

Chapter 13
Outlook on Theoretical, Research, and Application Efforts to Date

> *Just as the largest library, badly arranged, is not so useful as a very moderate one that is well arranged, so the greatest amount of knowledge, if not elaborated by our own thoughts, is worth much less than a far smaller volume that has been abundantly and repeatedly thought over.*
>
> Arthur Schopenhauer

Abstract This chapter serves as a review of each of the three main parts of this book in terms of coverage of theoretical, research, and application topics concerning the study of families with adolescents. The review of theoretical material focuses on this book's coverage of where we get our ideas about the families within which adolescents grow and develop. Special attention is given to both the generative and degenerative aspects of theories, as well as discussing the place of theoretical development in family-specific journals. The review of empirical material focuses on this book's coverage of the actual data that we have, which informs us about the families of adolescents. Issues requiring additional attention that are identified in this chapter include the need to incorporate more qualitative-oriented efforts, as well as greater attention being given to methods that allow multiple family member perspectives to be adequately accounted for in the gathering of family-oriented data. The review of application material focuses on our knowledge base about how to prevent problems in families with adolescents or otherwise how to intervene with adolescents and their families when difficulties arise. The reader's sensitivity to understanding how families can be viewed from quite different lenses when prevention and intervention efforts reflect activities are seen as something that are done "to" families in contrast to providing services "for families" and "with families."

13.1 Outlook of Theoretical Efforts to Understand Families with Adolescents

We began our focus on theoretical efforts with the question: Where do we get our ideas about the families within which adolescents grow and develop? The theoretical frameworks used to understand families with adolescents reviewed within this book included family development theory, family systems theory, ecological theory, attachment theory, and social learning theory. The five functions of theory (descriptive, sensitizing, integrative, explanatory, and value) discussed by Knapp (2009) were used to discuss what each of these conceptual frameworks offer scholars who are interested in families with adolescents. Obviously, there is a great wealth of information from each of these theories that contributes to ideas about the families within which adolescents grow and develop.

Although these five functions point to the generative nature of theory, Knapp (2009) also provided warnings about their potential degenerative characteristics. This is especially thought to be the case when theories are developed in "monological" fashion. That is to say, sometimes a conceptual framework is treated in isolation and therefore is not subjected to any sort of comparison or contrast with other theoretical perspectives. Often as not, this contributes to a theory veiling and obscuring as much as it reveals and brings to light.

Knapp (2009) argues for a "critical theorizing" approach to combat the more degenerative aspects of theory building (and research). This is thought to be especially important for the family field. In Knapp's (2009) own words:

> Attention to methodological rigor without an accompanying emphasis on theoretical rigor in the form of critical and dialogical theorizing will therefore likely result in the creation of multiple theories and research outcomes that *coexist in indifference* with each other and other alternative perspectives. Perhaps some will object, but this seems to describe quite well the state of much work in the family field (p. 138).

Although this is a criticism lodged against the family field in general, the very same thing can be said about the more specific theoretical literature regarding families with adolescents. Very little information exists that would allow readers to engage in a comparison and contrast of theoretical approaches. While there are instances of multiple theories being used in a blended approach, the side-by-side assessment of any two theoretical approaches does not appear in a single refereed journal article published over the last 15 years that was uncovered for the purposes of this book.

Thus, one area that is crying out for further development is exactly this sort of evaluative work with the five theoretical perspectives contained in this book. However, lest we forget there are other conceptual frameworks from the family field – including especially social exchange theory and symbolic interaction theory – that also have been used to describe families with adolescents in past scholarly efforts. While these theories rarely if ever receive mention in any of the scholarly work published over the past 15 years, they certainly can become part of the "critical theorizing" work suggested by Knapp (2009).

13.1 Outlook of Theoretical Efforts to Understand Families with Adolescents

As well, there are certain "mid-range" family frameworks that more recently have received some empirical attention in the literature on families with adolescents, yet also were not covered in the theory part of this book. Most prominently perhaps is the boundary ambiguity framework, which has been used to conceptualize everything from uncertainties surrounding life in a cohabiting household (Brown & Manning, 2009) to the stressors coming from truncated contact with an incarcerated parent (Bocknek, Sanderson, & Britner, 2009). Also, there are some other theoretical perspectives mentioned in the research part of this book that are not family theories per se, but certainly could become more impactful if greater attention was paid to their family-oriented conceptualizations. One such example discussed below is that of Crosswhite and Kerpelman (2009a), who write about the parental and family underpinnings of social control theory.

Because these and other family-based theories not reviewed more thoroughly in this book's theoretical part could in fact offer rich insights about families with adolescents; scholars with an affinity to these frameworks are urged to renew their efforts to provide theoretical guidance to scholars who are studying these families. As well, theorists and researchers alike should redouble their efforts to build and test propositions from all of these family theory frameworks that are directly applicable to families with adolescents.

Great hope for theoretical advances in the family field comes from the 2009 launch of the *Journal of Family Theory and Review*. Although the family field's main professional organization – the National Council on Family Relations – already maintains two journals (*Journal of Marriage and the Family* and *Family Relations*), this new periodical fills a basic need that largely has gone unmet by any other family-focused journal to date; that is, to publish works on theory and the methods by which theory development is advanced (Milardo, 2009, 2010). In fact, the work of Knapp (2009) that has been used so liberally above can be found in this journal.

In the more general sense, this journal has been seen as holding the promise of creating a forum for all family scholars both to increase the explanatory power of family theories and to critically investigate their biases and shortcomings. More specifically, however, this new journal already has generated some exciting and innovative theoretical approaches that speak directly to an audience interested in the theoretical treatment of families with adolescents.

For example, Ashbourne (2009) presents a dialogic approach to understanding the parent–adolescent relationship. By focusing attention on the communication (dialogue) that takes place between parents and adolescents, this theorist draws attention to the intergenerational "gaps" that exist between the lived experiences of these family members, and how these differences are negotiated. Particular consideration is given to the dynamic tension that exists within dialectics such as the responsiveness–demandingness concerns addressed in the parenting literature, as well as the separateness–connectedness issues that are contained within the family process literature. Clearly, the field will benefit from more theoretical work that fosters links between concepts used to describe parenting behaviors and family system dynamics.

As referenced above, Crosswhite and Kerpelman (2009b) provide a treatment of a classic criminology theory – social control theory (Gottfredson & Hirschi, 1990) – within a more parent and family-based approach. Part of this effort involves the systematic review of evidence that supports the established thinking of those parenting behaviors linked to adolescent antisocial behavior within the social control perspective. Here, parent–adolescent attachment, parental monitoring/supervision/knowledge, parental recognition and punishment of deviant activities all are acknowledged as having an important impact on adolescent problem behaviors.

As well, however, these authors assert that a host of other well-documented parent and family-based predictors of antisocial behavior are not accounted for in social control theory. Special attention in this regard is given to concepts and variables contained within the social learning and social information processing theories. Their call for the expansion of theoretical perspectives to be based on available research evidence is exactly the direction that family scholars need to take with other family theories.

In sum, readers should get the sense that there is a groundswell of support for making sure that ideas about families and data from families become better connected. Much of the family theory work that has been done with regard to families with adolescents has laid a foundation for this sort of work to occur. It is now up to the present generation of scholars to advance these efforts. To paraphrase the work of White (2005), it is high time for the family field's "context of justification" to be better linked to its "context of discovery."

13.2 Outlook on Empircal Efforts to Understand Families with Adolescents

We began our focus on empirical efforts with the question: What data do we have that informs us about the families of adolescents? This book's review of the empirical literature on families with adolescents offered a selection of articles that were meant to provide a representative sample of the types of studies that have been conducted over the last decade and a half. Clearly, there is an enormous amount of empirical information that informs the field about the families of adolescents.

While researchers still routinely assess the impact of parenting behaviors in the most recent of studies reviewed here, the last 15 years have seen a clear emergence of interest in family processes. Over a decade ago, Cox and Paley (1997) noted that:

> Much of family research has focused on the patterns of interaction within and across family subsystems (e.g., marital and parent-child, parent-child and sibling, parent-child and individual). Less research has focused on the impact of larger units in the family (triadic and whole family), perhaps because conceptualizing and measuring characteristics of the whole system has been difficult (pp. 246–247).

Several themes can be discerned from those articles that are related to the field's general progression toward more complex and sophisticated approaches to the study of these family processes, including attention being given to the impact of siblings, the overlapping influences of marital and parent-adolescent conflict, and the interactive effects of family and other social context variables.

At the same time, there are several interesting areas of family-based research that did not receive attention in this book, but nonetheless deserve some mention here. This includes the growing body of work that examines issues that concern adolescents in stepfamilies, including stepsibling influences (Tillman, 2008a, 2008b; Wallerstein & Lewis, 2007), as well as adolescents with same-sex parents (Baumrind, 1995; Gershon, Tschann, & Jemerin, 1999; Wainright, Russell, & Patterson, 2004). Also, the role of grandparents in the lives of adolescents has been the focus of studies throughout the time period covered in this book (King & Elder, 1997, 1998a, 1998b), as have other extended family networks (Pallock & Lamborn, 2006). Clearly, these areas can and should be investigated in future studies.

The increased attention given to racial, ethnic, and cultural considerations in the family also has given rise to a number of studies that have examined "familism," or the sense in which family values assume a position of ascendance over the interests of individual family members. Much of this work is being done in samples of Hispanic families (German, Gonzales, Bonds, Dumka, & Millsap, 2009; Umaña-Taylor, Updegraff, & Gonzales-Backen, 2011; Umaña-Taylor & Guimond, 2010; Updegraff, McHale, Whiteman, Thayer, & Delgado, 2005), although the familism construct can be found in studies of families with other racial and ethnic backgrounds (Ghazarian, Supple, & Plunkett, 2008). As researchers continue to examine issues of diversity, the familism construct in particular may help advance work in this area of inquiry.

In addition to race, ethnicity, and cultural variation, other studies reviewed in this book paid attention to potential variation as a function of other demographic variables such as gender and socioeconomic status. In the latter case, there are other important demographic characteristics linked to family economic circumstances that did not receive much coverage in this book that deserve mention here. This includes studies regarding the impact of family mobility (South, Haynie, & Bose, 2005), family economic stressors (Barrera et al., 2002) and socioeconomic circumstances (Conger, Conger, & Martin, 2010), the neighborhood conditions in which families reside (Henry, Merten, Plunkett, & Sands, 2008; Roche, Ensminger, & Cherlin, 2007; Roche & Leventhal, 2009; Upchurch, Aneshensel, Sucoff, & Levy-Storms, 1999), and the geographic location of families (Ball & Wiley, 2005; Elder, King, & Conger, 1996; Freeman & Anderman, 2005; King, Elder, & Whitbeck, 1997; Vicary, Snyder, & Henry, 2000; Wiley, Bogg, & Ho, 2005). The addition of these demographically oriented factors to future research efforts will help to shed further light on the broader social context in which families with adolescents are situated.

The review of the research literature in this book regarding the linkage between family factors and adolescent outcomes was limited to four aspects of adolescent problem behaviors (delinquency, mental health, substance use, and sexual activity) and two areas of potential adolescent assets (education and social competency).

A variety of topics related to adolescent outcomes were not covered at all, and could be given consideration in future research efforts that seek to understand how families impact adolescent development and well-being.

One area of inquiry that seems especially promising is the family's impact on adolescent identity development (Mullis, Brailsford, & Mullis, 2003; Mullis, Graf, & Mullis, 2009; Mullis, Mullis, Schwartz, Pease, & Shriner, 2007), including ethnic identity formation (Gonzales-Backen & Umaña-Taylor, 2010; Kiang & Fuligni, 2009). Another growing area of inquiry surrounds studies that are examining the relationship between family factors and adolescent health issues, including conditions such as asthma (Wood et al., 2008), diabetes (Naar-King, Podolski, Ellis, Frey, & Templin, 2006), and obesity (Fulkerson, Strauss, Neumark-Sztainer, Story, & Boutelle, 2007). Other emergent work surrounds the impact of religion on family processes (Stokes, 2008; Stokes & Regnerus, 2009).

Further, it is important to note that there has been a considerable rise in the number and types of longitudinal studies that have been conducted in the last 15 years, including the use of large and nationally representative databases containing information about families with adolescents. And as been mentioned earlier in this section, the field has witnessed the development of more sophisticated statistical methods for dealing with the complexities of these databases on dyads and larger systems (Lyons & Sayer, 2005). Clearly, the field has profited from these efforts, as the results of these large scale representative studies are more generalizable to larger segments of the population. As well, those empirical efforts that have adopted longitudinal designs have become more causal in their orientation, in that the measurement of set of variables at one time point allows researchers to discuss their consequential effects on variables at subsequent points in time.

The vast majority of studies covered in this book are of a more quantitative nature, meaning that great emphasis has been placed on studies that revolve around the statistical analysis of numerically-based data. At the same time, more recently, the families with adolescents' literature has witnessed an upsurge in the publication of studies that are more qualitative in nature. Here, greater attention is given to text-based data that is used to search for patterns and uncover meanings and interpretations related to participant experiences. It is asserted here that greater attention to such qualitatively-based work would provide a helpful parallel effort to the quantitative studies covered in the present text, research efforts that tend to lack the thickness of description often necessitated in interpreting results for practitioners. Even better, more mixed methods studies of families with adolescents also could be advanced, whereby quantitative and qualitative data gathering and analysis efforts could be combined.

Excellent recent examples of more qualitatively-based work include studies on parent-adolescent dyadic topics such as communication about sex (Afifi, Joseph, & Aldeis, 2008; O'Sullivan, Meyer-Bahlburg, & Watkins, 2001) more general parent-adolescent communication (Richardson, 2004), adolescent-to-parent abuse (Cottrell & Monk, 2004), and parent and adolescent choices made about spending time together (Ashbourne & Daly, 2010). Fatherhood issues more specifically also have received increased attention by qualitative researchers, including topics such as the fatherhood experiences of violent inner-city youth (Wilkinson, Magora, Garcia & Khurana, 2009) and court-involved Mexican-origin teenage fathers (Parra-Cardona, Sharp, & Wampler, 2008), father–daughter relationships in low-¥income minority families (Way & Gillman, 2000), and adolescent and young adult males' expectations about future fatherhood issues (Marsiglio, Hutchinson, & Cohan, 2000). Still other qualitative work on families with adolescents includes a focus on the family dynamics of immigrant families (Qin, 2008), attachment and individuation issues (Bell et al., 2007), family contributions to adolescent resilience (Ungar, 2004), and the experience of being in family therapy (Sheridan, Peterson, & Rosen, 2010).

Finally, while enormous empirical gains clearly have been made over the past 15 years, it must be said that the literature on families with adolescents continues to suffer from an overreliance on the adolescent's perspective. In a similar vein, whenever a parent's perspective is utilized in a study, more often than not it is that of the mother. Although these predilections exist throughout the family literature (Aquilino, 1999; Dadds, 1995; Phares, 1999), the continued reliance on adolescent only and mother only perspectives in research on families with adolescents is thought to be particularly problematical, especially when the focus becomes the assessment of some aspect of family functioning (Mathijssen, Koot, Verhulst, De Bruyn, & Oud, 1997; Sabatelli & Bartle, 1995).

Bogenschneider and Pallock (2008) raised these sorts of questions about the use of family member perspectives in a study of parental responsiveness using the reports of 440 adolescents in the 8th–12th grades, and their mothers and fathers. One part of this study was a reaction to previous research efforts that asserted a preference for using adolescents' perspectives on parenting behaviors when predicting adolescent outcomes (cf. Fletcher, Steinberg, & Williams-Wheeler, 2004). A second component of this research focused on the relative similarities or discrepancies between parent and adolescent reports, something that also has been related to adolescent outcomes in previous research (Ohannessian, Lerner, Lerner, & von Eye, 2000). A third objective of this study attended to the relative degree to which parent and adolescent reports operated in an independent fashion from one another.

Overall, the findings from this study provided strong support for the notion that all three perspectives – adolescent, mother, and father – were important sources of information about the adolescent outcome variables (grades, substance use, delinquent activity, and internal distress as reported by the adolescents only). Some evidence also was generated regarding the association between dissimilar scores and poor adolescent outcomes, at least in terms of internal stress, and the analyses also hinted at some complex and nonindependent relationships among the reports of the three family members.

Bogenschneider and Pallock (2008) raised a number of important methodological issues in light of their findings that have applicability beyond the parochial study of parental responsiveness. Of significant interest here was their rejection of the notion that any one family member could generate a "better" report than the others, instead noting that each perspective was unique and valuable. Also, these scholars argued against the combination of family member scores in any manner that could potentially obscure important differences among raters.

These are exactly the types of methodological issues that provoke questions regarding the unit of analysis that is employed in any family-based research effort. Readers will recall that the empirical part of this book regarded empirical efforts to be family-based under any of four circumstances: the single intergenerational dyad, the adolescent's nonspecific relationship to parents, the adolescent's family as a totality, and the family with adolescents as the combination of various dyads (adolescent–father, adolescent–mother, adolescent–sibling, etc.). While these four different forms of "family" were given equal treatment in the research section, the assertion is made here that these different approaches are not equally sophisticated in their approach to the study of family variables.

The difficulty with a single intergenerational dyad approach is axiomatic. By definition, it does not reflect the family as a whole, unless the empirical effort is meant to describe the more atypical case where a given household contains only one adult and one adolescent. In turn, the main problem with the nonspecific parent–adolescent relationship and the family as a totality is what might best be described as questions regarding "regression to the mean." For instance, when the researcher does not discriminate between parents, what happens to adolescents' answers about the relationships with their parents when their relationship with their mother is extremely warm while their relationship with their father is slightly cold? In the situation where the family as a totality approach is adopted, in addition to potentially different relationships between the adolescent and each parent, how does an adolescent judge the overall emotional climate of her/his family when relationships with siblings might vary as much or more?

In fact, it is only when the family is seen or measured as the combination of various dyads that the researcher is able to acquire that specificity of measurement, and therefore gains a more precise way of describing what is occurring within the various dyads of those families (Bartle-Haring & Gavazzi, 1996). Hence, it is believed that future research efforts not only should incorporate multiple family member perspective wherever possible, but also should focus questions at a dyadic level.

This means that adolescents should be asked to report about their relationship with their mother in a separate fashion from how they would report on their relationship with their father. In turn, mothers and fathers each would report on their own individual relationship with their son or daughter. And most importantly, such data would be analyzed with statistical procedures that retain and attend to the dyadic qualities of this information. There are a number of ways that researchers can handle dyadic data of this nature, and the number and use of these sophisticated statistical procedures continues to expand rapidly in the family field (Lyons and Sayer, 2005; Whiteman & Loken, 2006).

That being said, there is at least one approach to family-oriented data – the Social Relations Model (SRM: Kenny & La Voie, 1984) – that holds great promise for future studies of families with adolescents. SRM allows for the conceptualization and analysis at all three units of analysis: individual, dyadic, and family system levels. This is accomplished through the isolation of four unique sources of information – an actor effect, a partner effect, a relationship effect, and a family effect – that each account for a certain portion of the variance regarding a variable of interest to researchers (Cook, 2001a, 2001b).

To explain, consider first the adolescent's (let's call her Susie) perspective regarding her family's problem-solving skills. There is an "actor effect" that is used to describe how Susie thinks each of her family members is able to solve problems in general (Susie thinks that her Dad and Mom are pretty good problem solvers, but her older sister Tina is the best problem solver of all). There is also a "partner effect" that is used to indicate how Susie thinks that each family member elicits problem solving abilities from others (Mom seems to help everyone do their best problem solving, for instance).

Further, there is a "relationship effect" that speaks to what happens in specific dyads (for some reason, Tina just cannot seem to problem solve well with Susie as she can with other family members). And finally, the "family effect" is an indication of overall similarities or differences among family members (compared to all other families in the sample, Susie's family members solve problems very well). Now add in Dad, Mom, and Tina's perceptions of each family member's problem-solving abilities in the same manner – which gives you the ability to look specifically at "rater effects" as well – and you get a snapshot of what the SRM approach is capable of generating for researchers (Cook, 2005).

The Bartle-Haring, Kenny, and Gavazzi (1999) study on family differentiation that was reviewed in the research portion of the book above provides one illustration of the SRM's use in research that specifically targets families with adolescents. Another excellent example is a study by Buist, Dekovic, Meeus, and van Aken (2004), whereby the SRM approach was used to examine attachment relationships in families with adolescents. Still other examples of the SRM approach's use in research on families with adolescents can be found in an excellent review conducted by Eichelsheim, Dekovic, Buist, and Cook (2009). From a methodological standpoint, the sophisticated nature of these studies provides ample evidence to suggest that substantial consideration should be given to utilizing this particular way of framing research on families with adolescents. In essence, the reader gains access to information about potential similarities and differences at multiple levels of analysis: individual, dyadic, and family system.

13.3 Outlook on Application Efforts Targeting Families with Adolescents

We began the application focus of this book with the question: What is our knowledge base about how to prevent problems in families with adolescents, or otherwise what do we know about how to intervene with adolescents and their families when difficulties arise? There is in fact a substantial knowledge base about how to intervene with adolescents and their families when difficulties arise, and there is a considerable literature that informs the practice of preventing problems in families with adolescents as well. The family-based prevention and intervention efforts reviewed in the application part of this book represent a praiseworthy collection of best practices and promising approaches to work with the families of adolescents. On the whole, the developers of these initiatives are to be commended for their attention to both theoretical and empirical rigor.

Similar to the theoretical and empirical parts of this book, readers must be cautioned that the literature covered in the application part was not exhaustive. Rather, the studies covered here were meant to serve as a solid representation of some of the best prevention and intervention efforts that target families with adolescents. Bodies of work not covered in this book that readers might find interesting and informative include the empirical literature surrounding new treatment approaches in the health care arena, including the adolescent's response to illness in other family members (Davey, Gulish, Askew, Godette, & Childs, 2005; Faulkner & Davey, 2002). As well, other application work having arisen more recently in response to contemporary issues eventually may make an important contribution to the evidence-based literature on working with families of adolescents, including those dealing with hurricane destruction (Rowe & Liddle, 2008), war (Taft, Schumm, Panuzio, & Proctor, 2008), violence (Bonomi & Kelleher, 2007), homelessness (Gewirtz, 2007), having adolescents who come out as gay, lesbian, or bisexual (Saltzburg, 2007), HIV risks (Gangamma, Slesnick, Toviessi, & Serovich, 2008), and dealing with issues revolving around cybersex (Delmonico & Griffin, 2008).

In addition, the present limitations of the work covered within this book give us plenty of clues about the direction that future application-based work targeting families with adolescents ought to take. Much of the course of action can be extracted directly from the effectiveness principles (Kumpfer & Alvarado, 1998; Small, Cooney & O'Connor, 2009; Small & Huser, in press) covered in the application part of this book. That is, future work in this area should intensify present efforts to be guided by explicit theoretical principles, to offer comprehensive activities for family members to take part in together that are developmentally appropriate, to attend to culturally specific issues in the design and implementation phases of the initiative, to use the latest methodological advances in research and evaluation efforts surrounding the initiative, and to have all of this offered by well-trained professionals in a manual-driven format that attends closely to issues of fidelity.

All of that said, it is important to increase the reader's sensitivity to understanding how families can be viewed from quite different lenses within the context of this literature on application. Often as not, prevention and intervention efforts reflect activities that are done "to" families. Here, families are the recipients or "consumers" of the efforts. In contrast, calls have been made to direct the field's attention toward efforts that provide services "for families" and "with families" (Hoagwood, 2005).

In essence, families viewed in this latter manner are more likely to be seen as "partners" in the delivery of services to their members. This is a difference that can truly make a difference in application efforts targeting families with adolescents. For this reason, developers of prevention and intervention-based work with this population would do well to attend to a number of efforts that seek to create these sorts of partnerships within a collaborative context of working "for" and "with" family members.

Family empowerment, both as an activity and as a measurable construct, is one important contribution to the discussion of such partnerships with families. The use of a family empowerment perspective focuses attention on how family members are able to experience a sense of control over their lives and the situations that they are facing in their lives together (Koren, DeChillo, & Friesen, 1992). In a similar vein, family empowerment has been discussed as an effort to give family members "voice and choice" in the types and amounts of services that they receive (Scheer & Gavazzi, 2009).

Often as not, family empowerment efforts focus on information-sharing and decision-making actions taken for and with adult caregivers that surround the provision of some sort of services for adolescent (and younger age) family members (Kalafat, 2004; McCammon, Spencer, & Friesen, 2001; Singh et al., 1997). As such, family empowerment becomes a process of considering families within concepts of wellness, competence, and strengths rather than illness, deficits and weaknesses (Perkins & Zimmerman, 1995). Such efforts coexist with more individualized efforts to foster "adolescent empowerment" as well (Chinman & Linney, 1998).

Studies generally have indicated that family empowerment efforts are linked to positive outcomes for children, adolescents, and their families. For instance, Resendez, Quist, and Matshazi (2000) reported significant associations between family empowerment, satisfaction with mental health services, and the functioning levels of adolescents and children. Graves and Shelton (2007) reported that the relationship between those same functioning levels and being involved in family-centered care is mediated by family empowerment levels. Further, family empowerment training efforts developed by Bickman and colleagues (Bickman, Heflinger, Northrup, Sonnichsen, & Schilling, 1998; Heflinger, Bickman, Northrup, Sonnichsen, & Schilling, 1998) have been shown to generate significant gains for families whose adolescents and children are receiving services from mental health systems.

The idea of giving family members greater "voice and choice" in terms of the services they receive is not an unfamiliar concept in the literature on family-based interventions. For example, a study of the family empowerment component of MST (multisystemic therapy as reviewed in the family intervention chapter above) was undertaken by Cunningham, Henggeler, Brondino, and Pickrel (1999) using a sample of 118 families with substance using and court-involved adolescents between the ages of 12 and 17 (average age of 15.7 years). Families enrolled in MST displayed significantly greater family empowerment levels as compared to the treatment as usual control group. Also, results indicated that higher family empowerment levels were significantly associated with a range of individual, dyadic, and family system variables.

Dembo, Schmeidler, and Wotke (2003) report on the use of a family empowerment intervention (FEI) with 278 families of adolescents (average age of 14.5 years) arrested on either misdemeanor or felony charges. Latent growth analyses indicated that youth from families enrolled in FEI displayed significantly lower levels of delinquent behavior over a 3-year period in comparison to the control group. These findings are built on earlier evidence of the FEI's impact after 1 year (Dembo, Ramirez-Garnica, et al., 2000; Dembo, Seeberger, et al., 2000).

Seeing family members as partners instead of (or at least alongside of) the view that families are consumers or customers, has great potential to refashion how application efforts move forward. Hence, scholars interested in this type of alternative framework may do well to attend to family empowerment issues in their work with adolescents and their families. As well, there may be similar efforts to change lenses underway in other application areas that also may bear watching, perhaps most notably including the social justice approach that is being advanced in both the prevention (Hage & Kenny, 2009; Kenny & Hage, 2009) and intervention realms (Bowling, Kearney, Lumadue, & St. Germain, 2002; McDowell & Shelton, 2002; McGoldrick et al., 1999).

Chapter 14
The Need to Integrate Theory, Research, and Application Efforts

> *If you want a happy ending, that depends, of course, on where you stop your story.*
>
> Orson Welles

Abstract The knowledge base created about families with adolescents over the past 15 years has been organized in the present book as three separate parts according to work done on theory, research, and application topics, respectively. At the same time, the natural overlap of these theoretical, empirical, and application literatures was discussed wherever possible. The present chapter makes the case for more systematic attempts to highlight the interconnectedness of these oft-separated scholarly works. Harkening back over 3 decades ago in the family literature, David Olson's "triple threat" model for bridging theory, research, and application efforts is brought forward for consideration by scholars who think about, observe, and work with families with adolescents. This chapter begins by briefly reviewing some of the key points made in this earlier work, and is followed by a discussion of some of the key factors that have served as barriers to the unification of these academic activities. This is followed by some concluding thoughts as to why the "triple threat" model is both applicable and advantageous to those scholars who study families with adolescents.

> Emily, Gordon, and Pat started graduate school at the same time 2 years ago, and had taken all of the same classes together during their first year of coursework. During their second year, however, each of these students had elected to take very different paths in pursuit of their individual interests. Emily had loaded up on every theory-based class that she could take throughout the university, whereas Gordon spent most of his second year sitting in research methods and statistics classes. Pat was enrolled in the clinical scholar track, so she had started her internship in the program's family clinic on campus at the same time that she had sat through a series of therapy techniques courses.

> These three budding scholars all ran into each other in the local coffee shop just prior to the start of classes for the year. Now entering their third year of graduate work, these students had a bit more flexibility in the scheduling of classes. Much to their mutual delight, they discovered that they all had decided to take the same class on families with adolescents.
>
> "I can't wait to hear what Professor Intégrez is going to talk about in terms of doing therapy with adolescents and their families," Pat exclaimed. "I have been working with so many families with teenagers this past year, and honestly I think they are my hardest cases. There are just so many problems going on in those families. Funny enough, though, I think that I have helped out most when we have spent more time identifying their family's strengths instead of talking about their problems."
>
> "My understanding is that the class is going to start with theory, Pat, so you're going to have to be patient," noted Gordon. "Besides, I bet the best part of the class is going to be the section on research. Professor Intégrez may be trained as a family therapist, but his track record as a researcher is pretty impressive. I hope he spends a lot of time talking about structural equation modeling techniques and multiple family member perspectives."
>
> "Ugggh. Both of you are going to have to chill out a bit," Emily said. "And Gordon, you're right, Professor Intégrez is going to start out with theory, which is exactly where any class should start anyway. You guys can't do good research or clinical practice without a sound theoretical grounding, right?"
>
> "Yeah, but come on, how much theory did you read in the last journal article you read?" asked Gordon. "And I sure don't see a lot of theory in Professor Intégrez's publications." Emily countered, "That's because you're only reading his research articles." "It's not his fault that journal editors keeping reducing the amount of space dedicated to theory."
>
> "Well, it will be interesting to see how all of this is handled in class," Pat said. "The only reason I took this course was because I thought that Professor Intégrez would be able to keep us talking about the practical implications of all this theory and research stuff you both are so hopped up about."

The last vignette in this book features students who are engaged in a dialogue that surrounded issues related to creating linkages between ideas, data, and application. Actual students (and professionals who train those students, for that matter) may recognize certain features of this hypothetical conversation in their own educational experiences. How many readers can relate most to Emily, or Gordon, or Pat? And how many more can relate to what Professor Intégrez might be up to in terms of designing a course that would cover the theory, research, and application literature on families with adolescents?

Your author had exactly these types of students and educators in mind when the goals and objectives of the present text were formulated. Overall, this book set out to cover the knowledge base that has been created about families with adolescents by organizing the literature according to work done (especially over the last 15 years) within the realms of theory, research, and application topics. It is anticipated that even a casual glance at the breadth and depth of material generated over these past 15 years would create a rather stunning portrait of our knowledge base about these families. Hopefully, after reading through all three major parts of this book it becomes even more clear that the field has developed a substantial knowledge base about families with adolescents as a result of the distinct activities within these three areas.

At the same time, it should be noted that this book also promised to cover the "natural overlap" between the theoretical, empirical, and application parts wherever possible. To a reasonable extent, this objective was achieved. Readers will observe that a significant portion of the empirical studies covered in the research portion of this book were designated as having been based on specific theoretical approaches, for instance. Also, the majority of prevention and intervention efforts reviewed in the application part were attached to some sort of theoretical framework. That being the case, the family field in general, and certainly the literature concerning families with adolescents more specifically, still has ways to go in terms of making clear, consistent, and simultaneous connections between theory, research, and application.

Is it meaningful (much less realistic) to imagine a family field that makes these linkages in a coherent and dependable manner? The answer to that question, stemming back at least 3 decades ago in the family literature, is decidedly in the affirmative.

The roots of this type of effort were set down over 3 decades ago in the family literature. Most notably, Olson (1976) wrote about the "triple threat" of bridging theory, research, and application efforts as something to which all family-based professionals were supposed to aspire. Similar sentiments also were expressed by Sprenkle (1976) in that same year, and have been echoed in the 1980s (Volk, 1989), the 1990s (Lavee & Dollahite, 1991), and in the present decade as well (Hawley & Gonzalez, 2005; Karem & Sprenkle, 2010; McWey et al., 2002).

These final thoughts begin by briefly reviewing some of the key points made in these earlier contributions. Next, some of the key factors that have served as barriers to the unification of these academic activities are discussed. This is followed by some concluding thoughts as to why the "triple threat" is both applicable and advantageous to those scholars who study families with adolescents.

14.1 Original Thoughts About the Need for a "Triple Threat" Model

Stressing the importance of making connections between theory, research, and application efforts can seem almost axiomatic, at least on the surface. The present state of the literature, however, hardly makes for any sort of "Manifest Destiny" regarding the comprehensive integration of these scholarly activities. So it might well be asked: Are these potential connections mutually advantageous to theorists, researchers, and practitioners?

Olson (1976) wrote as if the answer to that question was an unqualified affirmative response, delineating the favorable contributions that each linkage rendered. Highlights of these benefits for practitioners (mainly therapists in this article, as this was a chapter in a clinically oriented book that he edited) included the assertion that greater connectedness to researchers would foster the formulation of more precise operational definitions regarding therapeutic concepts, dimensions, and goals. Also, researchers were thought to be in a trustworthy position to supply practitioners with enhanced tools for both the initial assessment of family functioning and the measurement of change (especially in terms of treatment impact), as well as providing a platform for comparing family-based issues as they manifest themselves inside both clinical and nonclinical samples.

Reciprocally, Olson (1976) noted that researchers were thought to benefit from practitioners by gaining access to actual families involved in therapeutic interventions. Here, the ability to have contact with families dealing with authentic life situations and events were seen as having the potential to stimulate new and more complex hypotheses about how family dynamics play out in actual practice. In related fashion, researchers who were gathering data in the real life settings provided by practitioners were thought to have a huge advantage in terms of establishing increased validity claims about their empirical assertions.

All of this connects well to various calls that have been made to get beyond the sterile confines of therapeutic efficacy studies conducted in controlled research laboratories and out into the real world studies of therapeutic effectiveness (Pinsof & Wynne, 2000). In the most classic sense, the documentation of therapeutic efficacy revolves around the impact that a family-based treatment would have within a highly controlled setting such as a university research lab or hospital setting. And "controlled" is the operative word here, in that the main purpose of such research is to regulate and restrict any and all variation in outcomes due to influences beyond the treatment model itself.

In contrast, the documentation of therapeutic effectiveness involves the use of that same family-based treatment in an actual clinic or other location where families typically receive such services. The purpose of this type of research is much different, in that one of its main objectives surrounds the gathering of information about how well a given family-based treatment model works under "normal circumstances." It is overly simplistic and philosophically divisive to portray efficacy and effectiveness studies as dichotomous approaches to clinically based research, however. Instead, the documentation of efficacy and effectiveness should be seen as existing on a continuum that allows researchers and clinicians to compare and contrast findings from both "sides" of this empirical spectrum.

Olson (1976) also cataloged the potential contributions of theorists to both researchers and practitioners. The theorist–researcher relationship was portrayed as the strongest of all linkages in the triple threat model, in that historically a considerable amount of attention has been given to the testing of theoretically derived hypotheses in the family field. That said, there are various accounts of how otherwise sound empirical studies in the family field often avoid mention of any sort of specific theoretical grounding (cf. Lavee & Dollahite, 1991).

The theorist–practitioner relationship, in turn, was depicted by Olson (1976) as the "weakest link" of all, although the grounded theory approach was noted as providing perhaps the best opportunity for some scholarly connectedness. In brief, the grounded theory approach sorts and interprets qualitative data in ways that help researchers to identify overarching themes or categories of participant responses (Strauss & Corbin, 1998). In fact, very recent examples of a grounded theory approach have been used to guide effective practices in work with adolescents and their families (cf. Schmied & Walsh, 2010a, 2010b). In any event, theorists are thought to offer to both researchers and practitioners the ability to condense and refine their knowledge base through the development of fundamental and interrelated propositions about the phenomena under study.

In sum, these potential linkages all seem like "win–win" relationships here. Practitioners working with researchers could launch more rigorous comparisons and contrasts between different family therapy approaches, as well as examining potential within-group differences among clinicians working inside of a single modality of family-based treatment. Researchers working with practitioners in turn could gain access to real world settings that would increase both the complexity and validity of their work. And theorists working with both researchers and practitioners would enhance the explanatory power of these empirical and applied efforts through an emphasis on deductive reasoning.

14.2 Key Factors That Serve as Barriers to Unification

If the "triple threat" family scientist is deemed to be a constructive notion, then what is preventing such an intention from becoming fully realized? There are at least three major stumbling blocks that have arisen along the way. The first barrier to integration has been the perceptions (real or imagined) of the "split" between family researchers and family therapists. As first discussed above in the family-based interventions chapter of this book, it was noted that there has been some lessening of the divisions between family therapists and family researchers in more recent years.

To this day, however, those who claim to be "researcher clinicians" (or scientist-practitioners) remain a distinct minority in the family field (Crane, Wampler, Sprenkle, Sandberg, & Hovestadt, 2002), despite the fact that the main regulating body of the profession – the American Association for Marriage and Family Therapy (AAMFT) – states specifically its vested interest in promoting empirical knowledge and practice (Lee & Nichols, 2010). This lack of empirical grounding among members is evidenced by the relatively low numbers of practicing clinicians who are open to collaboration with researchers (Sandberg, Johnson, Robila, & Miller, 2002), the fairly small numbers of clinical faculty engaged in publishing research (Hawley & Gonzalez, 2005), and the infrequent emphasis on empirical work as a requirement of graduate training programs (McWey et al., 2002).

A second barrier to integration concerns the "ghettoization" of the family-based journals. Even a cursory examination of the three main family journals – all of which are amply represented in the articles covered in this book – reveals a rather acute isolation of scholarly activities. The *Journal of Marriage and the Family*, for instance, remains most intensively focused on empirical activity in an attempt to remain the "flagship journal for family research" (Demo, 2008). While some of the more recent articles have included at least some mention of the theoretical underpinnings of the studies published in *JMF*, this is not representative of the majority of articles contained in this journal. As well, there is scant mention of information that would be of interest to practitioners.

Family Relations, in contrast, historically has published empirical work that consistently highlights the implication of findings for practitioners. As noted in its mission statement, this journal "emphasizes family research with implications for intervention, education, and public policy." While the theoretical foundations of certain scholarly contributions periodically are discussed in the articles published in *FR*, this is by no means a consistent pattern of activities. And as noted above in the theory part of this book, the launch of the *Journal of Family Theory and Review* was meant to fulfill the need for a publication outlet for works on theory and the methods by which theory development is advanced.

A third barrier to integration, and perhaps the biggest culprit of all, is the subtle and obvious pressures that begin in graduate school to become more of a specialist and, therefore, less of a generalist. Volk (1989) railed against this tendency in his own attempt to make a call for the integration of theory, research, and application efforts, stating that "those in the applied domain (should) pursue training in advanced family research methodologies and statistical analysis ... and that theorists and researchers address the practical relevance of their work in all published materials" (p. 221). This may go a long way toward helping readers to understand the first stumbling block discussed above regarding the lack of emphasis on research in the family therapy field. To wit, although this relative newcomer to the mental health service delivery system seemingly would be under pressure to generate supportive empirical evidence, many of the professionals within the field simply do not have the proper training to meet the simultaneous demands for conducting appropriately sophisticated research activities alongside the provision of high quality clinical services.

Therefore, integration (or the lack thereof) of theory, research, and application efforts has its proper beginning in graduate training programs. Presently, however, there does indeed seem to be a set of demands, perhaps even an unwritten code of conduct, which guides students and new professionals toward the adoption of a more singular area of expertise. There certainly is something to be said for that sort of specialization. At the very least, it helps to define one's identity and clarify one's purpose and direction in her or his scholarship. As well, specialization tracks help departments and colleges set themselves apart from one another as they market their graduate programs to interested students.

And yet, to be an expert in one particular area does not automatically disqualify anyone from being conversant in other areas. In fact, just the opposite is the case. Theorists and researchers who state that they do not need each other's wares have little or no understanding of the scientific process. And intervention-based professionals who declare that they do not need theory or data to do their work are naïve at best and downright dangerous at worst.

In practice, the solution requires a "both/and" approach, where change takes place in both graduate programs and the journals. Yes, graduate programs need to do a better job by ensuring that their clinically trained students also are well-trained in theory and research methods. Likewise, more theoretically and empirically driven programs also need to create opportunities for graduate students to better understand the real world (i.e., real family) applicability of the material they are covering. At the same time, there needs to be more material covered in the flagship family journals that integrates information about theory, research, and practice. After all, if that sort of information is present in the journals, the graduate programs undoubtedly will teach it. And finally, all of these efforts over time should naturally produce more young professionals within the field who will self-identify as scientist-practitioners.

14.3 The Importance of Integration in the Study of Families with Adolescents

The "triple threat" model is ideally suited for scholars focused on families with adolescents. In large part, this model seems so relevant because the literature already contains so many excellent examples of exactly this sort of work. This is particularly true with regard to the sophisticated articles that published in the applied realm, the content that were reviewed in this book's application part.

Numerous examples of this type of work can be found in the family-based interventions chapter of this book, for instance. Here, readers were exposed to a number of application-based efforts (cf. Brief Strategic Family Therapy, Functional Family Therapy, Multidimensional Family Therapy, and Multisystemic Therapy) that retained high degrees of theoretical and empirical rigor. Hence, the scholarly efforts that surround these family-based interventions are shining examples of the triple threat model in action.

In turn, the better integration of theoretical, empirical, and practice-based material related to families with adolescents creates an opportunity for leadership in the social sciences. Most specifically, this ability to lead would surround the fulfillment of the tripartite mission of the university system itself, or at least those institutions of higher learning that operate under the land grant tradition of teaching, research, and service.

This ideal borrows loosely from a vision put forward by MacKenzie (1998) to deal with crime in the twenty-first century in the same way as agricultural issues were dealt with in previous generations. By targeting scholarship on families with adolescents in a similar manner, the field could bring needed *simultaneous* attention to what we know theoretically about these families, the amount of scientific evidence we have accrued in support of our concepts and propositions, and how to apply all of this information in the most practical sense possible. In an era when greater accountability is being demanded of publically funded universities and its faculty members, this would seem like an ideal time to be seen as leading the way in terms of accomplishing the core missions of higher learning institutions.

The logical outcome of such efforts would be reflected in a rather radically altered conversation between Emily, Gordon, and Pat, the fictional graduate students we first met at the beginning of this chapter. For starters, these students would not have "lost touch" with each other in their second year of graduate studies, in large part because they would have continued to have been enrolled in many of the same classes. Emily could remain most excited about the theoretical aspects of an upcoming class on families with adolescents, Gordon might still long for an extended empirical treatment of this area of inquiry, and Pat could continue to search for the practical application of various theoretical and research aspects of the class content. However, none of these graduate students would appear to be as disconnected from each other's main interests to the degree that they are portrayed currently in the opening vignette. And finally, instructors such as Professor Intégrez would be the rule, not the exception. At least at some future point, professionals trained in the "triple threat" tradition would begin to take their place within academia, and in so doing would forever change the face of family sciences, especially in terms of the study of families with adolescents.

14.4 Coda

So these final thoughts end on the hopeful note that a book such as this, one that contains all three components – theory, research, and application – might in some way make a small, but significant contribution to a more general approach to understanding and working with families with adolescents. Thus, my final thoughts are part of an appeal for scholars to do a better job of bringing their work together under a common umbrella. In essence, a call is being made here for all parties involved to commit to an effort that makes the different aspects of how we understand, observe, and work with families containing adolescent members more unified and seamless.

References

Abbey, A., Pilgrim, C., Hendrickson, P., & Buresh, S. (2000). Evaluation of a family-based substance abuse prevention program targeted for the middle school years. *Journal of Drug Education, 30*, 213–228.

Ackerman, N. W. (1966). *Treating the troubled family*. New York: Basic Books.

Ackerman, N. J. (1980). The family with adolescents. In E. A. Carter & M. McGoldrick (Eds.), *The family life cycle: A framework for family therapy* (pp. 147–170). New York: Gardner Press.

Adams, R. E., & Laursen, B. (2007). The correlates of conflict: Disagreement is not necessarily determinental. *Journal of Family Psychology, 21*, 445–458.

Adelman, H. S., & Taylor, L. (2003). Creating school and community partnerships for substance abuse prevention programs. *The Journal of Primary Prevention, 23*, 329–369.

Afifi, T. D., Joseph, A., & Aldeis, D. (2008). Why can't we just talk about it? An observational study of parents' and adolescents' conversations about sex. *Journal of Adolescent Research, 23*, 689–721.

Ainsworth, M. D. S., Blehar, M. C., Waters, E., & Wall, S. (1978). *Patterns of attachment: A psychological study of the strange situation*. Hillsdale, NJ: Lawrence Erlbaum.

Akers, R. L. (1998). *Social learning and social structure: A general theory of crime and deviance*. Boston, MA: Northeastern University Press.

Akers, R. L. (2000). *Criminological theories. Introduction, evaluation, and application* (3rd ed.). Los Angeles, CA: Roxbury.

Akers, R. L., Krohn, M. D., Lanza-Kaduce, L., & Radosevich, M. (1979). Social learning and deviant behavior: A specific test of a general theory. *American Sociological Review, 44*, 636–655.

Akers, R. L., & Lee, G. (1996). A longitudinal test of social learning theory: Adolescent smoking. *Journal of Drug Issues, 26*, 317–343.

Akers, R. L., & Lee, G. (1999). Age, social learning, and social bonding in adolescent substance use. *Deviant Behavior, 20*, 1–25.

Aktan, G. B. (1999). A cultural consistency evaluation of a substance abuse prevention program with inner city African-American families. *The Journal of Primary Prevention, 19*, 227–239.

Aldous, J. (2006). Family, ethnicity, and immigrant youths' educational achievements. *Journal of Family Issues, 27*, 1633–1667.

Alexander, J. F., Barton, C., Schiavo, R. S., & Parsons, B. V. (1976). Systems-behavioral intervention with families of delinquents: Therapist characteristics, family behavior, and outcome. *Journal of Consulting and Clinical Psychology, 44*, 656–664.

Alexander, J. F., & Parsons, B. V. (1973). Short term behavior interventions with delinquent families: Impact on family process and recidivism. *Journal of Abnormal Psychology, 81*, 219–225.

Alexander, J. F., & Parsons, B. V. (1982). *Functional family therapy*. Monterey, CA: Brooks/Cole.

Alfaro, E. C., Umaña-Taylor, A. J., & Bámaca, M. Y. (2006). The influence of interpersonal support on Latino adolescents' academic motivation. *Family Relations, 55*, 279–291.

Allen, J. P., Philliber, S., Herrling, S., & Kuperminc, G. P. (1997). Preventing teen pregnancy and academic failure: Experimental evaluation of a developmentally based approach. *Child Development, 64*, 729–742.

Allison, B., & Schultz, J. (2004). Parent–adolescent conflict in early adolescence. *Adolescence, 39*, 100–119.

Allen, J. P., & Hauser, S. T. (1996). Autonomy and relatedness in adolescent-family interactions as predictors of young adults' states of mind regarding attachment. *Development and Psychopathology, 8*, 793–809.

Allen, J. P., Moore, C., Kuperminc, G., & Bell, K. (1998). Attachment and adolescent psychosocial functioning. *Child Development, 69*, 1406–1419.

Amato, P. R., & Fowler, F. (2002). Parenting practices, child adjustment, and family diversity. *Journal of Marriage and Family, 64*, 703–716.

Ambert, A. (1992). *The effects of children on their parents*. Binghampton, NY: Haworth.

Antonishak, J., Sutfin, E. L., & Reppucci, N. D. (2005). Community influence on adolescent development. In T. P. Gullotta & G. Adams (Eds.), *Handbook of adolescent behavior problems* (pp. 57–78). New York: Springer.

Anderson, S. A., & Sabatelli, R. M. (1990). Differentiating differentiation and individuation: Conceptual and operational challenges. *American Journal of Family Therapy, 18*, 32–50.

Anderson, S. A., & Sabatelli, R. M. (2006). *Family interaction* (4th ed.). Boston: Allyn & Bacon.

Aquilino, W. (1999). Two views of one relationship: Comparing parents' and young adult children's reports of the quality of intergenerational relations. *Journal of Marriage and the Family, 61*, 858–870.

Arcia, E., Reyes-Blanes, M. E., & Vasquez-Montilla, E. (2000). Constructions and reconstructions: Latino parents' values for children. *Journal of Child and Family Studies, 9*, 333–350.

Arditti, J. A. (1999). Rethinking relationships between divorced mothers and their children: Capitalizing on family strengths. *Family Relations, 48*, 109–120.

Ardelt, M., & Day, L. (2002). Parents, siblings, and peers: Close social relationships and adolescent deviance. *Journal of Early Adolescence, 22*, 310–349.

Arnett, J. J. (2010). *Adolescence and emerging adulthood: A cultural approach* (4th ed.). New York: Prentice Hall.

Ashbourne, L. M. (2009). Reconceptualizing parent-adolescent relationships: A Dialogic Model. *Journal of Family Theory and Review, 1*, 211–222.

Ashbourne, L. M., & Daly, K. J. (2010). Parents and adolescents making time choices: Choosing a relationship. *Journal of Family Issues, 31*, 1419–1441.

Bagwell, C. L., Newcomb, A. F., & Bukowski, W. M. (1998). Preadolescent friendship and peer rejection as predictors of adult adjustment. *Child Development, 69*, 140–153.

Bahr, S. J., Maughan, S. L., Marcos, A. C., & Li, B. (1998). Family, religiosity, and the risk of adolescent drug use. *Journal of Marriage and Family, 60*, 979–992.

Bao, W. N., Whitbeck, L. B., Hoyt, D. R., & Conger, R. D. (1999). Perceived parental acceptance as a moderator of religious transmission among adolescent boys and girls. *Journal of Marriage and Family, 61*, 362–374.

Ball, A., & Wiley, A. (2005). The aspirations of farm parents and pre-adolescent children for generational succession of the family farm. *Journal of Agricultural Education, 46*, 36–46.

Bandura, A. (1977). *Social learning theory*. New York: General Learning Press.

Bandura, A. (1986). *Social foundations of thought and action: A social cognitive theory*. Englewood Cliffs, NJ: Prentice-Hall.

Bandura, A. (2001). Social cognitive theory: An agentic perspective. *Annual Review of Psychology, 52*, 1–26.

Bank, L., Burraston, B., & Snyder, J. (2004). Sibling conflict and ineffective parenting as predictors of adolescent boys' antisocial behavior and peer difficulties: Additive and interactional effects. *Journal of Research on Adolescence, 14*, 99–125.

Barber, B. K. (1997). Adolescent socialization in context: The role of connection, regulation, and autonomy in the family. *Journal of Adolescent Research, 12*, 5–11.

Barber, B. K. (1996). Parental psychological control: Revisiting a neglected construct. *Child Development, 67*, 3296–3319.
Barber, B. K., & Buehler, C. (1996). Family cohesion and enmeshment: Different constructs, different effects. *Journal of Marriage and the Family, 58*, 433–441.
Baril, M. E., Crouter, A. C., & McHale, S. M. (2007). Processes linking adolescent well-being, marital love, and coparenting. *Journal of Family Psychology, 21*, 645–654.
Barnes, G. M., Hoffman, J. H., Welte, J. W., Farrell, M. P., & Dintcheff, B. A. (2006). Effects of parental monitoring and peer deviance on substance use and delinquency. *Journal of Marriage and Family, 68*, 1084–1104.
Barnes, G. M., Reifman, A. S., Farrell, M. P., & Dintcheff, B. A. (2000). The effects of parenting on the development of adolescent alcohol misuse: A six-wave latent growth model. *Journal of Marriage and Family, 62*, 175–186.
Barrera, M., Prelow, H. M., Dumka, L. E., Gonzales, N. A., Knight, G. P., Michaels, M. L., et al. (2002). Pathways from family economic conditions to adolescents' distress: Supportive parenting, stressors outside the family, and deviant peers. *Journal of Community Psychology, 30*, 135–152.
Bartle-Haring, S. E., & Gavazzi, S. M. (1996). Multiple views on family data: The sample case of adolescent, maternal, and paternal perspectives on family differentiation levels. *Family Process, 35*, 457–472.
Bartle-Haring, S. E., Kenny, D. A., & Gavazzi, S. M. (1999). Multiple perspectives on family differentiation: Analyses by Multitrait Multimethod Matrix and Triadic Social Relations Models. *Journal of Marriage and the Family, 61*, 491–503.
Barton, C., Alexander, J. F., Waldron, H., Turner, C. W., & Warburton, J. (1985). Generalizing treatment effects of functional family therapy: Three replications. *American Journal of Family Therapy, 13*, 16–26.
Baumrind, D. (1978). Parent disciplinary patterns and social competence in children. *Youth and Society, 9*, 239–276.
Baumrind, D. (1995). Commentary on sexual orientation: Research and social policy implications. *Developmental Psychology, 31*, 130–136.
Bean, R. A., Barber, B. K., & Crane, D. R. (2003). Parent support, behavioral control, and psychological control among African American youth: The relationships to academic grade, delinquency, and depression. *Journal of Family Issues, 27*, 1335–1355.
Bean, R. A., Bush, K. R., McKenry, P. C., & Wilson, S. M. (2003). The impact of parental support, behavioral control, and psychological control on the academic achievement and self-esteem of African American and European American adolescents. *Journal of Adolescent Research, 18*, 523–541.
Bell, D. C. (2009). Attachment without fear. *Journal of Family Theory and Review, 1*, 177–197.
Bell, L. G., Bell, D. C., & Nakata, Y. (2001). Triangulation and adolescent development in the US and Japan. *Family Process, 40*, 173–186.
Bell, L. G., Meyer, J., Rehal, D., Swope, C., Martin, D. R., & Lakhani, A. (2007). Connection and individuation as separate and independent processes: A qualitative analysis. *Journal of Family Psychotherapy, 18*, 43–59.
Belsky, J. (1981). Early human experience: A family perspective. *Developmental Psychology, 17*, 3–23.
Benda, B. B., & Corwyn, R. F. (1997). Religion and delinquency: The relationship after considering family and peer influences. *Journal for the Scientific Study of Religion, 36*, 81–92.
Bengston, V. L., & Allen, K. R. (1993). The life course perspective applied to families over time. In P. G. Boss, W. J. Doherty, R. LaRossa, W. R. Schumm, & S. K. Steinmetz (Eds.), *Sourcebook of family theories and methods* (pp. 469–499). New York: Plenum.
Bengston, V. L., Acock, A. C., Allen, K. R., Dilworth-Anderson, P., & Klein, D. M. (2005). *Sourcebook of family theory and research*. Thousand Oaks, CA: Sage.
Benson, M. J. (2005). Parent-adolescent relationships: Integrating attachment and Bowenian family systems theories. In V. L. Bengston, A. C. Acock, K. R. Allen, P. Dilworth-Anderson, &

D. M. Klein (Eds.), *Sourcebook of family theory and research* (pp. 382–385). Thousand Oaks, CA: Sage.

Bianchi, S. M., & Casper, L. M. (2005). Explanations of family change: A family demographic perspective. In V. L. Bengston, A. C. Acock, K. R. Allen, P. Dilworth-Anderson, & D. M. Klein (Eds.), *Sourcebook of family theory and research* (pp. 93–103). Thousand Oaks, CA: Sage.

Bickman, L., Heflinger, C. A., Northrup, D., Sonnichsen, S., & Schilling, S. (1998). Longterm outcomes to family caregiver empowerment. *Journal of Child and Family Studies, 7*, 269–282.

Bloom, M. (2000). Twenty years of the Journal of Primary Prevention: A collage. *The Journal of Primary Prevention, 20*, 189–255.

Blume, L. B. (2009). Books still matter: A note from the book review editor. *Journal of Family Theory and Review, 1*, 54–55.

Blumenkrantz, D. G., & Gavazzi, S. M. (1993). Guiding transitional events for children and adolescents through a modern day rite of passage. *Journal of Primary Prevention, 13*, 199–212.

Bocknek, E. L., Sanderson, J., & Britner, P. A. (2009). Ambiguous loss and posttraumatic stress in school-age children of prisoners. *Journal of Child and Family Studies, 18*, 323–333.

Bogenschneider, K. (1996). An ecological risk/protective theory for building prevention programs, policies, and community capacity to support youth. *Family Relations, 45*, 127–138.

Bogenschneider, K., & Pallock, L. (2008). Responsiveness in parent-adolescent relationships: Are influences conditional? Does the reporter matter? *Journal of Marriage and Family, 70*, 1015–1029.

Bogenschneider, K., Small, S. A., & Tsay, J. C. (1997). Child, parent, and contextual influences on perceived parenting competence among parents of adolescents. *Journal of Marriage and Family, 59*, 345–362.

Bonomi, A. E., & Kelleher, K. J. (2007). Dating violence, sexual assault and suicide attempts in urban adolescents: Ending the silence. *Archives of Pediatrics and Adolescent Medicine, 161*, 609–610.

Booth, A., Scott, M. E., & King, V. (2010). Father residence and adolescent problem behavior: Are youth always better off in two-parent families? *Journal of Family Issues, 31*, 585–605.

Borduin, C. M., Henggeler, S. W., Blaske, D. M., & Stein, R. (1990). Multisystemic treatment of adolescent sexual offenders. *International Journal of Offender Therapy and Comparative Criminology, 34*, 105–113.

Borduin, C. M., Schaeffer, C. M., & Heiblum, N. (2009). A randomized clinical trial of multisystemic therapy with juvenile sexual offenders: Effects on youth social ecology and criminal activity. *Journal of Consulting and Clinical Psychology, 77*, 26–37.

Bornstein, M. H. (1995). *Handbook of parenting: Vol. 3. Status and social conditions of parenting*. Mahwah, NJ: Erlbaum.

Bosco, G. L., Renk, K., Dinger, T. M., Epstein, M. K., & Phares, V. (2003). The connections between adolescents' perceptions of parents, parental psychological symptoms, and adolescent functioning. *Applied Developmental Psychology, 24*, 179–200.

Boss, P. G., Doherty, W. J., LaRossa, R., Schumm, W. R., & Steinmetz, S. K. (1993). *Sourcebook of family theories and methods*. New York: Plenum.

Bowlby, J. (1969). *Attachment and loss*. New York: Basic Books.

Bowling, S. W., Kearney, L. K., Lumadue, C. A., & St. Germain, N. R. (2002). Considering justice: An exploratory study of family therapy with adolescents. *Journal of Marital and Family Therapy, 28*, 213–223.

Bowen, M. (1978). *Family therapy in clinical practice*. New York: Aronson.

Bradshaw, C. P., Glaser, B. A., Calhoun, G. B., & Bates, J. M. (2006). Beliefs and practices of the parents of violent and oppositional adolescents: An ecological perspective. *The Journal of Primary Prevention, 27*(3), 245–263.

Breivik, K., & Olweus, D. (2006). Adolescents' adjustment in four post-divorce family structures: Single mother, stepfather, joint physical custody and single father families. *Journal of Divorce and Remarriage, 44*, 99–124.

Broderick, C. B. (1993). *Understanding family process*. Thousand Oaks, CA: Sage.

Brody, G. H., & Ge, X. (2001). Linking parenting practices and self-regulation to psychological functioning and alcohol use during early adolescence. *Journal of Family Psychology, 15*, 82–94.

Brody, G. H., Kogan, S. M., Chen, Y-f, & Murry, V. M. (2008). Long-term effects of the Strong African American Families program on youths' conduct problems. *Journal of Adolescent Health, 43*, 474–481.

Brody, G. H., Murry, V. M., Gerrard, M., Gibbons, F. X., McNair, L., Brown, A. C., et al. (2006). The Strong African American Families program: Prevention of youths' high-risk behavior and a test of a model of change. *Journal of Family Psychology, 20*, 1–11.

Bronfenbrenner, U. (1979). *The ecology of human development.* Cambridge, MA: Harvard University Press.

Bronfenbrenner, U. (1995). Developmental ecology through space and time: A future perspective. In P. Moen, G. H. Elder, & K. Luscher (Eds.), *Examining lives in context: Perspectives on the ecology of human development* (pp. 619–647). Washington, DC: American Psychological Association.

Bronfenbrenner, U., & Morris, P. A. (1998). The ecology of developmental processes. In W. Damon, & R. M. Lerner (Eds.), *Handbook of child psychology, Vol. 1: Theoretical models of human development* (5th ed., pp. 993–1023). New York: Wiley.

Bronte-Tinkew, J., Moore, K. A., & Carrano, J. (2006). The father-child relationship, parenting styles, and adolescent risk behaviors in intact families. *Journal of Family Issues, 27*, 850–881.

Brown, S. A., & Landry-Meyer, L. (2007). An ecological approach to high school students' school food choice. *Journal of Family and Consumer Sciences Education, 25*, 34–44.

Brown, S. L., & Manning, W. D. (2009). Family boundary ambiguity and the measurement of family structure: The significance of cohabitation. *Demography, 46*, 85–101.

Brown, S. L., & Rinelli, L. N. (2010). Family structure, family processes, and adolescent smoking and drinking. *Journal of Research on Adolescence, 20*, 259–273.

Bubolz, M. M., & Sontag, M. S. (1993). Human ecology theory. In P. G. Boss, W. J. Doherty, R. LaRossa, W. R. Schumm, & S. K. Steinmetz (Eds.), *Sourcebook of family theories and methods* (pp. 419–468). New York: Plenum.

Bucx, F., van Wel, F., Knijn, T., & Hagendoorn, L. (2008). Intergenerational contact and the life course status of young adult children. *Journal of Marriage and Family, 70*, 144–156.

Budney, A. J., & Higgins, S. T. (1998). *A community reinforcement plus vouchers approach: Treating cocaine addiction* (NIH Publication No. 98-4309). Rockville, MD: National Institute on Drug Abuse.

Buehler, C., Franck, K. L., & Cook, E. C. (2009). Adolescents' triangulation in marital conflict and peer relations. *Journal of Research on Adolescence, 19*, 669–689.

Buehler, C., Krishnakumar, A., Stone, G., Anthony, C., Pemberton, S., Gerard, J., et al. (1998). Interparental conflict styles and youth problem behaviors: A two-sample replication study. *Journal of Marriage and the Family, 60*, 119–132.

Buist, K. L., Dekovic, M., Meeus, W., & van Aken, M. A. G. (2002). Developmental patterns in adolescent attachment to mother, father and sibling. *Journal of Youth and Adolescence, 31*, 167–176.

Buist, K. L., Dekovic, M., Meeus, M. H., & van Aken, M. A. G. (2004). Attachment in adolescence: A social relations model analysis. *Journal of Adolescent Research, 19*(6), 826–850.

Burkhead, E. J., & Wilson, L. M. (1995). The family as a developmental system: Impact on the career development of individuals with disabilities. *Journal of Career Development, 21*, 187–199.

Bush, K. R., & Peterson, G. W. (2007). Family influences on child development. In T. P. Gullotta & G. M. Blau (Eds.), *Handbook of childhood behavioral issues* (pp. 43–67). New York: Routledge.

Butler, J. M., Skinner, M., Gelfand, D., Berg, C. A., & Wiebe, D. J. (2007). Maternal parenting style and adjustment in adolescents with Type I diabetes. *Journal of Pediatric Psychology, 32*, 1227–1237.

Byng-Hall, J. (1995). Creating a secure attachment base: Some implications of attachment theory for family therapy. *Family Process, 34*, 45–58.

Caffery, T., & Erdman, P. (2000). Conceptualizing parent-adolescent conflict: Applications from systems and attachment theories. *Family Journal, 8*, 14–21.

Campbell, F. A., Pungello, E. P., & Miller-Johnson, S. (2002). The development of perceived scholastic competence and global self-worth in African American adolescents from low-income families: The roles of family factors, early educational intervention, and academic experience. *Journal of Adolescent Research, 17*, 277–302.

Capaldi, D. M., & Stoolmiller, M. (1999). Co-occurrence of conduct problems and depressive symptoms in early adolescent boys: III. Prediction to young-adult adjustment. *Development and Psychopathology, 11*, 59–84.

Carlson, M. J. (2006). Family structure, father involvement, and adolescent behavioral outcomes. *Journal of Marriage and Family, 68*, 137–154.

Carson, D. K., Chowdhury, A., Perry, C. K., & Pati, C. (1999). Family characteristics and adolescent competence in India: Investigation of youth in Southern Orissa. *Journal of Youth and Adolescence, 28*, 211–233.

Carter, E. A., & McGoldrick, M. (1980). *The family life cycle: A framework for family therapy.* New York: Gardner.

Carter, E. A., & McGoldrick, M. (1989). *The changing family life cycle: A framework for family therapy.* Boston: Allyn & Bacon.

Cashwell, C. S., & Vacc, N. A. (1996). Familial influences on adolescent delinquent behavior. *Family Journal, 4*, 217–225.

Cassidy, J., & Shaver, P. R. (1999). *Handbook of attachment: Theory, research, and clinical applications.* New York: Guilford.

Catalano, R. F., Kosterman, R., Hawkins, J. D., Newcomb, M. D., & Abbott, R. D. (1996). Modeling the etiology of adolescent substance use: A test of the Social Development Model. *Journal of Drug Issues, 26*, 429–455.

Catalano, R. F., Kosterman, R., Haggerty, K. P., Hawkins, J. D., & Spoth, R. (1998). A Universal intervention for the prevention of substance abuse: Preparing for the drug free years. In *Drug abuse prevention through family interventions* (pp. 130–159). Rockville, MD: National Institute on Drug Abuse.

Catanzaroa, S. J., & Laurent, J. (2004). Perceived family support, negative mood regulation expectancies, coping, and adolescent alcohol use: Evidence of mediation and moderation effects. *Addictive Behaviors, 29*, 1779–1797.

Cavanagh, S. E. (2008). Family structure history and adolescent adjustment. *Journal of Family Issues, 29*, 944–980.

Cavanagh, S. E., & Huston, A. C. (2008). The timing of family instability and children's social adjustment. *Journal of Marriage and Family, 70*, 1258–1270.

Chao, R. (2001). Extending research on the consequences of parenting style for Chinese Americans and European Americans. *Child Development, 72*, 1832–1843.

Chamberlain, P., & Reid, J. (1998). Comparison of two community alternatives to incarceration for chronic juvenile offenders. *Journal of Consulting and Clinical Psychology, 6*, 624–633.

Chamberlain, P., & Rosicky, J. G. (1995). The effectiveness of family therapy in the treatment of adolescents with conduct disorders and delinquency. *Journal of Marital and Family Therapy, 21*, 441–459.

Chen, Z. Y., & Kaplan, H. B. (2005). Intergenerational transmission of constructive parenting. In T. R. Chibucos & R. W. Leite (Eds.), *Readings in family theory* (pp. 118–136). Thousand Oaks, CA: Sage.

Cherlin, A. J., Kiernan, K. E., & Chase-Lansdale, P. L. (1995). Parental divorce in childhood and demographic outcomes in young adulthood. *Demography, 32*, 299–318.

Chibucos, T. R., & Leite, R. W. (2005). *Readings in family theory.* Thousand Oaks, CA: Sage.

Chinman, M. J., & Linney, J. A. (1998). Toward a model of adolescent empowerment: Theoretical and empirical evidence. *The Journal of Primary Prevention, 18*, 393–413.

Chun, Y. J., & MacDermid, S. M. (1997). Perceptions of family differentiation, individuation, and self-esteem among Korean adolescents. *Journal of Marriage and the Family, 59*, 451–462.

References

Chung, G. H., Flook, L., & Fuligni, A. (2009). Daily family conflict and emotional distress among adolescents from Latin American, Asian, and European backgrounds. *Developmental Psychology, 45*, 1406–1415.

Clarke-Stewart, A. (2006). What we have learned: Proof the families matter, policies for families and children, prospects for future research. In A. Clarke-Stewart & J. Dunn (Eds.), *Families count* (pp. 321–336). New York: Cambridge University Press.

Clausson, E., & Berg, A. (2008). Family intervention sessions: One useful way to improve schoolchildren's mental health. *Journal of Family Nursing, 14*, 289–313.

Cleveland, M. J., Feinberg, M. E., & Greenberg, M. T. (2010). Protective families in high-and low-risk environments: Implications for adolescent substance use. *Journal of Youth and Adolescence, 39*, 114–126.

Coatsworth, J. D., Pantin, H., & Szapocznik, J. (2002). Familias Unidas: A family-centered ecodevelopmental intervention to reduce risk for problem behavior among Hispanic adolescents. *Clinical Child and Family Psychology Review, 5*, 113–132.

Coatsworth, J. D., Santisteban, D. A., McBride, C. K., & Szapocznik, J. (2001). Brief strategic family therapy versus community control: Engagement, retention, and an exploration of the moderating role of adolescent symptom severity. *Family Process, 40*, 313–332.

Cobb, C. L. H. (1996). Adolescent-parent attachments and family problem-solving styles. *Family Process, 35*, 57–82.

Cobb, N. (2006). *Adolescence: Continuity, change, and diversity* (6th ed.). New York: McGraw Hill.

Cohen, E. A., Vasey, M. W., & Gavazzi, S. M. (2003). Family differentiation as individuality and intimacy tolerance: Multiple family perspectives and the dimensionality of family distance regulation. *Journal of Family Issues, 24*, 99–123.

Colan, N. B., Mague, K. C., Cohen, R. S., & Schneider, R. J. (1994). Family education in the workplace: A prevention program for working parents and school-age children. *Journal of Primary Prevention, 15*, 161–172.

Collins, W. A., & Laursen, B. (2004). Changing relationships, changing youth: Interpersonal contexts of adolescent development. *The Journal of Early Adolescence, 24*, 55–62.

Collins, W. A., Laursen, B., Mortenson, N., Luebker, C., & Ferreira, M. (1997). Conflict processes and transitions in parent and peer relationships: Implications for autonomy and regulation. *Journal of Adolescent Research, 12*, 178–198.

Conger, R. D., Conger, K. J., & Martin, M. J. (2010). Socioeconomic status, family processes, and individual development. *Journal of Marriage and the Family, 72*, 685–704.

Conger, K. J., Conger, R. D., & Scaramella, L. V. (1997). Parents, siblings, psychological control, and adolescent adjustment. *Journal of Adolescent Research, 12*(1), 113–138.

Conger, R. D., Patterson, G. R., & Ge, X. (1995). It takes two to replicate: A meditational model for the impact of parents' stress on adolescent adjustment. *Child Development, 66*, 80–97.

Connell, A. M., Dishion, T. J., Yasui, M., & Kavanagh, K. (2007). An adaptive approach to family intervention: Linking engagement in family-centered intervention to reductions in adolescent problem behavior. *Journal of Consulting and Clinical Psychology, 75*, 568–579.

Cook, L. S. (2001a). Adolescent addiction and delinquency in the family system. *Issues in Mental Health Nursing, 22*, 151–157.

Cook, W. L. (2000). Understanding attachment security in family context. *Journal of Personality and Social Psychology, 78*, 285–294.

Cook, W. L. (2001b). Interpersonal influence in family systems: A Social Relations Model analysis. *Child Development, 72*, 1179–1197.

Cook, W. L. (2005). The SRM approach to family assessment: An introduction and case example. *European Journal of Psychological Assessment, 21*, 216–225.

Corcoran, J. (1999). Ecological factors associated with adolescent pregnancy: A review of the literature. *Adolescence, 34*, 603–619.

Corwyn, R. F., & Bradley, R. H. (2005). Socioeconomic status and child externalizing behaviors. In V. L. Bengston, A. C. Acock, K. R. Allen, P. Dilworth-Anderson, & D. M. Klein (Eds.), *Sourcebook of family theory and research* (pp. 469–483). Thousand Oaks, CA: Sage.

Cottrell, B., & Monk, P. (2004). Adolescent-to-parent abuse: A qualitative overview of common themes. *Journal of Family Issues, 25*, 1072–1095.

Coulton, C., Korbin, J., Su, M., & Chow, J. (1995). Community level factors and child maltreatment rates. *Child Development, 66*, 1262–1276.

Cox, M., & Harter, K. S. M. (2003). Parent-child relationships. In M. H. Bornstein, L. Davidson, C. L. M. Keyes, K. A. Moore, & The Center for Child Well-being (Eds.), *Well-being: Positive development across the life course* (pp. 191–204). Mahwah, NJ: Lawrence Erlbaum.

Cox, M. J., & Paley, B. (1997). Families as systems. *Annual Review of Psychology, 4*, 243–267.

Crane, D. R., Wampler, K. S., Sprenkle, D. H., Sandberg, J. G., & Hovestadt, A. J. (2002). The scientist-practitioner model in marriage and family therapy programs. *Journal of Marital and Family Therapy, 28*, 75–83.

Cretzmeyer, S. (2003). Attachment theory applied to adolescents. In P. Erdman & T. Caffery (Eds.), *Attachment and family systems* (pp. 65–77). New York: Brunner-Routledge.

Crockett, L. J., Bingham, C. R., Chopak, J. S., & Vicary, J. R. (1996). Timing of first sexual intercourse: The role of social control, social learning, and problem behavior. *Journal of Youth and Adolescence, 25*, 89–111.

Crosbie-Burnett, M., & Lewis, E. A. (1993). Theoretical contributions from social and cognitive behavioral psychology. In P. G. Boss, W. J. Doherty, R. LaRossa, W. R. Schumm, & S. K. Steinmetz (Eds.), *Sourcebook of family theories and methods* (pp. 531–558). New York: Plenum.

Crosnoe, R. (2004). Social capital and the interplay of families and schools. *Journal of Marriage and the Family, 66*, 267–280.

Crosnoe, R., & Cavanagh, S. E. (2010). Families with children and adolescents: A review, critique, and future agenda. *Journal of Marriage and the Family, 72*, 594–611.

Crosnoe, R., & Elder, G. H. (2004). Family dynamics, supportive relationships, and educational resilience during adolescence. *Journal of Family Issues, 25*, 571–602.

Crosswhite, J. M., & Kerpelman, J. (2009a). Coercion theory, self-control, and social information processing: Understanding potential mediators for how parents influence deviant behaviors. *Deviant Behaviors, 30*, 611–646.

Crosswhite, J. M., & Kerpelman, J. (2009b). Critiquing the general theory of crime's empirical evidence: Does the evidence support the theory? *Journal of Family Theory and Review, 1*, 146–163.

Crouter, A. C. (2006). Mothers and fathers at work. In A. Clarke-Stewart & J. Dunn (Eds.), *Families count* (pp. 135–154). New York: Cambridge University Press.

Cui, M., Conger, R. D., Bryant, C. M., & Elder, G. H. (2002). Parental behavior and the quality of adolescent friendships: A social-contextual perspective. *Journal of Marriage and Family, 64*, 676–689.

Cui, M., Donnellan, M. B., & Conger, R. D. (2007). Reciprocal influences between parents' marital problems and adolescent internalizing and externalizing behavior. *Developmental Psychology, 43*, 1544–1552.

Cunningham, P. B., Henggeler, S. W., Brondino, M. J., & Pickrel, S. G. (1999). Testing underlying assumptions of the family empowerment perspective. *Journal of Child and Family Studies, 8*, 437–449.

Dadds, M. R. (1995). *Families, children, and the development of dysfunction*. Thousand Oaks, CA: Sage.

Darling, N. (2007). Ecological systems theory: The person in the center of the circles. *Research in Human Development, 4*, 203–217.

Darling, N., & Steinberg, L. D. (1993). Parenting styles as context: An integrative model. *Psychological Bulletin, 113*, 487–496.

Davey, M., Gulish, L., Askew, J., Godette, K., & Childs, N. (2005). Adolescents coping with mom's breast cancer: Developing family intervention programs. *Journal of Marital and Family Therapy, 31*, 247–258.

David, C., Steele, R., Forehand, R., & Armistead, L. (1996). The role of family conflict and marital conflict in adolescent functioning. *Journal of Family Violence, 11*, 81–91.

References

Davidson, M. (1983). *Uncommon sense: The life and thought of Ludwig Von Bertalanffy.* Los Angeles, CA: J. P. Tarcher.

Davies, P. T., & Forman, E. M. (2002). Children's patterns of preserving emotional security in the interparental subsystem. *Child Development, 73,* 1880–1903.

Day, R. D. (2010). Stephen Gavazzi: Strong families, successful students: Helping teenagers reach their full academic potential. *Journal of Youth and Adolescence, 39,* 704–705.

Day, R. D., Gavazzi, S., & Acock, A. (2001). Compelling family processes. In A. Thornton (Ed.), *The well-being of children and families: Research and data needs* (pp. 103–126). Ann Arbor, MI: University of Michigan Press.

Day, R. D., Gavazzi, S. M., Miller, R., & Langeveld, A. (2009). Compelling family processes. *Marriage and Family Review, 45,* 116–128.

De Goede, I. H. A., Branje, S. J. T., Delsing, M. J. M. H., & Meeus, W. H. J. (2009). Linkages over time between adolescents' relationships with parents and friends. *Journal of Youth and Adolescence, 38,* 1304–1315.

Delmonico, D. L., & Griffin, E. J. (2008). Cybersex and the e-teen: What marriage and family therapists should know. *Journal of Marital and Family Therapy, 34,* 431–444.

Deković, M., Buist, K. L., & Reitz, E. (2004). Stability and changes in problem behavior during adolescent latent growth analysis. *Journal of Youth and Adolescence, 33,* 1–12.

Deković, M., Janssens, J. M. A. M., & van As, N. M. C. (2003). Parental predictors of antisocial behavior in adolescence. *Family Process, 42,* 223–235.

Dembo, R., Ramirez-Garnica, G., Rollie, M., Schmeidler, J., Livingston, S., & Hartsfield, A. (2000). Youth recidivism 12 months after a family empowerment intervention: Final report. *Journal of Offender Rehabilitation, 31,* 29–65.

Dembo, R., Schmeidler, J., & Wotke, W. (2003). Impact of a family empowerment intervention on delinquent behavior: A latent growth model analysis. *Journal of Offender Rehabilitation, 37,* 17–41.

Dembo, R., Seeberger, W., Shemwell, M., Schmeidler, J., Klein, L., Rollie, M., et al. (2000). Psychosocial functioning among juvenile offenders 12 months after family empowerment intervention. *Journal of Offender Rehabilitation, 32,* 1–56.

Demo, D. H. (2008). From the editor. *Journal of Marriage and Family, 70,* 1–2.

Demo, D. H., & Acock, A. C. (1996). Family structure, family process, and adolescent well-being. *Journal of Research on Adolescence, 6,* 457–488.

Demo, D. H., Aquilino, W. S., & Fine, M. A. (2005). Family composition and family transitions. In V. L. Bengston, A. C. Acock, K. R. Allen, P. Dilworth-Anderson, & D. M. Klein (Eds.), *Sourcebook of family theory and research* (pp. 119–134). Thousand Oaks, CA: Sage.

Diamond, G. S., Reis, B. F., Diamond, G. M., Siqueland, L., & Isaacs, L. (2002). Attachment Based Family Therapy for depressed adolescents: A treatment development study. *Journal of the American Academy of Child and& Adolescent Psychiatry, 47,* 1190–1196.

Diamond, G. S., Siqueland, L., & Diamond, G. M. (2003). Attachment-based family therapy: A program of treatment development research. *Clinical Child Family Psychology Review, 6,* 107–128.

Diamond, G. S., Wintersteen, M. B., Brown, G. K., Diamond, G. M., Gallop, R., Shelef, K., & Levy, S. (2010). Attachment-Based Family Therapy for adolescents with suicidal ideation: A randomized controlled trial. *Journal of the American Academy of Child and Adolescent Psychiatry, 49,* 122–131.

Dilworth-Anderson, P., Burton, L. M., & Klein, D. M. (2005). Contemporary and emerging theories in studying families. In V. L. Bengston, A. C. Acock, K. R. Allen, P. Dilworth-Anderson, & D. M. Klein (Eds.), *Sourcebook of family theory and research* (pp. 35–50). Thousand Oaks, CA: Sage.

Dishion, T. J., Eddy, J. M., Haas, E., Li, F., & Spracklin, K. M. (1997). Friendships and violent behavior during adolescence. *Social Development, 6,* 207–225.

Dishion, T. J., Kavanagh, K., Schneiger, A., Nelson, S., & Kaufman, N. (2002). Preventing early adolescent substance use: A family-centered strategy for the public middle-school ecology. *Prevention Science, 3*, 191–201.

Dishion, T. J., Nelson, S. E., & Kavanagh, K. (2003). The family check-up for high-risk adolescents: Preventing early-onset substance use by parent monitoring. *Behavior Therapy, 34*, 553–571.

Dixon, S. V., Graber, J. A., & Brooks-Gunn, J. (2008). The roles of respect for parental authority and parenting practices in parent-child conflict among African American, Latino, and European American families. *Journal of Family Psychology, 22*, 1–11.

Dorius, C. J., Bahr, S. J., Hoffmann, J. P., & Harmon, E. L. (2004). Parenting practices as moderators of the relationship between peers and adolescent marijuana use. *Journal of Marriage and Family, 66*, 163–178.

Dotterer, A. M., Hoffman, L., Crouter, A. C., & McHale, S. M. (2008). A longitudinal examination of the bidirectional links between academic achievement and parent-adolescent conflict. *Journal of Family Issues, 29*, 762–779.

Dumka, L. E., Gonzales, N. A., Bonds, D., & Millsap, R. (2009). Academic success in Mexican origin adolescent boys and girls: The role of mothers' and fathers' parenting and cultural orientation. *Sex Roles, 60*, 588–599.

Dumka, L. E., Gonzales, N., Woods, J., & Formoso, D. (1998). Using qualitative methods to develop contextually relevant measures and preventive interventions: An illustration. *American Journal of Community Psychology, 26*, 600–633.

Dusenbury, L. (2000). Family-based drug abuse prevention programs: A review. *The Journal of Primary Prevention, 20*, 337–352.

Duvall, E. M. (1957). *Family development*. Philadelphia: Lippincott.

East, P. L. (1996). The younger sisters of childbearing adolescents: Their attitudes, expectations, and behaviors. *Child Development, 67*, 267–282.

East, P., & Khoo, S. T. (2005). Longitudinal pathways linking family factors and sibling relationship qualities to adolescent substance use and sexual risk behaviors. *Journal of Family Psychology, 19*, 571–580.

Eccles, J. S., Midgley, C., Wigfield, A., Buchanan, C. M., Reuman, D., Flanagan, C., et al. (1993). Development during adolescence: The impact of stage–environment fit on adolescents' experiences in schools and families. *American Psychologist, 48*, 90–101.

Eddy, J. M., & Chamberlain, P. (2000). Family management and deviant peer association as mediators of the impact of treatment condition on youth antisocial behavior. *Journal of Consulting and Clinical Psychology, 68*, 857–863.

Eichelsheim, V. I., Dekovic, M., Buist, K. L., & Cook, W. L. (2009). The Social Relations Model in family studies: A systematic review. *Journal of Marriage and Family, 71*, 1052–1069.

Eiden, R. D., Teti, D. M., & Corns, K. M. (1995). Maternal working models of attachment, marital adjustment, and the parent-child relationship. *Child Development, 66*, 1504–1518.

Eitle, D. (2005). The moderating effects of peer substance use on the family structure–adolescent substance use association: Quantity versus quality of parenting. *Addictive Behaviors, 30*, 963–980.

Elder, G. H., Jr., King, V., & Conger, R. D. (1996). Attachment to place and migration prospects: A developmental perspective. *Journal of Research on Adolescence, 6*, 397–425.

Ellis, D. A., Frey, M. A., Naar-King, S., Templin, T., Cunningham, P., & Cakan, N. (2005). Use of multisystemic therapy to improve regimen adherence among adolescents with type 1 diabetes in chronic poor metabolic control: A randomized controlled trial. *Diabetes Care, 28*, 1604–1610.

Ellis, D. A., Naar-King, S., Frey, M. A., Rowland, M., & Greger, N. (2003). Case study: Feasibility of multisystemic therapy as a treatment for urban adolescents with poorly controlled type 1 diabetes. *Journal of Pediatric Psychology, 28*, 287–294.

Eng, S., Kanitkar, K., Cleveland, H. H., Herbert, R., Fischer, J., & Wiersma, J. (2008). School achievement differences among Chinese and Filipino American students: Acculturation and family factors. *Educational Psychology, 28*, 535–550.

Eng, S., Mulsow, M., Cleveland, H. H., & Hart, S. (2009). Academic achievement among adolescents in Cambodia: Does maternal trauma matter? *Journal of Community Psychology, 37*, 754–768.

Erikson, E. H. (1950). *Childhood and society*. New York: Norton.

Erikson, E. H. (1968). *Identity: Youth and crisis*. New York: Norton.

Faber, A. J., Edwards, A. E., Bauer, K. S., & Wetchler, J. L. (2003). Family structure: Its effects on adolescent attachment and identity formation. *American Journal of Family Therapy, 31*, 243–255.

Faulkner, R. A., & Davey, M. (2002). Children and adolescents of cancer patients: The impact of cancer on the family. *American Journal of Family Therapy, 30*, 63–72.

Feeney, J. A., & Nollar, P. (1996). *Adult attachment*. Thousand Oaks, CA: Sage.

Feinberg, M., & Hetherington, E. M. (2001). Differential parenting as a within-family variable. *Journal of Family Psychology, 15*, 22–37.

Fisher, L., Kokes, R. F., Ransom, D. C., Philips, S. L., & Rudd, P. (1985). Alternative strategies for creating relational family data. *Family Process, 24*, 213–224.

Fletcher, A. C., Steinberg, L., & Sellers, E. B. (1999). Adolescents' well-being as a function of perceived interparental consistency. *Journal of Marriage and Family, 61*, 599–610.

Fletcher, A. C., Steinberg, L., & Williams-Wheeler, M. (2004). Parental influences on adolescent problem behavior: Revisiting Stattin and Kerr. *Child Development, 75*, 781–796.

Fosco, G. M., & Grych, J. H. (2008). Emotional, cognitive, and family systems mediators of children's adjustment to interparental conflict. *Journal of Family Psychology, 22*, 843–854.

Fosco, G. M., & Grych, J. H. (2010). Adolescent triangulation into parental conflicts: Longitudinal implications for appraisals and adolescent-parent relations. *Journal of Marriage and Family, 72*, 254–266.

Foshee, V. A., Bauman, & Linder, G. F. (1999). Family violence and the perpetration of adolescent dating violence: Examining social learning and social control processes. *Journal of Marriage and Family, 61*, 331–342.

Foshee, V. A., Linder, F., MacDougall, J. E., & Bangdiwala, S. (2001). Gender differences in the longitudinal predictors of adolescent dating violence. *Preventive Medicine, 32*, 128–141.

Forehand, R., Biggar, H., & Kotchick, B. A. (1998). Cumulative risk across family stressors: Short- and long-term effects for adolescents. *Journal of Abnormal Child Psychology, 26*, 119–128.

Franck, K. L., & Buehler, C. (2007). A family process model of marital hostility, parental depressive affect, and early adolescent problem behavior: The roles of triangulation and parental warmth. *Journal of Family Psychology, 21*, 614–625.

Freeman, T. M., & Anderman, L. H. (2005, January 12). Changes in mastery goals in urban and rural middle school students. *Journal of Research in Rural Education, 20*(1). Retrieved May 23, 2010, from http://www.umaine.edu/jrre/20-1.pdf

Frisco, M. L. (2005). Parental involvement and young women's contraceptive use. *Journal of Marriage and the Family, 67*, 110–121.

Frisco, M. L., Muller, C., & Frank, K. A. (2007). Familystructure change and adolescents' school performance: A propensity score approach. *Journal of Marriage and the Family, 69*, 721–741.

Fristad, M. A., Gavazzi, S. M., & Mackinaw-Koons, B. (2003). Family psychoeducation: An adjunctive intervention for children with early onset bipolar disorder. *Biological Psychiatry, 53*, 1000–1008.

Fristad, M. A., Goldberg-Arnold, J. S., & Gavazzi, S. M. (2002). Multifamily psychoeducation groups for families of children with bipolar disorder. *Journal of Bipolar Disorders, 4*, 254–262.

Fuligni, A. J., Hughes, D. L., & Way, N. (2009). Ethnicity and immigration. In R. M. Lerner & L. Steinberg (Eds.), *andHandbook of adolescent psychology* (3rd ed.). New York: Wiley.

Fulkerson, J. A., Strauss, J., Neumark-Sztainer, D., Story, M., & Boutelle, K. (2007). Correlates of psychosocial well-being among overweight adolescents: The role of the family. *Journal of Consulting and Clinical Psychology, 75*, 181–186.

Fuhrman, T., & Holmbeck, G. N. (1995). A contextual moderator analysis of emotional autonomy and adjustment in adolescence. *Child Development, 66*, 793–811.

Furstenberg, F. F., Cook, T. D., Eccles, J., Elder, G. H., Jr., & Sameroff, A. (1999). *Managing to make it: Urban families and adolescent success*. Chicago: University of Chicago Press.

Gagne, M. H., Drapeau, S., Melancon, C., Saint-Jacques, M. C., & Lepine, R. (2007). Links between parental psychological violence, other family disturbances, and children's adjustment. *Family Process, 46*, 523–542.

Gangamma, R., Slesnick, N., Toviessi, P., & Serovich, J. (2008). Comparison of HIV risks among gay, lesbian, bisexual and heterosexual homeless youth. *Journal of Youth and Adolescence, 37*, 456–464.

Garber, J., Robinson, N. S., & Valentiner, D. (1997). The relation between parenting and adolescent depression: Self-worth as a mediator. *Journal of Adolescent Research, 12*, 12–33.

Garcia, F., & Gracia, E. (2009). Is always authoritative the optimum parenting style? Evidence from Spanish families. *Adolescence, 44*, 101–131.

Gardner, F., Connell, A., Trentacosta, C. J., Shaw, D. S., Dishion, T. J., & Wilson, M. N. (2009). Moderators of outcome in a brief family-centered intervention for preventing early problem behavior. *Journal of Consulting and Clinical Psychology, 77*, 543–553.

Gavazzi, S. M. (1993). The relation between family differentiation levels in families with adolescents and the severity of presenting problems. *Family Relations, 42*, 463–468.

Gavazzi, S. M. (1995). The Growing Up FAST: Families and Adolescents Surviving and Thriving™ Program. *Journal of Adolescence, 18*, 31–47.

Gavazzi, S. M. (2003). Family strengthening programs for families with adolescents. In T. P. Gullotta & M. Bloom (Eds.), *The encyclopedia of primary prevention and health promotion* (pp. 486–492). New York: Kluwer/Plenum.

Gavazzi, S. M. (2006). Gender, ethnicity, and the family environment: Contributions to assessment efforts within the realm of juvenile justice. *Family Relations, 55*, 190–199.

Gavazzi, S. M., & Blumenkrantz, D. G. (1993). Facilitating clinical work with adolescents and their families through the Rite of Passage Experience Program. *Journal of Family Psychotherapy, 4*, 47–67.

Gavazzi, S. M., Bostic, J. M., Lim, J. Y., & Yarcheck, C. M. (2008). Examining the impact of gender, race/ethnicity, and family factors on mental health issues in a sample of court-involved youth. *Journal of Marital and Family Therapy, 34*, 353–368.

Gavazzi, S. M., & Law, J. C. (1997). Therapeutic utility of the Growing Up FAST program. *Journal of Family Psychotherapy, 8*, 21–39.

Gavazzi, S. M., Reese, M. J., & Sabatelli, R. M. (1998). Conceptual development and empirical use of the Family Intrusiveness Scale. *Journal of Family Issues, 19*, 65–74.

Gavazzi, S. M., Russell, C. M., & Khurana, A. (2009). Predicting educational risks among court-involved Black males: Family, peers and mental health issues. *Negro Educational Review, 60*, 99–114.

Gavazzi, S. M., & Sabatelli, R. M. (1990). Family system dynamics, the individuation process and psychosocial development. *Journal of Adolescent Research, 5*, 499–518.

Gavazzi, S. M., Wasserman, D., Partridge, C., & Sheridan, S. (2000). The Growing Up FAST diversion program: An example of juvenile justice program development for outcome evaluation. *Aggression and Violent Behavior, 5*, 159–175.

Gavazzi, S. M., Yarcheck, C. M., Rhine, E. E., & Partridge, C. (2003). Building bridges between parole officers and the families of serious juvenile offenders. *International Journal of Offender Therapy and Comparative Criminology, 47*, 291–308.

Gavazzi, S. M., Slade, D., Buettner, C. K., Partridge, C., Yarcheck, C. M., & Andrews, D.W. (2003). Toward conceptual development and empirical measurement of global risk indicators in the lives of court-involved youth. *Psychological Reports, 92*, 599–615.

References

Gavazzi, S. M., Yarcheck, C. M., Sullivan, J. M., Jones, S. C., & Khurana, A. (2008). Global risk factors and the prediction of recidivism rates in a sample of first-time misdemeanant offenders. *International Journal of Offender Therapy and Comparative Criminology, 52*, 330–345.

Geist, R., Heinmaa, M., Stephens, D., Davis, R., & Katzman, D. K. (2000). Comparison of family therapy and family group psychoeducation in adolescents with anorexia nervosa. *Canadian Journal of Psychiatry, 45*, 173–178.

Gerard, J. M., Buehler, C., Franck, K., & Anderson, O. (2005). In the eyes of the beholder: Cognitive appraisals as mediators of the association between interparental conflict and youth maladjustment. *Journal of Family Psychology, 19*, 376–384.

German, M., Gonzales, N. A., Bonds, D. D., Dumka, L. E., & Millsap, R. E. (2009). Familism values as a protective factor for Mexican-origin adolescents exposed to deviant peers. *Journal of Early Adolescence, 29*, 16–42.

Gershon, T. D., Tschann, J. M., & Jemerin, J. M. (1999). Stigmatization, self-esteem, and coping among the adolescent children of lesbian mothers. *Journal of Adolescent Health, 24*, 437–445.

Gewirtz, A. H. (2007). Promoting children's mental health in family supportive housing: A community-university partnership for formerly homeless children and families. *Journal of Primary Prevention, 28*(3–4), 359–374.

Ghazarian, S. R., & Buehler, C. (2010). Interparental conflict and academic achievement: An examination of mediating and moderating factors. *Journal of Youth and Adolescence, 39*, 23–32.

Ghazarian, S. R., Supple, A. J., & Plunkett, S. W. (2008). Familism as a predictor of parent-adolescent relationships and developmental outcomes for adolescents in Armenian American families. *Journal of Child and Family Studies, 17*, 599–613.

Glick, P. C. (1947). The life cycle of the family. *Marriage and Family Living, 17*, 3–9.

Gonzales, N. A., Dumka, L. E., Deardorff, J., JacobsCarter, S., & McCray, A. (2004). Preventing poor mental health and school dropout of Mexican-American adolescents following the transition to junior high school. *Journal of Adolescent Research, 19*, 113–131.

Gonzales-Backen, M. A., & Umaña-Taylor, A. J. (2010). The Role of Physical Appearance on Ethnic Identity Formation Processes among Latino Adolescents. *Journal of Adolescence, 34*, 151–162.

Goodnow, J. J. (2006). Research and policy: Second looks at development, families, and communities, and at translations into practice. In A. Clarke-Stewart & J. Dunn (Eds.), *Families count* (pp. 3337–3360). New York: Cambridge University Press.

Goodson, P., Evans, A., & Edmunson, E. (1996). Female adolescents and onset of sexual intercourse: A theory-based review of research from 1984 to 1994. *Journal of Adolescent Health, 21*, 147–156.

Gordon, D. A. (2000). Parent training via CD-ROM: Using technology to disseminate effective prevention practices. *Journal of Primary Prevention, 21*, 227–251.

Gordon, D. A., Arbuthnot, J., Gustafson, K. E., & McGreen, P. (1988). Home-based behavioral systems family therapy with disadvantaged juvenile delinquents. *American Journal of Family Therapy, 16*(3), 243–255.

Gorman-Smith, D., Tolan, P. H., Zelli, A., & Huesmann, L. R. (1996). The relation of family functioning to violence among inner-city minority youths. *Journal of Family Psychology, 10*, 115–129.

Gottfredson, M. R., & Hirschi, T. (1990). *A general theory of crime*. Stanford, CA: Stanford University Press.

Gottlieb, G., & Halpern, C. (2002). A relational view of causality in normal and abnormal development. *Development and Psychopathology, 14*, 421–435.

Granic, I., Dishion, T. J., & Hollenstein, T. (2006). The Family ecology of adolescence: A dynamic systems perspective on normative development. In G. R. Adams & M. D. Berzonsky (Eds.), *Blackwell handbook of adolescence* (pp. 60–91). Malden, MA: Blackwell.

Granic, I., & Patterson, G. R. (2006). Toward a comprehensive model of antisocial development: A dynamic systems approach. *Psychological Review, 113*, 101–131.

Graves, K. N., & Shelton, T. L. (2007). Family empowerment as a mediator between family-centered systems of care and changes in child functioning: Identifying an important mechanism of change. *Journal of Child and Family Studies, 16*, 556–566.

Greenstein, T. N. (2006). *Methods of family research* (2nd ed.). Thousand Oaks, CA: Sage.

Griffin, K. W., Botvin, G. J., Scheier, L. M., Diaz, T., & Miller, N. L. (2000). Parenting practices as predictors of substance use, delinquency, and aggression among urban minority youth: Moderating effects of family structure. and gender. *Psychology of Addictive Behaviors, 14*, 174–184.

Grotevant, H. D. (1997). Family processes, identity development, and behavioral outcomes for adopted adolescents. *Journal of Adolescent Research, 12*, 139–161.

Grych, J. H., Raynor, S. R., & Fosco, G. M. (2004). Family processes that shape the impact of interparental conflict on adolescents. *Development and Psychopathology, 16*, 649–665.

Gutman, L. M., & Eccles, J. E. (2007). Stage–environment fit during adolescence: Trajectories of family relations and adolescent outcomes. *Developmental Psychology, 43*, 522–537.

Hage, S. M., & Kenny, M. E. (2009). Promoting a social justice approach to prevention: Future directions for training, practice, and research. *Journal of Primary Prevention, 30*, 75–87.

Hair, E. C., Moore, K. A., Garrett, S. B., Ling, T., & Cleveland, K. (2008). The continued importance of quality parent–adolescent relationships during late adolescence. *Journal of Research on Adolescence, 18*, 187–200.

Haj-Yahia, M., & Dawud-Noursi, S. (1998). Predicting the use of different conflict tactics among Arab siblings in Israel: A study based on social learning theory. *Journal of Family Violence, 13*, 81–103.

Haley, J. (1978). Ideas which handicap therapists. In M. M. Berger (Ed.), *Beyond the double bind* (pp. 65–82). New York: Bruner/Mazel.

Halgunseth, L. C., Ispa, J. M., & Rudy, D. (2006). Parental control in Latino families: An integrated review in the literature. *Child Development, 77*(5), 1282–1297.

Halpern-Meekin, S., & Tach, L. (2008). Heterogeneity in two-parent families and adolescent well-being. *Journal of Marriage and Family, 70*, 435–451.

Hamilton, C. E. (2000). Continuity and discontinuity of attachment from infancy to adolescence. *Child Development, 71*, 690–694.

Hardy, S. A., Carlo, G., & Roesch, S. C. (2010). Links between adolescents' expected parental reactions and prosocial behavioral tendencies: The mediating role of prosocial values. *Journal of Youth and Adolescence, 39*, 84–95.

Harold, G. T., & Conger, R. D. (1997). Marital conflict and adolescent distress: The role of adolescent awareness. *Child Development, 68*, 333–350.

Harper, N. J., & Russell, K. C. (2008). Family involvement and outcome in adolescent wilderness treatment: A mixed-methods evaluation. *International Journal of Child and Family Welfare, 1*, 19–36.

Hauser, S. T., Powers, S. I., & Noam, G. G. (1991). *Adolescents and their families*. New York: Free Press.

Havighurst, R. J. (1944). *Who shall be educated? The challenge of unequal opportunities*. New York: Harper.

Havighurst, R. J. (1972). *Developmental tasks and education*. New York: McKay.

Hawkins, J. D., Catalano, R. F., Kosterman, R., Abbott, R. D., & Hill, K. G. (1999). Preventing adolescent health-risk behaviors by strengthening protection during childhood. *Archives of Pediatrics and Adolescent Medicine, 153*, 226–234.

Hawley, D. R., & Geske, S. (2000). The use of theory in family therapy research: A content analysis of family therapy journals. *Journal of Marital and Family Therapy, 26*, 17–22.

Hawley, D. R., & Gonzalez, C. (2005). Publication patterns of faculty in commission on accreditation for marriage and family therapy education programs. *Journal of Marital and Family Therapy, 31*, 89–98.

Heard, H. E. (2007). The family structure trajectory and adolescent school performance. *Journal of Family Issues, 28*, 319–354.

Heatherington, E. M. (2006). The influence of conflict, marital problem solving and parenting on children's adjustment in nondivorced, divorced, and remarried families. In A. Clarke-Stewart & J. Dunn (Eds.), *Families count* (pp. 203–237). New York: Cambridge University Press.

Henderson, C. E., Rowe, C. L., Dakof, G. A., Hawes, S. W., & Liddle, H. A. (2009). Parenting practices as mediators of treatment effects in an early-intervention trial of Multidimensional Family Therapy. *The American Journal of Drug and Alcohol Abuse, 35*, 220–226.

Heflinger, C. A., Bickman, L., Northrup, D., Sonnichsen, S., & Schilling, S. (1998). A theory-driven intervention and evaluation to explore family caregiver empowerment. *Journal of Emotional and Behavioral Disorders, 57*, 184–191.

Henggeler, S. W., & Borduin, C. M. (1990). *Family therapy and beyond: A multisystemic approach to treating the behavior problems of children and adolescents*. Pacific Grove, CA: Brooks/Cole.

Henggeler, S. W., Clingempeel, W. G., Brondino, M. J., & Pickrel, S. G. (2002). Four-year follow-up of multisystemic therapy with substance-abusing and substance dependent juvenile offenders. *Journal of the American Academy of Child and Adolescent Psychiatry, 41*, 868–874.

Henggeler, S. W., Halliday-Boykins, C. A., Cunningham, P. B., Randall, J., Shapiro, S. B., & Chapman, J. E. (2006). Juvenile drug court: Enhancing outcomes by integrating evidence-based treatments. *Journal of Consulting and Clinical Psychology, 74*, 42–54.

Henggeler, S. W., Pickrel, S. G., & Brondino, M. J. (1999). Multisystemic treatment of substance abusing and dependent delinquents: Outcomes, treatment fidelity, and transportability. *Mental Health Services Research, 1*, 171–184.

Henggeler, S. W., Pickrel, S. G., Brondino, M. J., & Crouch, J. L. (1996). Eliminating (almost) treatment dropout of substance abusing or dependent delinquents through home-based multisystemic therapy. *American Journal of Psychiatry, 153*, 427–428.

Henggeler, S. W., Rowland, M. D., Randall, J., Ward, D. M., Pickrel, S. G., Cunningham, P. B., et al. (1999). Home-based multisystemic therapy as an alternative to the hospitalization of youths in psychiatric crisis: Clinical outcomes. *Journal of the American Academy of Child and Adolescent Psychiatry, 38*, 1331–1339.

Henggeler, S. W., & Sheidow, A. J. (2003). Conduct disorder and delinquency. *Journal of Marital and Family Therapy, 29*, 505–522.

Henggeler, S. W., Schoenwald, S. K., Borduin, C. M., Rowland, M. D., & Cunningham, P. B. (1998). *Multisystemic treatment of antisocial behavior in children and adolescents*. New York: Guilford.

Hennan, M. R., Dornbusch, S. M., Herron, M. C., & Herting, J. R. (1997). The influence of family regulation, connection, and psychological autonomy on six measures of adolescent functioning. *Journal of Adolescent Research, 12*, 34–67.

Henry, C. S., Huey, E. L., Robinson, L. C., & Neal, R. A. (2006). Adolescent perceptions of family system functioning and parental behaviors. *Journal of Child and Family Studies, 15*, 308–318.

Henry, C. S., Merten, M. J., Plunkett, S. W., & Sands, T. (2008). Neighborhood, parenting, and adolescent factors and academic achievement in Latino adolescents from immigrant families. *Family Relations, 57*, 579–590.

Henry, C. S., Sager, D. W., & Plunkett, S. W. (1996). Adolescents' perceptions of family system characteristics, parent-adolescent dyadic behaviors, adolescent qualities, and adolescent empathy. *Family Relations, 45*, 283–292.

Herman, K. C., Ostrander, R., & Tucker, C. M. (2007). Do family environments and negative cognitions of adolescents with depressive symptoms vary by ethnic group? *Journal of Family Psychology, 21*, 325–330.

Hernandez, D. J. (1993). *America's Children: Resources from family, government, and the economy*. New York: Russell Sage Foundation.

Hernandez, D. J. (1997). Child development and the social demography of childhood. *Child Development, 68*, 149–169.

Hernandez, D. J. (2003). Changing family circumstances. In R. P. Weissberg, H. J. Walberg, M. U. O'Brien, & C. B. Kuster (Eds.), *Long-term trends in the well-being of children and youth* (pp. 115–179). Washington, DC: Child Welfare League of America Press.

Hill, K. G., Hawkins, J. D., Catalano, R. F., Abbott, R. D., & Guo, J. (2005). Family influences on the risk of daily smoking initiation. *Journal of Adolescent Health, 37*, 202–210.

Hinde, R. A. (2006). Prognosis: Policy and process. In A. Clarke-Stewart & J. Dunn (Eds.), *Families count* (pp. 361–370). New York: Cambridge University Press.

Hoagwood, K. E. (2005). Family-based services in children's mental health: A research review and synthesis. *Journal of Child Psychology and Psychiatry, 47*, 690–713.

Hogben, M., & Byrne, D. (1998). Using social learning theory to explain individual differences in human sexuality. *Journal of Sex Research, 35*, 58–71.

Huang, B., Kosterman, R., Catalano, R. F., Hawkins, J. D., & Abbot, R. D. (2001). Modeling mediation in the etiology of violent behavior in adolescence: A test of the social development model. *Criminology, 39*, 75–108.

Hughes, E. K., & Gullone, E. (2008). Internalizing symptoms and disorders in families of adolescents: A review of family systems literature. *Clinical Psychology Review, 28*, 92–117.

Jacobvitz, D., Hazen, N., & Leon, K. (2006). Does expectant mothers' unresolved/disorganized trauma predict frightening/frightened maternal behavior? Risk and protective factors. *Development and Psychopathology, 18*, 363–379.

Johnson, L. N., Ketring, S. A., Rohacs, J., & Brewer, A. L. (2006). Attachment and the therapeutic alliance in family therapy. *The American Journal of Family Therapy, 34*, 205–218.

Johnson, S. M., Maddeaux, C., & Blouin, J. (1998). Emotionally focused family therapy for bulimia: Changing attachment patterns. *Psychotherapy, 25*, 238–247.

Johnson, V. K. (2010). From early childhood to adolescence: Linking family functioning and school behavior. *Family Relations, 59*, 313–325.

Jory, B., Rainbolt, E., Xia, Y., Karns, J., Freeborn, A., & Greer, C. (1996). Communication patterns and alliances between parents and adolescents during a structured problem solving task. *Journal of Adolescence, 19*, 339–346.

Kalafat, J. (2004). Enabling and empowering practices of Kentucky's school-based family resource centers: A multiple case study. *Evaluation and Program Planning, 27*, 65–78.

Kan, M. L., McHale, S. M., & Crouter, A. C. (2008). Interparental incongruence in differential treatment of adolescent siblings: Links with marital quality. *Journal of Marriage and Family, 70*, 466–479.

Karem, E. A., & Sprenkle, D. H. (2010). The research-informed clinician: A guide to training the next-generation MFT. *Journal of Marital and Family Therapy, 36*, 307–319.

Kenny, D. A., & La Voie, L. (1984). The Social Relations Model. In L. Berrowitz (Ed.), *Advances in experimental social psychology* (Vol. 18, pp. 142–182). San Diego, CA: Academic.

Kenny, M. E., & Hage, S. M. (2009). The next frontier: Prevention as an instrument of social justice. *Journal of Primary Prevention, 30*, 1–10.

Kerns, K. A., & Stevens, A. C. (1996). Parent-child attachment in late adolescence: Links to social relations and personality. *Journal of Youth and Adolescence, 25*, 323–342.

Kerr, D. C. R., Leve, L. D., & Chamberlain, P. (2009). Pregnancy rates among juvenile justice girls in two randomized controlled trials of Multidimensional Treatment Foster Care. *Journal of Consulting and Clinical Psychology, 77*, 588–593.

Kerr, M. E., & Bowen, M. (1988). *Family evaluation*. New York: Norton.

Kerr, M., & Stattin, H. (2000). What parents know, how they know it and several forms of adolescent adjustment: Further support for a reinterpretation of monitoring. *Developmental Psychology, 36*(3), 366–380.

Khurana, A., & Gavazzi, S. M. (2010). Juvenile delinquency and adolescent fatherhood. *International Journal of Offender Therapy and Comparative Criminology*.

Khurana, A., Cooksey, E. C., & Gavazzi, S. M. (in press). Juvenile Delinquency and teenage pregnancy: A comparison of ecological risk profiles among Midwestern European and African American female juvenile offenders. *Psychology of Women's Quarterly*.

Kiang, L., & Fuligni, A. J. (2009). Ethnic identity and family processes among adolescents from Latin American, Asian, and European backgrounds. *Journal of Youth and Adolescence, 38*, 228–241.

Kim, J. E., Hetherington, E. M., & Reiss, D. (1999). Associations among family relationships, antisocial peers, and adolescents' externalizing behaviors: Gender and family type differences. *Child Development, 70*, 1209–1230.

King, V. (2006). The antecedents and consequences of adolescents' relationships with stepfathers and nonresident fathers. *Journal of Marriage and Family, 68*, 910–928.

King, V. (2009). Stepfamily formation: Implications for adolescent ties to mothers, nonresident fathers, and stepfathers. *Journal of Marriage and Family, 71*, 954–968.

King, V., & Elder, G. H., Jr. (1997). The legacy of grandparenting: Childhood experiences with grandparents and current involvement with grandchildren. *Journal of Marriage and the Family, 59*, 848–859.

King, V., & Elder, G. H., Jr. (1998a). Education and grandparenting roles. *Research on Aging, 20*, 450–474.

King, V., & Elder, G. H., Jr. (1998b). Perceived self-efficacy and grandparenting. *Journal of Gerontology: Social Sciences, 53*, 249–S257.

King, V., Elder, G. H., Jr., & Whitbeck, L. B. (1997). Religious involvement among rural youth: An ecological and life course perspective. *Journal of Research on Adolescence, 7*, 431–456.

King, V., & Sobolewski, J. M. (2006). Nonresident fathers' contributions to adolescent well-being. *Journal of Marriage and Family, 68*, 537–557.

Klein, D. M. (1994). *Theory as data: An investigation of ourselves.* Paper presented at the National Council on Family Relations Conference Theory Construction and Research Methodology Workshop, November, Minneapolis, MN.

Klein, N., Alexander, J., & Parsons, B. (1977). Impact of family systems intervention on recidivism and sibling delinquency: A model of primary prevention and program evaluation. *Journal of Consulting and Clinical Psychology, 45*, 469–474.

Knapp, S. J. (2009). Critical theorizing: Enhancing theoretical rigor in family research. *Journal of Family Theory and Review, 1*, 133–145.

Koerner, S. S., Jacobs, S. L., & Raymond, M. (2000). When mothers turn to their adolescent daughters: Predicting daughters' vulnerability to negative adjustment outcomes. *Family Relations, 49*, 301–309.

Koerner, S. S., Rankin, L. A., Kenyon, D. B., & Korn, M. (2004). Mothers re-partnering after divorce: Diverging perceptions of mothers and adolescents. *Journal of Divorce and Remarriage, 41*, 25–38.

Kohli, M. (2007). The institutionalization of the life course: Looking back to look ahead. *Research in Human Development, 4*, 253–271.

Koman, S. L., & Stechler, G. (1985). Making the jump to systems. In M. P. Mirkin & S. L. Koman (Eds.), *Handbook of adolescents and family therapy* (pp. 1–20). Boston: Allyn & Bacon.

Komro, K. A., Perry, C. L., Veblen-Mortenson, S., Farbakhsh, K., Kugler, K. C., Alfano, K. A., et al. (2006). Cross-cultural adaptation and evaluation of a home-based program for alcohol use prevention among urban youth: The "Slick Tracy Home Team Program". *Journal of Primary Prevention, 27*, 135–154.

Koren, P. E., DeChillo, N., & Friesen, B. J. (1992). Measuring empowerment in families whose children have emotional disabilities: A brief questionnaire. *Rehabilitation Psychology, 37*, 305–320.

Kowal, A., Krull, J., & Kramer, L. (2004). How the differential treatment of siblings is linked with parent-child relationship quality. *Journal of Family Psychology, 18*, 658–665.

Kowal, A. K., & Blinn-Pike, L. (2004). Sibling influences on adolescents' attitudes toward safe sex practices. *Family Relations, 53*, 377–384.

Kratochwill, T. R., McDonald, L., Levin, J. R., Bear-Tibbetts, H. Y., & Demaray, M. K. (2004). Families and schools together: An experimental analysis of a parent-mediated multi-family group program for American Indian children. *Journal of School Psychology, 42*, 359–383.

Krautter, T. H., & Lock, J. (2004). Treatment of anorexia nervosa using family-based manualized treatment. *Clinical Case Studies, 3*, 107–123.

Krohn, M. D., Hall, G. P., & Lizotte, A. J. (2009). Family transitions and later delinquency and drug use. *Journal of Youth and Adolescence, 38*, 466–480.

Kuendig, H., & Kuntsche, E. (2006). Family bonding and adolescent alcohol use: Moderating effect of living with excessive drinking parents. *Alcohol and Alcoholism, 41*, 464–471.

Kumpfer, K. L., & Alvarado, R. (1998). *Effective family strengthening interventions*. Washington, DC: US Department of Justice, Office of Justice Programs, Office of Juvenile Justice and Delinquency Prevention.

Kumpfer, K. L., Alvarado, R., Smith, P., & Bellamy, N. (2002). Cultural sensitivity and adaptation in family-based prevention interventions. *Prevention Science, 3*, 241–246.

Kumpfer, K. L., & Tait, C. M. (2000). *Family skills training for parents and children*. Washington, DC: US Department of Justice, Office of Justice Programs, Office of Juvenile Justice and Delinquency Prevention.

L'Abate, L., & Colondie, G. (1987). The emperor has no clothes! Long live the emperor! A critique of family systems thinking and a reductionistic proposal. *American Journal of Family Therapy, 15*, 19–33.

Laible, D. J., Carlo, G., & Raffaelli, M. (2000). The differential relations of parent and peer attachment to adolescent adjustment. *Journal of Youth and Adolescence, 29*, 45–59.

Lamborn, S. D., Dornbusch, S. M., & Steinberg, L. (1996). Ethnicity and community context as moderators of the relations between family decision making and adolescent adjustment. *Child Development, 67*, 283–301.

Langenkamp, A. G., & Frisco, M. L. (2008). Family transitions and adolescent severe emotional distress: The salience of family context. *Social Problems, 55*, 238–253.

Laub, J. H. (2002). A century of delinquency research and delinquency theory. In M. K. Rosenbaum, F. E. Zimring, D. S. Tanenhaus, & B. Dohrn (Eds.), *A century of juvenile justice* (pp. 179–205). Chicago: University of Chicago Press.

Lavee, Y., & Dollahite, D. C. (1991). The linkage between theory and research in family science. *Journal of Marriage and the Family, 53*, 361–373.

Lavoie, F., Hebert, M., Tremblay, R., Vitaro, F., Vezina, L., & McDuff, P. (2002). History of family dysfunction and perpetration of dating violence by adolescent boys: A longitudinal study. *Journal of Adolescent Health, 30*, 375–383.

Law, J. C., & Gavazzi, S. M. (1999). Definitions of adulthood: From the voices of parents and adolescents. *Family Science Review, 11*, 318–335.

Lee, G., Akers, R. L., & Borg, M. J. (2004). Social learning and structural factors in adolescent substance use. *Western Criminology Review, 5*, 17–34.

Lee, R. E., & Nichols, W. C. (2010). The doctoral education of professional marriage and family therapists. *Journal of Marital and Family Therapy, 36*, 259–269.

Lemmon, C. R., & Josephson, A. M. (2001). Family therapy for eating disorders. *Child and Adolescent Psychiatry Clinics of North America, 10*, 519–542.

Lengua, L., Roosa, M. W., Shupak, E., Michaels, M., Berg, C., & Ayers, T. (1992). The role of focus groups in the development of community-based parenting intervention programs. *Family Relations, 41*, 163–168.

Lerner, R. M. (2002). *Adolescence: Development, diversity, context, and application*. New York: Prentice-Hall.

Lerner, R. M., & Overton, W. F. (2008). Exemplifying the integrations of the relational developmental system: Synthesizing theory, research, and application to promote positive development and social justice. *Journal of Adolescent Research, 23*, 245–255.

Lerner, R. M., von Eye, A., Lerner, J. V., & Lewin-Bizan, S. (2009). Exploring the foundations and functions of adolescent thriving within the 4-H study of positive youth development: A view of the issues. *Journal of Applied Developmental Psychology, 30*, 567–570.

Levesque, R. J. R. (2007). Book reviews and the need to take books more seriously. *Journal of Youth and Adolescence, 36*, 1086–1088.

Lewis, M., Feiring, C., & Rosenthal, S. (2000). Attachment over time. *Child Development, 71*, 707–720.

Levy, K. N., Blatt, S. J., & Shaver, P. R. (1998). Attachment styles and parental representations. *Journal of Personality and Social Psychology, 74*, 407–419.

Lian, T. C., & Yusooff, F. (2009). Effects of family functioning on self-esteem of children. *European Journal of Social Sciences, 9*, 643–650.
Liddle, H. A. (1991). Empirical values and the culture of family therapy. *Journal of Marital and Family Therapy, 17*, 327–348.
Liddle, H. A. (1996). Family-based treatment for adolescent problem behaviors: Overview of contemporary developments and introduction to the special section. *Journal of Family Psychology, 10*, 3–11.
Liddle, H. A. (2004). Family-based therapies for adolescent alcohol and drug use: Research contributions and future research needs. *Addiction, 99*, 76–92.
Liddle, H. A., Dakof, G. A., & Diamond, G. (1991). Adolescent substance abuse: Multidimensional Family Therapy in action. In E. Kaufman & P. Kaufmann (Eds.), *Family therapy of drug and alcohol abuse* (2nd ed., pp. 120–171). Needham Heights, MA: Allyn & Bacon.
Liddle, H. A., & Dakof, G. A. (1995). Efficacy of family therapy for drug abuse: Promising but not definitive. *Journal of Marital and Family Therapy, 21*, 511–543.
Liddle, H. A., Dakof, G. A., Henderson, C., & Rowe, C. (in press). Implementation outcomes of Multidimensional Family Therapy – detention to community: A reintegration program for drug-using juvenile detainees. *International Journal of Offender Therapy and Comparative Criminology*.
Liddle, H. A., Dakof, G. A., Parker, K., Diamond, G. S., Barrett, K., & Tejeda, M. (2001). Multidimensional Family Therapy for adolescent substance abuse: Results of a randomized clinical trial. *American Journal of Drug and Alcohol Abuse, 27*, 651–687.
Liddle, H. A., Dakof, G. A., Turner, R. M., Henderson, C. E., & Greenbaum, P. E. (2008). Treating adolescent drug abuse: A randomized trial comparing Multidimensional Family Therapy and cognitive behavior therapy. *Addiction, 103*, 1660–1670.
Liddle, H. A., Jackson-Gilfort, A., & Marvel, F. A. (2006). An empirically-supported and culturally specific engagement and intervention strategy for African-American adolescent males. *American Journal of Orthopsychiatry, 76*, 215–225.
Liddle, H. A., Rowe, C. L., Dakof, G., & Lyke, L. (1998). Translating parenting research into clinical interventions for families of adolescents. *Clinical Child Psychology and Psychiatry, 3*, 419–443.
Liddle, H. A., Rowe, C. L., Dakof, G. A., Henderson, C. E., & Greenbaum, P. E. (2009). Multidimensional Family Therapy for young adolescent substance abuse: Twelve-month outcomes of a randomized controlled trial. *Journal of Consulting and Clinical Psychology, 77*, 12–25.
Liddle, H. A., Rowe, C. L., Diamond, G. M., Sessa, F., Schmidt, S., & Ettinger, D. (2000). Towards a developmental family therapy: The clinical utility of adolescent development research. *Journal of Marital and Family Therapy, 26*, 491–505.
Liddle, H. A., & Schwartz, S. J. (2002). Attachment and family therapy: Clinical utilization of adolescent-family attachment research. *Family Process, 41*, 457–478.
Lochman, J. E. (2000). Parent and family skills training in targeted prevention programs for at-risk youth. *The Journal of Primary Prevention, 21*, 253–265.
Lochman, J. E. (2004). Contextual factors in risk and prevention research. *Merrill-Palmer Quarterly, 50*, 311–325.
Longmore, M. A., Manning, W. D., & Giordano, P. C. (2001). Preadolescent parenting strategies and teens' dating and sexual initiation: A longitudinal analysis. *Journal of Marriage and the Family, 63*, 322–335.
Loomis, L. S., & Booth, A. (1995). Multigenerational caregiving and well-being: The myth of the beleaguered sandwich generation. *Journal of Family Issues, 16*, 131–148.
Lopez, F. G. (1995). Attachment theory as an integrative framework for family counseling. *The Family Journal, 3*, 11–17.
Luthar, S., & Cicchetti, D. (2000). The construct of resilience: Implications for interventions and social policies. *Development and Psychopathology, 12*, 857–885.
Lyons, K. S., & Sayer, A. G. (2005). Longitudinal dyad models in family research. *Journal of Marriage and Family, 67*, 1048–1060.
Maccoby, E., & Martin, J. (1983). Socialization in the context of the family: Parent-child interaction. In E. M. Hetherington (ed.), *Handbook of child psychology: Socialization, personality, and social development* (Vol. 4, pp. 1–101). New York: Wiley.

MacKenzie, D. L. (1998). Using the US land-grant system as a model to attack this nation's crime problem. *The Criminologist, 23,* 1–4. Accessed July 12, 2010, from http://www.asc41.com/March-April%201998.htm

MacMillan, R., & Copher, R. (2005). Families in the life course: Interdependency of roles, role configurations, and pathways. *Journal of Marriage and Family, 67,* 858–879.

Madison, S. M., McKay, M. M., Paikoff, R., & Bell, C. C. (2000). Basic research and community collaboration: Necessary ingredients for the development of a family-based HIV prevention program. *AIDS Education and Prevention, 12,* 281–298.

Main, M., Kaplan, N., & Cassidy, J. (1985). Security in infancy, childhood, and adulthood: A move to the level of representation. Growing points of attachment theory and research. *Monographs of the Society for Research in Child Development, 50,* 66–104.

Maio, G. R., Fincham, F. D., & Lycett, E. J. (2000). Attitudinal ambivalence toward parents and attachment style. *Personality and Social Psychology Bulletin, 26,* 1451–1464.

Matjasko, Jl, & Paz, K. A. (2005a). The role of families in developmental continuity and change in adolescence. In V. L. Bengston, A. C. Acock, K. R. Allen, P. Dilworth-Anderson, & D. M. Klein (Eds.), *Sourcebook of family theory and research* (pp. 385–387). Thousand Oaks, CA: Sage.

Marvel, F., Rowe, C., Colon-Perez, L., DiClemente, R. J., & Liddle, H. A. (2009). Multidimensional Family Therapy HIV/STD risk reduction intervention: An integrative family-based model for drug-involved juvenile offenders. *Family Process, 48,* 69–84.

Manning, W. D., & Lamb, K. A. (2003). Adolescent well-being in cohabiting, married, and single-parent families. *Journal of Marriage and the Family, 65,* 876–893.

Marek, L. I., Brock, D. J. P., & Sullivan, R. (2006). Cultural adaptations to a family life skills program: Implementation in rural Appalachia. *The Journal of Primary Prevention, 27,* 113–133.

Markiewicz, D., Doyle, A. B., & Brengdon, M. (2001). The quality of adolescents' friendships: Associations with mothers' interpersonal relationships, attachment to parents and friends, and prosocial behavior. *Journal of Adolescence, 24,* 429–445.

Matjasko, J. L., Grunden, L. N., & Ernst, J. L. (2007). Structural and dynamic process family risk factors: Consequences for holistic adolescent functioning. *Journal of Marriage and Family, 69,* 654–674.

Matjasko, J. L., & Paz, K. A. (2005b). The role of families in developmental continuity and change during adolescence. In V. L. Bengston, A. C. Acock, K. R. Allen, P. Dilworth-Anderson, & D. M. Klein (Eds.), *Sourcebook of family theory and research* (pp. 385–387). Thousand Oaks, CA: Sage.

Mattessich, P., & Hill, R. (1987). Life cycle and family development. In M. B. Sussman & S. K. Steinmetz (Eds.), *Handbook of marriage and the family* (pp. 437–469). New York: Plenum.

Manzi, C., Vignoles, V. L., Regalia, C., & Scabini, E. (2006). Cohesion and enmeshment revisited: Differentiation, identity, and well-being in two European cultures. *Journal of Marriage and the Family, 68,* 673–689.

Marsiglio, W., Hutchinson, S., & Cohan, M. (2000). Envisioning fatherhood: A social psychological perspective on young men without kids. *Family Relations, 49,* 133–142.

Masten, A. S., & Shaffer, A. (2006). How families matter in child development. In A. Clarke-Stewart & J. Dunn (Eds.), *Families count* (pp. 5–25). New York: Cambridge University Press.

Matsumoto, D., Kudoh, T., & Takeuchi, S. (1996). Changing patterns of individualism and collectivism in the United States and Japan. *Culture and Psychology, 2,* 77–107.

Mathijssen, J. J. J. P., Koot, H. M., Verhulst, F. C., De Bruyn, E. E. J., & Oud, J. H. L. (1997). Family functioning and child psychopathology: Individual versus composite family scores. *Family Relations, 46,* 247–255.

McCammon, S. L., Spencer, S. A., & Friesen, B. J. (2001). Promoting family empowerment through multiple roles. In D.A. Dosser, D. Handron, S. McCammon, & J. Y. Powell (Eds.), *Child mental health: Exploring systems of care in the new millennium* (pp. 1–24). New York: Haworth.

McDowell, T., & Shelton, D. (2002). Valuing social justice in MFT curriculum. *Contemporary Family Therapy, 24*, 313–331.

McDonald, L., & Frey, H. E. (1999). *Families and schools together: Building relationships.* Washington, DC: US Department of Justice, Office of Justice Programs, Office of Juvenile Justice and Delinquency Prevention.

McGoldrick, M., Almeida, R., Preto, N. G., Bibb, A., Sutton, C. E., Hudak, J., et al. (1999). Efforts to incorporate social justice perspectives into a family therapy training program. *Journal of Marital and Family Therapy, 25*, 191–209.

McHale, S. M., Crouter, A. C., & Whiteman, S. D. (2003). The family contexts of gender development in childhood and adolescence. *Social Development, 12*, 125–148.

McHale, S. M., Updegraff, K. A., Helms-Erikson, H., & Crouter, A. C. (2001). Sibling influences on gender development in middle childhood and early adolescence: A longitudinal study. *Developmental Psychology, 37*, 115–125.

McKay, M. M., Taberchasse, K., Paikoff, R., McKinney, L., Baptiste, D., Coleman, D., et al. (2004). Family-level impact of the CHAMP family program: A community collaborative effort to support urban families and reduce youth HIV risk exposure. *Family Process, 43*, 79–93.

McKenry, P. C., & Gavazzi, S. M. (1994). *Visions 2010: Adolescents and families.* Minneapolis, MN: National Council on Family Relations Publications.

McKeown, R. E., Garrison, C. Z., Jackson, K. L., Cuffe, S. P., Addy, C. L., & Waller, J. L. (1997). Family structure and cohesion, and depressive symptoms in adolescents. *Journal of Research on Adolescence, 7*, 267–281.

McWey, L. M., West, S. H., Ruble, N., Handy, A. K., Handy, D. G., Koshy, M., et al. (2002). The practice of clinical research in accredited marriage and family therapy programs. *Journal of Marital and Family Therapy, 28*, 85–92.

Melby, J., & Conger, R. D. (1996). Parental behaviors and adolescent academic performance: A longitudinal analysis. *Journal of Research on Adolescence, 6*, 113–137.

Meschke, L. L., Bartholomae, S., & Zentall, S. R. (2000). Adolescent sexuality and parent-adolescent processes: Promoting healthy teen choices. *Family Relations, 49*, 143–154.

Meyers, R. J., & Smith, J. E. (1995). *Clinical guide to alcohol treatment: The community reinforcement approach.* New York: Guilford.

Mihalic, S. W., & Elliott, D. (1997). A social learning theory model of marital violence. *Journal of Family Violence, 12*, 21–47.

Mihalic, S. W., Fagan, A., Irwin, K., Ballard, D., & Elliott, D. (2004). Blueprints for violence prevention. *National Criminal Justice Reference Service.* Retrieved May 15, 2010, from http://www.ncjrs.gov/pdffiles1/ojjdp/204274.pdf

Miklowitz, D. J., George, E. L., Axelson, D. A., Kim, E. Y., & Birmaher, B. (2004). Family-focused treatment for adolescents with bipolar disorder. *Journal of Affective Disorders, 82*, 113–128.

Miklowitz, D. J., Simoneau, T. L., George, E. L., Richards, J. A., Kalbag, A., Sachs-Ericsson, N., et al. (2000). Family-focused treatment of bipolar disorder: 1-year effects of a psychoeducational program in conjunction with pharmacotherapy. *Biological Psychiatry, 48*, 582–592.

Milardo, R. M. (2009). Editorial: Following a sociological imagination. *Journal of Family Theory and Review, 1*, 1–3.

Milardo, R. M. (2010). From the editor: Auguries of year two. *Journal of Family Theory and Review, 2*, 1–3.

Miller, B. C., Norton, M. C., Fan, X., & Christopherson, C. R. (1998). Parental discipline and control attempts in relation to adolescent sexual attitudes and behavior. *Journal of Marriage and the Family, 48*, 503–512.

Miller, K. S., Forehand, R., & Kotchick, B. A. (1999). Adolescent sexual behavior in two ethnic minority samples: The role of family variables. *Journal of Marriage and Family, 61*, 85–98.

Miller, W. R., & Rollnick, S. (2002). *Motivational interviewing: Preparing people for change* (2nd ed.). New York: Guilford.

Miller-Day, M. A. (2002). Parent-adolescent communication about alcohol, tobacco, and other drug use. *Journal of Adolescent Research, 17*, 604–616.

Minuchin, P. (1985). Families and individual development: Provocations from the field of family therapy. *Child Development, 56*, 289–302.

Minuchin, S., Rosman, B. L., & Baker, L. (1978). *Psychosomatic families.* Cambridge, MA: Harvard University Press.

Mitchell, K. S., Booth, A., & King, V. (2009). Adolescents with nonresident fathers: Are daughters more disadvantaged than sons? *Journal of Marriage and Family, 71*, 650–662.

Molgaard, V., & Spoth, R. (2001). The Strengthening Families Program for young adolescents: Overview and outcomes. *Residential Treatment for Children and Youth, 18*, 15–29.

Molgaard, V., Spoth, R. L., & Redmond, C. (2000). *Competency training: The Strengthening Families Program for parents and youth 10–14.* Washington, DC: US Department of Justice, Office of Justice Programs, Office of Juvenile Justice and Delinquency Prevention.

Molinari, L., Everri, M., & Fruggeri, L. (2010). Family microtransitions: Observing the process of change in families with adolescent children. *Family Process, 49*, 236–250.

Moore, K. A., & Lippman, L. (2005). *What do children need to flourish: Conceptualizing and measuring positive development.* New York: Springer.

Moore, K. A., McGroder, S. M., Hair, E. C., & Gunnoe, M. (1999). NLSY97 codebook supplement main file round 1. Appendix 9: Family process and adolescent outcomes measures. Bureau of Labor Statistics, US Department of Labor, from http://www.nlsinfo.org/

Mullis, R. L., Graf, S. C., & Mullis, A. K. (2009). Parental relationships, autonomy, and identity processes of high school students. *The Journal of Genetic Psychology, 170*, 326–338.

Mullis, A. K., Mullis, R. L., Schwartz, S. J., Pease, J. L., & Shriner, M. (2007). Relations among parental divorce, identity status, and coping strategies of college age women. *Identity: An International Journal of Theory and Research, 7*, 137–154.

Mullis, R. L., Brailsford, J. C., & Mullis, A. K. (2003). Relations between identity formation and family characteristics among young adults. *Journal of Family Issues, 24*, 966–980.

Naar-King, S., Podolski, C. L., Ellis, D. A., Frey, M. A., & Templin, T. (2006). Social ecological model of illness management in high-risk youths with Type 1 Diabetes. *Journal of Consulting and Clinical Psychology, 74*, 785–789.

Nelson, J., O'Brien, M., Blankson, N., Calkins, S., & Keane, S. (2009). Family stress and parental responses to children's negative emotions: Tests of the spillover, crossover, and compensatory hypotheses. *Journal of Family Psychology, 23*, 671–679.

Newcomb, M. D., & Loeb, T. B. (1999a). Poor parenting as an adult problem behavior: General deviance, deviant attitudes, inadequate family support and bonding, or just bad parents? *Journal of Family Psychology, 13*, 175–193.

Newcomb, M. D., & Loeb, T. B. (1999b). Poor parenting as an adult problem behavior: General deviance, deviant attitudes, inadequate family support and bonding, or just bad parents? *Journal of Family Psychology, 13*, 175–193.

Nichols, M. P., & Schwartz, R. C. (2006). *Family therapy: Concepts and methods* (7th ed.). Boston: Pearson.

Norman, E., & Turner, S. (1993). Adolescent substance abuse prevention programs: Theories, models, and research in the encouraging 80s. *Journal of Primary Prevention, 14*, 3–20.

O'Brien, M. (2005). Studying individual and family development: Linking theory and research. *Journal of Marriage and Family, 67*, 880–890.

O'Connor, T. G., Hetherington, E. M., & Clingepeel, W. G. (1997). Systems and bidirectional influences in families. *Journal of Social and Personal Relationships, 14*, 491–504.

O'Connor, T. G., Hetherington, E. M., & Reiss, D. (1998). Family systems and adolescent development: Shared and nonshared risk and protective factors in nondivorced and remarried families. *Development and Psychopathology, 10*, 353–375.

O'Donnell, E. H., Moreau, M., Cardemil, E. V., & Pollastri, A. (2010). Interparental conflict, parenting, and childhood depression in a diverse urban population: The role of general cognitive style. *Journal of Youth and Adolescence, 39*, 12–22.

Ohannessian, C. M. (2009). Does technology use moderate the relationship between parental alcoholism and adolescent alcohol and cigarette use? *Addictive Behaviors, 34*, 606–609.

Ohannessian, C. M., & Hesselbrock, V. (2005). The relationship between parental psychopathology and adolescent pychopathology: An examination of gender patterns. *Journal of Emotional and Behavioral Disorders, 13*(2), 67–76.

Ohannessian, C. M., & Hesselbrock, V. M. (2008). Paternal alcoholism and youth substance abuse: The indirect effects of negative affect, conduct problems, and risk taking. *Journal of Adolescent Health, 42*(2), 198–200.

Ohannessian, C. M., Lerner, R. M., Lerner, J. V., & von Eye, A. (2000). Adolescent-parent discrepancies in perceptions of family functioning and early adolescent self-competence. *International Journal of Behavioral Development, 24*, 362–372.

O'Keefe, M. (1997). Adolescents' exposure to community and school violence: Prevalence and behavioral correlates. *Journal of Adolescent Health, 20*, 368–376.

Olson, D. H. L. (1976). Bridging research, theory, and application: The triple threat in science. In D. H. L. Olson (Ed.), *Treating relationships* (pp. 565–579). Lake Mills, IA: Graphic Press.

Olson, D. H. L., & DeFrain, J. (2006). *Marriages and families* (5th ed.). New York: McGraw-Hill.

Osborne, C., & McLanahan, S. (2007). Partnership instability and child well-being. *Journal of Marriage and Family, 69*, 1065–1083.

O'Sullivan, L. F., Meyer-Bahlburg, H. F. L., & Watkins, B. X. (2001). Mother-daughter communication about sex Among urban African American and Latino families. *Journal of Adolescent Research, 16*, 269–292.

Paikoff, R. L., Parfenoff, S. H., Williams, S. A., & McCormick, A. (1997). Parenting, parent–child relationships, and sexual possibility situations among urban African American preadolescents: Preliminary findings and implications for HIV prevention. *Journal of Family Psychology, 11*, 11–22.

Pallock, L., & Lamborn, S. (2006). Beyond parenting practices: Extended kinship support and the academic adjustment of African American and European American teens. *Journal of Adolescence, 26*, 813–828.

Perkins, D. D., & Zimmerman, M. A. (1995). Empowerment theory, research, and application. *American Journal of Community Psychology, 23*, 569–579.

Padilla-Walker, L. M. (2007). Characteristics of mother-child interactions related to adolescents' positive values and behaviors. *Journal of Marriage and Family, 69*, 675–686.

Pagani, L. S., Tremblay, R. E., Nagin, D., Zoccolillo, M., Vitaro, F., & McDuff, P. (2004). Risk factor models for adolescent verbal and physical aggression toward mothers. *International Journal of Behavioral Development, 28*, 528–537.

Paley, B., Conger, R. D., & Harold, G. T. (2000). Parents' affect, adolescent cognitive representations, and adolescent social development. *Journal of Marriage and the Family, 62*, 761–776.

Park, J., Kosterman, R., Hawkins, J. D., Haggerty, K. P., Duncan, T. E., Duncan, S. C., et al. (2000). Effects of the "Preparing for the Drug Free Years" curriculum on growth in alcohol use and risk for alcohol use in early adolescence. *Prevention Science, 1*, 125–138.

Parra-Cardona, J. R., Sharp, E. A., & Wampler, R. S. (2008). "Changing for my kid": Fatherhood experiences of Mexican-origini teen fathers involved in the justice system. *Journal of Marital and Family Therapy, 34*, 369–387.

Paschall, M. J., Ringwalt, C. L., & Flewelling, R. L. (2003). Effects of parenting, father absence, and affiliation with delinquent peers on delinquent behavior among African-American male adolescents. *Adolescence, 38*, 15–34.

Patterson, G. R. (1982). *Coercive family process*. Eugene, OR: Castalia.

Patterson, G. R., Bank, L., & Stoolmiller, M. (1990). The preadolescent's contributions to disrupted family process. In R. Montemayor, G. R. Adams, & T. P. Gullotta (Eds.), *From childhood to adolescence* (pp. 107–133). Thousand Oaks, CA: Sage.

Patterson, G. R., & Yoerger, K. (1993). Developmental models for delinquent behavior. In S. Hodgins (Ed.), *Mental disorder and crime* (pp. 140–172). Newbury Park: Sage.

Peris, T. S., Cummings, E. M., Goeke-Morey, M. C., & Emery, R. E. (2008). Martial conflict and support seeking by parents in adolescence: Empirical support for the parentification construct. *Journal of Family Psychology, 22*, 633–642.

Peterson, G. W. (2005). Family influences on adolescent development. In T. P. Gullotta & G. Adams (Eds.), *Handbook of adolescent behavior problems* (pp. 27–55). New York: Springer.

Peterson, G. W., & Hann, D. (1999). Socializing children and parents in families. In M. B. Sussman, S. K. Steinmetz, & G. W. Peterson (Eds.), *Handbook of marriage and the family* (pp. 327–370). New York: Plenum.

Phares, V. (1999). *"Poppa" psychology: The role of fathers in childrens' mental well-being.* Westport, CT: Praeger.

Phares, V. (2002). Finding poppa in substance abuse research. *Addiction, 97*, 1119–1120.

Phares, V., Fields, S., & Kamboukos, D. (2009). Fathers' and mothers' involvement with their adolescents. *Journal of Child and Family Studies, 18*, 1–9.

Phares, V., Renk, K., Duhig, A. M., Fields, S., & Sly, J. (2009). Gender differences in positive and negative feelings between adolescents and their fathers and mothers. *Journal of Child and Family Studies, 18*, 213–218.

Pilgrim, C., Abbey, A., Hendrickson, P., & Lorenz, S. (1998). Implementation and impact of a family-based substance abuse prevention program in rural communities. *Journal of Primary Prevention, 18*, 341–361.

Pinsof, W. M., & Wynne, L. C. (1995a). The effectiveness and efficacy of marital and family therapy: Introduction to the special issue. *Journal of Marital and Family Therapy, 21*, 341–343.

Pinsof, W. M., & Wynne, L. C. (1995b). The effectiveness and efficacy of marital and family therapy: An empirical overview, conclusions, and recommendations. *Journal of Marital and Family Therapy, 21*, 341–343.

Pinsof, W. M., & Wynne, L. C. (2000). Toward progress research: Closing the gap between family therapy practice and research. *Journal of Marital and Family Therapy, 26*, 1–8.

Pinquart, M., & Silbereisen, R. K. (2005). Influences of parents and siblings on the development of children and adolescents. In V. L. Bengston, A. C. Acock, K. R. Allen, P. Dilworth-Anderson, & D. M. Klein (Eds.), *Sourcebook of family theory and research* (pp. 367–382). Thousand Oaks, CA: Sage.

Plunkett, S. W., & Henry, C. S. (1999). Adolescent perceptions of interparental conflict, stressors, and coping as predictors of adolescent family life satisfaction. *Sociological Inquiry, 69*, 599–620.

Pomerantz, E. M., & Wang, Q. (2009). The role of parental control in children's development in Western and East Asian Countries. *Current Directions in Psychological Science, 18*, 285–289.

Prado, G., Pantin, H., Briones, E., Schwartz, S. J., Feaster, D., Huang, S., et al. (2007). A randomized controlled trial of a parent-centered intervention in preventing substance use and HIV risk behaviors in Hispanic adolescents. *Journal of Consulting and Clinical Psychology, 75*, 914–926.

Prather, W., & Golden, J. A. (2009a). A behavioral perspective of childhood trauma and attachment issues: Toward alternative treatment approaches for children with a history of abuse. *International Journal of Behavioral Consultation and Therapy, 5*, 56–74.

Prather, W., & Golden, J. A. (2009b). Learning and thinking: A behavioral treatise on abuse and antisocial behavior in young criminal offenders. *International Journal of Behavioral Consultation and Therapy, 5*, 75–105.

Prather, W. (2007). Trauma and psychotherapy: Implications from a behavior analysis perspective. *International Journal of Behavioral Consultation and Therapy, 3*, 555–570.

Prelow, H. M., Loukas, A., & Jordan-Green, L. (2007). Socioenvironmental risk and adjustment in Latino youth: The mediating effects of family processes and social competence. *Journal of Youth and Adolescence, 36*, 465–476.

Preto, N. G. (1989). Transformation of the family system in adolescence. In E. A. Carter & M. McGoldrick (Eds.), *The changing family life cycle: A framework for family therapy* (pp. 255–284). Boston: Allyn & Bacon.
Preto, N. G., & Travis, N. (1985). The adolescent phase of the family life cycle. In M. P. Mirkin & S. L. Koman (Eds.), *Handbook of adolescents and family therapy* (pp. 52–69). Boston: Allyn & Bacon.
Price, S. (1994). Note from the series editor. In P. C. McKenry, & S. M. Gavazzi (eds.), *Visions 2010: Adolescents and Families* (p. i). Minneapolis, MN: National Council on Family Relations Publications.
Qin, D. B. (2008). Doing well vs. feeling well: Understanding family dynamics and the psychological adjustment of Chinese immigrant adolescents. *Journal of Youth and Adolescence, 37*, 22–35.
Raneri, L. G., & Wiemann, C. M. (2007). Social ecological predictors of repeat adolescent pregnancy. *Perspectives on Sexual and Reproductive Health, 39*, 39–47.
Rankin, S. H., & Weekes, D. P. (1989). Life-span development: A review of theory and practice for families with chronically ill members. *Scholarly Inquiry for Nursing Practice: An International Journal, 3*, 3–22.
Ream, G. L., & Savin-Williams, R. C. (2005). Reciprocal associations between adolescent sexual activity and quality of youth–parent interactions. *Journal of Family Psychology, 19*, 171–179.
Rende, R., Slomkowski, C., Lloyd-Richardson, E., & Niaura, R. (2005). Sibling effects on substance use in adolescence: Social contagion and genetic relatedness. *Journal of Family Psychology, 19*, 611–618.
Regnerus, M. D., & Luchies, L. B. (2006). The parent-child relationship and opportunities for adolescents' first sex. *Journal of Family Issues, 27*, 159–183.
Reis, H. T., Collins, W. A., & Berscheid, E. (2000). The relationship context of human behavior and development. *Psychological Bulletin, 126*, 844–872.
Resendez, M. G., Quist, R. M., & Matshazi, D. G. M. (2000). A longitudinal analysis of family empowerment and client outcomes. *Journal of Child and Family Studies, 9*, 449–460.
Reuter, M., & Conger, R. D. (1995). Antecedents of parent-adolescent disagreements. *Journal of Marriage and Family, 57*, 435–448.
Richardson, R. A. (2004). Early adolescence talking points: Questions that middle school students want to ask their parents. *Family Relations, 53*, 87–94.
Riggins-Caspers, K. M., Cadoret, R. J., Knutson, J. F., & Langbehn, D. (2003). Biology-environment interaction and evocative biology-environment correlation: Contributions of harsh discipline and parental psychopathology to problem adolescent behaviors. *Behavior Genetics, 33*, 205–220.
Robbins, M. S., Alexander, J. F., Newell, R. M., & Turner, C. W. (1996). The immediate effect of reframing on client attitude in family therapy. *Journal of Family Psychology, 10*, 28–34.
Robbins, M. S., Alexander, J. F., & Turner, C. W. (2000). Disrupting defensive family interactions in family therapy with delinquent adolescents. *Journal of Family Psychology, 14*, 688–701.
Robbins, M. S., Turner, C. W., Alexander, J. F., & Perez, G. A. (2003). Alliance and dropout in family therapy for adolescents with behavior problems: Individual and systemic effects. *Journal of Family Psychology, 17*, 534–544.
Roche, K. M., Ensminger, M. E., & Cherlin, A. J. (2007). Variations in parenting and adolescent outcomes among African American and Latino families living in low-income, urban areas. *Journal of Family Issues, 28*, 882–909.
Roche, K. M., Mekos, D., Alexander, C. S., Astone, N. M., Bandeen-Roche, K., & Ensminger, M. E. (2005). Parenting influences on early sex initiation among adolescents: How neighborhood matters. *Journal of Family Issues, 26*, 32–54.
Roche, K. M., & Leventhal, T. (2009). Beyond neighborhood poverty: Family management, neighborhood disorder, and adolescents' early sexual onset. *Journal of Family Psychology, 23*, 819–827.

Rodgers, R. H., & White, J. M. (1993). Family development theory. In P. G. Boss, W. J. Doherty, R. LaRossa, W. R. Schumm, & S. K. Steinmetz (Eds.), *Sourcebook of family theories and methods* (pp. 225–254). New York: Plenum.

Rohner, R. P., & Khaleque, A. (2009). Testing central postulates of Parental Acceptance-Rejection Theory (PARTheory): A meta-analysis of cross-cultural studies. *Journal of Family Theory and Review, 2*, 73–87.

Roisman, G. I., Madsen, S. D., Hennighausen, K. H., Sroufe, L. A., & Collins, W. A. (2001). The coherence of dyadic behavior across parent–child and romantic relationships as mediated by the internalized representation of experience. *Attachment and Human Development, 3*, 156–172.

Rosenfeld, R., Jacobs, B. A., & Wright, R. (2003). Snitching and the code of the street. *The British Journal of Criminology, 43*, 291–309.

Rosenstein, D. S., & Horowitz, H. A. (1996). Adolescent attachment and psychopathology. *Journal of Consulting and Clinical Psychology, 64*, 244–253.

Rowe, C. L., Gomez, L., & Liddle, H. A. (2006). Family therapy research: Empirical foundations and practice implications. In M. Nichols, & R. Schwartz (Eds.), *Family therapy: Concepts and methods* (7th ed., pp. 395–445). Boston: Allyn & Bacon.

Rowe, C. L., & Liddle, H. A. (2008). When the levee breaks: Treating adolescents and families in the aftermath of hurricane Katrina. *Journal of Marital and Family Therapy, 34*, 132–148.

Rubin, K. H., Dwyer, K. M., Booth-LaForce, C., Kim, A. H., Burgess, K. B., & Rose-Krasnor, L. (2004). Attachment, friendship, and psychosocial functioning in early adolescence. *The Journal of Early Adolescence, 24*, 326–356.

Russell, C. S. (1993). Family development theory as revised by Rodgers and White: Implications for practice. In Boss, Doherty, LaRossa, Schumm & Steinmetz (Eds.): *Source book of Family Theories and Methods: A Contextual Approach* (pp. 255–258). New York: Plenum.

Sabatelli, R. M., & Bartle, S. E. (1995). Survey approaches to the assessment of family functioning: Conceptual, operational, and analytical issues. *Journal of Marriage and the Family, 57*, 1025–1039.

Sagrestano, L. M., Paikoff, R. L., Holmbeck, G. N., & Fendrich, M. (2003). A longitudinal examination of familial risk factors for depression among inner-city African American adolescents. *Journal of Family Psychology, 17*, 108–120.

Saltzburg, S. (2007). Narrative therapy pathways for re-authoring with parents of adolescents coming-out as lesbian, gay, and bisexual. *Contemporary Family Therapy, 29*, 57–69.

Sameroff, A. J., & MacKenzie, M. J. (2003). Research strategies for capturing transactional models of development: The limits of the possible. *Development and Psychopathology, 15*, 613–640.

Sampson, R. J., & Laub, J. H. (1997). A life-course theory of cumulative disadvantage and the stability of delinquency. In T. P. Thornberry (ed.), *Advances in criminological theory: Developmental theories of crime and delinquency* (Vol. 7, pp. 133–161). New Brunswick, NJ: Transaction Publishers.

Sandberg, J. G., Johnson, L. N., Robila, M., & Miller, R. B. (2002). Clinician identified barriers to clinical research. *Journal of Marital and Family Therapy, 28*, 61–67.

Saner, H., & Ellickson, P. (1996). Concurrent risk factors for adolescent violence. *Journal of Adolescent Health, 19*, 94–103.

Santisteban, D. A., Coatsworth, J. D., Perez-Vidal, A., Kurtines, W. M., Schwartz, S. J., LaPerriere, A., et al. (2003). The efficacy of brief strategic/structural family therapy in modifying behavior problems and an exploration of the mediating role that family functioning plays in behavior change. *Journal of Family Psychology, 17*, 121–133.

Santisteban, D. A., Coatsworth, J. D., Perez-Vidal, A., Mitrani, V., Jean-Gilles, M., & Szapocznik, J. (1997). Brief structural strategic family therapy with African American and Hispanic high risk youth: A report of outcome. *Journal of Community Psychology, 25*, 453–471.

Santisteban, D. A., & Mena, M. P. (2009). Culturally informed and flexible family-based treatment for adolescents: A tailored and integrative treatment for Hispanic youth. *Family Process, 48*, 253–268.

Santisteban, D. A., Suarez-Morales, L., Robbins, M. S., & Szapocznik, J. (2006). Brief strategic family therapy: Lessons learned in efficacy research and new research directions on blending research and practice. *Family Process, 45*, 259–275.

Santisteban, D. A., Szapocznik, J., Perez-Vidal, A., Kurtines, W. M., Murray, E. J., & Laperriere, A. (1996). Efficacy of intervention for engaging youth and families into treatment and some variables that may contribute to differential effectiveness. *Journal of Family Psychology, 10*, 35–44.

Santrock, J. W. (2008). *Adolescence* (12th ed.). New York: McGraw-Hill.

Schmied, V., & Walsh, P. (2010a). Effective casework practice with adolescents: perspectives of statutory child protection practitioners. *Child and Family Social Work, 15*, 165–175.

Schneider, B. H., Atkinson, L., & Tardif, C. (2001). Child-parent attachment and children's peer relations: A quantitative review. *Developmental Psychology, 37*, 86–100.

Schoenrock, C. J., Bell, N. J., Sun, S., & Avery, A. W. (1999). Family correlates of adolescent self-monitoring and social competence. *Journal of Psychology, 133*, 377–393.

Schermerhorn, A. C., & Cummings, E. M. (2008). Transactional family dynamics: A new framework for conceptualizing family influence processes. *Advances in Child Development and Behavior, 36*, 187–250.

Schmidt, S. E., Liddle, H. A., & Dakof, G. A. (1996). Changes in parenting practices and adolescent drug abuse during Multidimensional Family Therapy. *Journal of Family Psychology, 10*, 12–27.

Schock-Giordano, A. M., & Gavazzi, S. M. (2010). Mental illness in a family context. In S. J. Price & C. A. Price (Eds.), *Families and change* (4th ed.). Newbury Park, CA: Sage.

Scott, M. E., Booth, A., King, V., & Johnson, D. R. (2007). Postdivorce father-adolescent closeness. *Journal of Marriage and Family, 69*, 1194–1209.

Sexton, T. L., & Alexander, J. F. (2002). Family-based empirically supported treatment interventions. *The Counseling Psychologist, 30*(2), 238–261.

Scheer, S. D., Borden, L. M., & Donnermeyer, J. F. (2000). The relationship between family factors and adolescent substance use in rural, suburban, and urban settings. *Journal of Child and Family Studies, 9*, 105–115.

Scheer, S. D., & Gavazzi, S. M. (2009). A qualitative examination of a state-wide initiative to empower families containing children and adolescents with behavioral health care needs. *Children and Youth Services Review, 31*, 370–377.

Schmied, V., & Walsh, P. (2010b). Effective casework practice with adolescents. Perspectives of statutory child protection practitioners. *Child and Family Social Work, 15*, 165–175.

Schunk, D. H. (2005). Self-regulated learning: The educational legacy of Paul R. Pintrich. *Educational Psychologist, 40*, 85–94.

Schwartz, S. J., Coatsworth, J. D., Pantin, H., Prado, G., Hiley, E. H., & Szapocznik, J. (2006). The role of ecodevelopmental context and self-concept in depressive and externalizing symptoms in Hispanic adolescents. *International Journal of Behavioral Development, 30*, 359–370.

Seltzer, M. M., Greenberg, J. S., Floyd, F. J., Pettee, Y., & Hong, J. (2001). Life course impacts of parenting a child with a disability. *American Journal on Mental Retardation, 106*, 265–286.

Sexson, S. B., Glanville, D. N., & Kaslow, N. J. (2001). Attachment and depression: Implications for family therapy. *Child and Adolescent Psychiatric Clinics of North America, 10*, 465–486.

Shanahan, L., McHale, S. M., Crouter, A. C., & Osgood, D. W. (2008). Parents' differential treatment and youth depressive symptoms and sibling relationships: Longitudinal linkages. *Journal of Marriage and the Family, 70*, 480–495.

Sheridan, M., Peterson, B. D., & Rosen, K. H. (2010). The experiences of parents of adolescents in family therapy: A qualitative investigation. *Journal of Marital and Family Therapy, 36*, 144–157.

Shields, C. G., Wynne, L. C., McDaniel, S. H., & Gawinski, B. A. (1994). The marginalization of family therapy: A historical and continuing problem. *Journal of Marital and Family Therapy, 20*, 117–138.

Simons, L. G., & Conger, R. D. (2007). Linking mother-father differences in parenting to a typology of family parenting styles and adolescent outcomes. *Journal of Family Issues, 28,* 212–241.

Simons, R. L., Chao, W., Conger, R. D., & Elder, G. H. (2001). Quality of parenting as mediator of the effect of childhood defiance on adolescent friendship choices and delinquency: A growth curve analysis. *Journal of Marriage and Family, 63,* 63–79.

Simons, R. L., Lin, K. H., & Gordon, L. C. (1998). Socialization in the family of origin and male dating violence: A prospective study. *Journal of Marriage and Family, 60,* 467–478.

Singh, N. N., Curtis, W. J., Cohen, R., Ellis, C. R., Best, A. M., & Wechsler, H. A. (1997). Empowerment status and families whose children have serious emotional disturbance and attention-deficit/hyperactivity disorder. *Journal of Emotional and Behavioral Disorders, 5,* 223–229.

Skinner, B. F. (1950). Are learning theories necessary? *Psychological Review, 57,* 193–216.

Skinner, B. F. (1989). The origins of cognitive thought. *American Psychologist, 44,* 13–18.

Slesnick, N., Erdem, G., Collins, J., Bantchevska, D., & Katafiasz, H. (in press). Predictors of treatment attendance among adolescent substance abusing runaways: A comparison of family and individual therapy modalities. *Journal of Family Therapy.*

Slesnick, N., & Prestopnik, J. L. (2005). Ecologically-based family therapy outcome with substance abusing runaway adolescents. *The Journal of Adolescence, 28,* 277–298.

Slesnick, N., & Prestopnik, J. L. (2009). Comparison of family therapy outcome with alcohol-abusing runaway adolescents. *Journal of Marital and Family Therapy, 35,* 255–277.

Slesnick, N., & Waldron, H. B. (1997). Interpersonal problem-solving interactions of depressed adolescents and their parents. *Journal of Family Psychology, 11,* 234–245.

Slomkowski, C., Rende, R., Conger, K. J., Simons, R. L., & Conger, R. D. (2001). Sisters, brothers, and delinquency: Evaluating social influence during early and middle adolescence. *Child Development, 72,* 271–283.

Small, S. A., Cooney, S., & O'Connor, C. (2009). Evidence-based program improvement: Using principles of effectiveness to enhance the quality and impact of youth and family-based prevention programs. *Family Relation, 58,* 1–13.

Small, S. A., & Huser, M. (in press). Family-based prevention programs. *Encyclopedia of Adolescence.* New York: Springer.

Smetana, J. G. (1995). Parenting styles and conceptions of parental authority during adolescence. *Child Development, 66,* 299–316.

Smetana, J. (2008). It's 10 o'clock: Do you know where your children are? Recent advances in understanding parental monitoring and adolescents' information management. *Child DevelopmentPerspectives, 2,* 19–25.

Smetana, J. G., Campione-Barr, N., & Metzger, A. (2006). Adolescent development in interpersonal and societal contexts. *Annual Review of Psychology, 57,* 255–284.

Smetana, J. G., Metzger, A., & Campione-Barr, N. (2004). African American adolescents' relationships with parents: Developmental transitions and longitudinal patterns. *Child Development, 75,* 932–947.

Snyder, J., Bank, L., & Burraston, B. (2005). The consequences of antisocial behavior in older male siblings for younger brothers and sisters. *Journal of Family Psychology, 19,* 643–653.

Soenens, B., Vansteenkiste, M., Luyckx, K., & Goossens, L. (2006). Parenting and adolescent problem behavior: An integrated model with adolescent self-disclosure and perceived parental knowledge as intervening variables. *DevelopmentalPsychology, 42,* 305–318.

South, S. J., Haynie, D. L., & Bose, S. (2005). Residential mobility and the onset of adolescent sexual activity. *Journal of Marriage and Family, 67,* 499–514.

Spera, C. (2005). A review of the relationship among parenting practices, parenting styles, and adolescent school achievement. *Educational Psychology Review, 17,* 125–146.

Spillman, B. C., & Pezzin, L. E. (2000). Potential and active family caregivers: Changing networks and the "sandwich generation.". *The Milbank Quarterly, 78,* 347–374.

Sprenkle, D. H. (1976). In my opinion: The need for integration among theory, research, and practice in the family field. *The Family Coordinator, 25,* 261–263.

St John, W., & Flowers, K. (2009). Working with families: From theory to clinical nursing practice. *Collegian, 16*, 131–138.
Stattin, H., & Kerr, M. (2000). Parental monitoring: A reinterpretation. *Child Development, 71*, 1072–1085.
Steinberg, L. (2007). *Adolescence* (8th ed.). New York: McGraw-Hill.
Steinberg, L., Blatt-Eisengart, I., & Cauffman, E. (2006). Patterns of competence and adjustment among adolescents from authoritative, authoritarian, indulgent, and neglectful homes: Replication in a sample of serious juvenile offenders. *Journal of Research on Adolescence, 16*, 47–58.
Steinberg, L., & Morris, A. S. (2001). Adolescent development. *Annual Review of Psychology, 52*, 83–110.
Steinberg, L. D., & Silk, J. S. (2002). Parenting adolescents. In M. Bornstein (Ed.), *Handbook of parenting* (2nd ed., Vol. 1, pp. 103–134). Mahwah, NJ: Erlbaum.
Stern, S. B., & Smith, C. A. (1995). Family processes and delinquency in an ecological context. *The Social Service Review, 69*, 703–731.
Stevens, J. W. (2001). The social ecology of the co-occurrence of substance use and early coitus among poor, urban black female adolescents. *Substance Use and Misuse, 36*, 421–446.
Stewart, S. D. (2003). Nonresident parenting and adolescent adjustment. *Journal of Family Issues, 24*, 217–244.
Steinmetz, S. K. (1999). Adolescence in contemporary families. In M. B. Sussman, S. K. Steinmetz, & G. W. Peterson (Eds.), *Handbook of marriage and the family* (pp. 371–424). New York: Plenum.
Stokes, C. E. (2008). The role of parental religiosity in high school completion. *Sociological Spectrum, 28*, 531–555.
Stokes, C. E., & Regnerus, M. D. (2009). When faith divides family: Religious discord and adolescent reports of parent-child relations. *Social Science Research, 38*, 155–167.
Stokols, D. (1996). Translating social ecological theory into guidelines for community health promotion. *American Journal of Health Promotion, 10*, 282–298.
Stoll, B. M., Arnaut, G. L., Fromme, D. K., & Felker-Thayer, J. A. (2005). Adolescents in stepfamilies: A qualitative analysis. *Journal of Divorce and Remarriage, 44*, 177–189.
Stolz, H., Barber, B. K., & Olsen, J. A. (2005). Toward disentangling fathering and mothering: An assessment of relative importance. *Journal of Marriage and Family, 67*, 1076–1092.
Stormshak, E. A., & Dishion, T. J. (2002). An ecological approach to child and family clinical and counseling psychology. *Clinical Child and Family Psychology Review, 5*, 197–215.
Storvoll, E. E., Wichstrom, L., & Pape, H. (2003). Gender differences in the association between conduct problems and other problems among adolescents. *Journal of Scandinavian Studies in Criminology and Crime Prevention, 3*, 194–209.
Stierlin, H. (1981). *Separating parents and adolescents*. New York: Aronson.
Strauss, A. L., & Corbin, J. M. (1998). *Basics of qualitative research: Techniques and procedures for developing grounded theory*. Thousand Oaks, CA: Sage.
Szapocznik, J., Hervis, O. E., & Schwartz, S. (2003). *Brief strategic family therapy manual. NIDA therapy manuals for drug addiction series*. Rockville, MD: National Institute on Drug Abuse.
Szapocznik, J., Perez-Vidal, A., Brickman, A., Foote, F. H., Santisteban, D., Hervis, O. E., et al. (1988). Engaging adolescent drug abusers and their families into treatment: A strategic structural systems approach. *Journal of Consulting and Clinical Psychology, 56*, 552–557.
Szapocznik, J., Santisteban, D., Rio, A., Perez-Vidal, A., Santisteban, D., & Kurtines, W. M. (1989). Family effectiveness training: An intervention to prevent drug abuse and problem behaviors in Hispanic adolescents. *Hispanic Journal of Behavioral Sciences, 11*, 4–27.
Szapocznik, J., & Williams, R. A. (2000). Brief Strategic Family Therapy: Twenty-five years of interplay among theory, research and practice in adolescent behavior problems and drug abuse. *Clinical Child and Family Psychology Review, 3*, 117–134.
Taft, C. T., Schumm, J. A., Panuzio, J., & Proctor, S. P. (2008). An examination of family adjustment among Operation Desert Storm veterans. *Journal of Consulting and Clinical Psychology, 76*, 648–656.

Talbot, J., & McHale, J. (2003). Family-level emotional climate and its impact on the flexibility of relationship representations. In P. Erdman & T. Caffery (Eds.), *Attachment and family systems* (pp. 31–61). New York: Brunner-Routledge.

Taylor-Seehafer, M., & Rew, L. (2000). Risky sexual behavior among adolescent women. *Journal for Specialists in Pediatric Nursing, 5*, 15–25.

Teachman, J. D. (2000). Diversity of family structure: Economic and social influences. In D. H. Demo, K. R. Allen, & M. A. Fine (Eds.), *Handbook of family diversity* (pp. 32–58). New York: Oxford University Press.

Thompson, R. A., & Raikes, H. A. (2003). Toward the next quarter-century: Conceptual and methodological challenges for attachment theory. *Development and Psychopathology, 15*, 691–718.

Tillman, K. H. (2008a). Co-resident sibling composition and the academic ability, expectations, and performance of youth. *Sociological Perspectives, 51*, 679–712.

Tillman, K. H. (2008b). Non-traditional siblings and the academic outcomes of adolescents. *Social Science Research, 37*, 88–108.

Tobler, N. S., & Stratton, H. H. (1997). Effectiveness of school-based prevention programs: A meta-analysis of the research. *Journal of Primary Prevention, 18*, 71–128.

Tudge, J. R. H., Mokrova, I., Hatfield, B., & Karnik, R. B. (2009). Uses and abuses of Bronfenbrenner's bioecological theory of human development. *Journal of Family Theory and Review, 1*, 189–210.

Turner, W. L. (2000). Cultural considerations in family-based primary prevention programs in drug abuse. *Journal of Primary Prevention, 21*, 285–303.

Umaña-Taylor, A. J., Updegraff, K. A., & Gonzales-Backen, M. A. (2011). Mexican-origin adolescent mothers' stressors and psychosocial functioning: Examining ethnic identity affirmation and familism as moderators. *Journal of Youth and Adolescence, 40*, 140–157.

Umaña-Taylor, A. J. & Guimond, A. (2010). A Longitudinal examination of parenting behaviors and perceived discrimination predicting latino adolescents' ethnic identity. *Developmental Psychology, 46*, 636–650.

Ungar, M. (2004). The importance of parents and other caregivers to the resilience of high-risk adolescents. *Family Process, 43*, 23–41.

Upchurch, D. M., Aneshensel, C. S., Sucoff, C. A., & Levy-Storms, L. (1999). Neighborhood and family contexts of adolescent sexual activity. *Journal of Marriage and the Family, 61*, 920–933.

Updegraff, K. A., McHale, S. M., Crouter, A. C., & Kupanoff, K. (2001). Parents' involvement in adolescents' peer relationships: A comparison of mothers' and fathers' roles. *Journal of Marriage and the Family, 63*, 655–668.

Updegraff, K. A., McHale, S. M., Whiteman, S. D., Thayer, S. M., & Crouter, A. C. (2006). The nature and correlates of Mexican American adolescents' time with parents and peers. *Child Development, 77*, 1470–1486.

Updegraff, K. A., McHale, S. M., Whiteman, S. D., Thayer, S. M., & Delgado, M. Y. (2005). Adolescents' sibling relationships in Mexican American families: Exploring the role of familism. *Journal of Family Psychology, 19*, 512–522.

Updegraff, K. A., Thayer, S. M., Whiteman, S. D., Denning, D. A., & McHale, S. M. (2005). Sibling relational aggression in adolescence: Links to parent-adolescent and sibling relationship quality. *Family Relations, 54*, 373–385.

Urberg, K., Goldstein, M. S., & Toro, P. A. (2005). Supportive relationships as a moderator of the effects of parent and peer drinking on adolescent drinking. *Journal of Research on Adolescence, 15*, 1–19.

van der Aa, N., Overbeek, G., Engels, R. C. M. E., Scholte, R. H. J., Meerkerk, G. J., & van den Eijnden, R. J. J. M. (2009). Daily and compulsive internet use and well-being in adolescence: A diathesis-stress model based on big five personality traits. *Journal of Youth and Adolescence, 38*, 765–776.

Vakalahi, H. F. (2002). Family-based predictors of adolescent substance use. *Journal of Child and Adolescent Substance Abuse, 11*, 1–15.
van den Eijnden, R. J. J. M., Spijkerman, R., Vermulst, A. A., van Rooij, T. J., & Engles, R. C. M. E. (2009). Compulsive internet use among adolescents: Bidirectional parent–child relationships. *Journal of Abnormal Child Psychology, 38*, 77–89.
Van Doorn, M. D., Branje, S. J. T., & Meeus, W. H. J. (2007). Longitudinal transmission of conflict resolution styles from marital relationships to adolescent-parent relationships. *Journal of Family Psychology, 21*, 426–434.
Vazsonyi, A., & Flannery, D. (1997). Early adolescent delinquent behaviors: Associations with family and school domains. *Journal of Early Adolescence, 17*, 271–293.
Vicary, J. R., Snyder, A. R., & Henry, K. L. (2000). The effects of family variables and personal competencies on the initiation of alcohol use by rural seventh grade students. *Adolescent and Family Health, 1*, 21–28.
Volk, R. J. (1989). The need for integration among theory, research, and application in family science: An update. *Family Relations, 38*, 220–222.
von Bertalanffy, L. (1968). *General system theory*. New York: George Braziller.
Vuchinich, S., Angelelli, J., & Gatherum, A. (1996). Context and development in family problem solving with preadolescent children. *Child Development, 67*, 1276–1288.
Wainright, J. L., Russell, S. T., & Patterson, C. J. (2004). Psychosocial adjustment, school outcomes, and romantic relationships of adolescents with same-sex parents. *Child Development, 75*, 1886–1898.
Wandersman, A., Morrissey, E., Davino, K., Seybolt, D., Crusto, C., Nation, M., et al. (1998). Comprehensive quality programming and accountability: Eight essential strategies for implementing successful prevention programs. *Journal of Primary Prevention, 19*, 3–30.
Wallerstein, J. S. (1991). The long-term effects of divorce on children: A review. *Journal of the American Academy for Child and Adolescent Psychiatry, 30*, 349–360.
Wallerstein, J. S., & Lewis, J. M. (2007). Sibling outcomes and disparate parenting and stepparenting after divorce: Report from a 25 year longitudinal study. *Psychoanlytic Psychology, 24*, 445–458.
Wallerstein, J. S., & Lewis, J. M. (2009). Divorced fathers and their adult offspring: Report from a 25 year study. *Family Law Quarterly, 42*, 695–711.
Waters, E., Crowell, J., Elliott, M., Corcoran, D., & Treboux, D. (2002). Bowlby's secure base theory and the social/personality psychology of attachment styles: Work(s) in progress. *Attachment and Human Development, 4*, 230–242.
Waters, E., Weinfield, N. S., & Hamilton, C. E. (2000). The stability of attachment security from infancy to adolescence to early adulthood: General discussion. *Child Development, 71*, 703–706.
Way, N., & Gillman, D. A. (2000). Early adolescent girls' perceptions of their relationships with their fathers: A qualitative investigation. *Journal of Early Adolescence, 20*, 309–331.
Weinfield, N. S., Sroufe, L. A., & Egeland, B. (2000). Attachment from infancy to early adulthood in a high-risk sample: Continuity, discontinuity, and their correlates. *Child Development, 71*, 695–702.
Weisner, M., Capaldi, D. M., & Patterson, G. R. (2003). Development of antisocial behavior and crime across the life-span from a social interactional perspective: The coercion model. In R. L. Akers & G. F. Jensen (Eds.), *Social learning theory and the explanation of crime* (pp. 317–337). New Brunswick, NJ: Transaction.
Weiss, L. H., & Schwartz, J. C. (1996). The relationship between parenting types and older adolescents' personality, academic achievement, adjustment, and substance use. *Child Development, 67*, 2101–2114.
Werner-Wilson, R. J., & Morrissey, K. M. (2005). Family influences on adolescent development. In T. P. Gullotta & G. Adams (Eds.), *Handbook of adolescent behavior problems* (pp. 79–100). New York: Springer.

White, J. M. (2005). *Advancing family theories*. Thousand Oaks, CA: Sage.

White, J. M., & Klein, D. M. (2008). *Family theories*. Thousand Oaks, CA: Sage.

Whitechurch, G. C., & Constantine, L. L. (1993). Systems theory. In P. G. Boss, W. J. Doherty, R. LaRossa, W. R. Schumm, & S. K. Steinmetz (Eds.), *Sourcebook of family theories and methods* (pp. 325–352). New York: Plenum.

Whiteman, S. D., & Loken, E. (2006). Comparing analytic techniques to classify dyadic relationships: An example using siblings. *Journal of Marriage and Family, 68*, 1370–1382.

Widmer, E. D. (1997). Influence of older siblings on initiation of sexual intercourse. *Journal of Marriage and the Family, 59*, 928–938.

Wiley, A. R., Bogg, T., & Ho, M. R. (2005). The influence of parental socialization factors on family farming plans of preadolescent children: An exploratory analysis. *Journal of Research in Rural Education, 20*, from http://www.umaine.edu/jrre/20-11.htm

Wilkinson, D. L., Magora, A., Garcia, M., & Khurana, A. (2009). Fathering from the margins of society. *Journal of Family Issues Volume, 30*, 945–967.

Wiium, N., & Wold, B. (2009). An ecological system approach to adolescent smoking behavior. *Journal of Youth and Adolescence, 38*, 1351–1363.

Wood, B. L., Lim, J., Miller, B. D., Cheah, P., Zwetch, T., Ramesh, S., et al. (2008). Testing the biobehavioral family model in pediatric asthma: Pathways of effect. *Family Process, 47*, 21–40.

Woolfork, A. (2010). *Educational Psychology*. Upper Saddle River, NJ: Merrill/Pearson.

Wu, L. L., & Thomson, E. (2001). Race differences in family experiences and early sexual initiation: Dynamic models of family structure and family change. *Journal of Marriage and Family, 63*, 682–696.

Wynne, L. C. (1983). Family research and family therapy: A reunion? *Journal of Marital and Family Therapy, 9*, 113–117.

Wysocki, T., Harris, M. A., Buckloh, L. M., Mertlich, D., Lochrie, A. S., Taylor, A., et al. (2006). Effects of behavioral family systems therapy for diabetes on adolescents' family relationships, treatment adherence, and metabolic control. *Journal of Pediatric Psychology, 31*, 928–938.

Yu, J. J., & Gamble, W. C. (2008). Familial correlates of overt and relational aggression between young adolescent siblings. *Journal of Youth and Adolescence, 37*, 655–673.

Yuan, A. S., Vogt, H., & Hayley, A. (2006). Stepfather involvement and adolescent well-being: Do mothers and nonresidential fathers matter? *Journal of Family Issues, 27*, 1191–1213.

Zhang, W., & Fuligni, A. J. (2006). Authority, autonomy, and family relationships among adolescents in urban and rural China. *Journal of Research on Adolescence, 16*, 527–537.

Index

A

AAMFT. *See* American association for marriage and family therapy
Adolescent outcomes
  associations, family, 18
  attachment theory, 54
  authoritative parents, 69, 71
  "conditional" influence, family variable, 16–17
  delinquency and violence, 44
  families impact
    delinquency and conduct disorders, 94–96
    demographic variables, 94
    educational issues, 103–107
    externalizing and internalizing problem behaviors, 93
    global risk factors and GRAD, 93
    mental health, 96–99
    parent-adolescent disagreement, 92
    processes and parental behaviors, 93–94
    sexual activity, 101–103
    social competence, 107–109
    substance use, 99–101
  prevention and intervention programs, 20
  research literature, 5
  step-family formation, 80
  transactional family effects model, 17
  variables measurement, 6
American association for marriage and family therapy (AAMFT), 155
Analysis
  child–mother–father triad, reciprocal influences, 52
  family-based research
    families with adolescents, 19
    parent–adolescent dyad, 19
    relational family data, 20
    "unit of analysis", 18
    SRM, 146–147
    unit of analysis, family-based research effort, 146
  variance mentality, 39
Anna Karenina, 14
Attachment theory
  ambivalent/preoccupied and avoidant/dismissing attachment, 52
  child–mother–father triad, 52–53
  families with adolescents
    dyads, 53
    explanatory function, 55
    internalizing and externalizing problem, 54
    multiple attachment relationships, 54
    parental coalitions and boundary maintenance, 53–54
    therapeutic alliance, 54
    value function, 54–55
  gender, 53
  internal working models, 51
  mother-infant dyadic relationship, 50
  multiple attachments, 53
  relationship, mother, 52
  relative stability, 52
  secure attachment, 51
  strong emotional connections, 51
  well-adjusted individuals, 51

B

The Bridges to High School Program, 130
Brief strategic family therapy (BSFT)
  approach and treatment, 117
  description, 116
  engagement and retention improvement, 117
  family pattern diagnosis, 117
  substance use, 116–117
BSFT. *See* Brief strategic family therapy

C

CHAMP. *See* The Chicago HIV Prevention and Adolescent Mental Health Project
The Chicago HIV Prevention and Adolescent Mental Health Project (CHAMP), 130–131
Conduct disorders
  BSFT, 117
  disrupted family processes, 95–96
  gender-related differences, 95
  "inept" parenting behaviors, 94
  positive parenting, 94–95
  review articles, family therapy, 115–116
  siblings, 95

D

Delinquency
  adolescent and families impact
    "inept" parenting behaviors, 94
    intermediary influences, 96
    males *vs.* females, 95
    peer associations, 96
    siblings role, 95
    social learning and ecological approach, 94–95
  adolescent outcomes, 44
  FEI, 149–150

E

Ecological theory
  child effects models, 44
  "compulsive internet use", 45
  contributing factor, Naomi's situation, 43–44
  ecosystem levels, 42–43
  exosystem and macrosystem, 43
  families with adolescents
    "advanced" form, 46
    dynamic systems, 45
    empirical literature, adolescent development, 46
    explanatory function, 46
    PPCT model, 47
    prevention programs, 46
    sensitizing function, 46
  family context, 44
  mesosystem and microsystem, 43
  neighborhood and media, 44
  peers, 44–45
  social contexts, 44

Educational issues
  adolescent, family impact
    academic motivation, 106
    Asian and African American backgrounds, 106–107
    competent and problematic behaviors, school, 103
    conflict, amounts and types, 105
    "contextual model", 104
    harshness and classroom behavior, 106
    outcomes, 107
    parent-adolescent relationship, conflict, 104–105
    race/ethnicity, 106
    social capitals and mesolevel interactions, 105
    structure change and academic performance, 104
  HIV/AIDS transmission, 131
  safety, 132
"Epigenetic principle", 26

F

Familias Unidas/United Families, 131
Families. *See also* Families with adolescents; Polyadic research
  adolescents
    interventions, 6
    members, 4
    peers, 3
    positive outcomes, 5
    theorizing, 5
  coercive family processes, negative reinforcement cycle, 60
  conflict (*see* Family conflict)
  demographic shifts, factors, 3–4
  development theory (*see* Family development theory)
  differentiation levels, 35–36
  distance regulation (*see* Family distance regulation)
  empirical studies, 4
  impoverished neighborhood, 44
  instructors, development courses, 7
  interactions, 5
  intergenerational caring, 68
  Journal of Marriage and the Family's decade review, 70
  life events, 52
  microsystem, 43

multiple attachments, 53
observational techniques, 73
research
   empirical work, 15
   "happiness" and "unhappiness", 14
   models, 14–18
   theory classification, 14
   "unit of analysis", 14–15, 18
social learning theory
   dyadic relationships, 63–64
   family level factors, 62
   integrative function, 62–63
   Multidimensional Treatment Foster Care, 62
   psychological mechanisms, 63
   social development model, 62
   substance use and abuse, 63
   triangulation processes, 62
theory
   child, adolescent and adult, 10
   definition, 11–12
   dictionary definitions, 12
   "emerging adulthood", 11
   "families with adolescents", 9
   functions, 13–14
   intergenerational nurturing, 12
   merits, frameworks, 13
   variations, definitions, 10
   young children, adolescents and adult offspring, 11
therapy (*see* Family therapy)
The Families and Schools Together Program, 131
The Families in Action Program, 131–132
Families with adolescents. *See also* Attachment theory; Ecological theory
   application efforts
      effectiveness principles, 148
      FEI, 149–150
      health care arena, 148
      "partners", 148–149
      problem prevention, 147
      social justice approach, 150
   empirical efforts
      demographic variables, 143
      dyadic topics, 144–145
      evidence, 145
      "familism", 143
      identity development, 144
      intergenerational dyad approach, 146
      longitudinal studies, 144
      methodological issues, 145–146
      parenting behaviors, 142
      problem behaviors and assets, 143–144
      problem-solving skills, 147
      reliance, adolescent, 145
      specificity, measurement, 146
      SRM, 146–147
      stepsibling influences, 143
   family development theory, 30–32
   theoretical efforts
      boundary ambiguity framework, 141
      "critical theorizing" approach, 140
      dialogic approach, 141
      functions, 140
      Journal of Family Theory and Review, 141
      social control theory, 141, 142
      social learning and information processing, 142
Families with Adolescents Surviving and Thriving Program, 132
Family-based application efforts
   adolescents, understanding
      effectiveness principles, 148
      FEI, 149–150
      health care arena, 148
      "partners", 148–149
      problem prevention, 147
      social justice approach, 150
   forms, 20
   intergenerational criterion, 20
   "selective prevention", 21
Family-based interventions
   "adolescent outcome" orientation, 20
   adolescents
      amelioration, 122
      eating disorders, 123
      treatment, 122–123
   ecologically-based family therapy, 123
   Multidimensional Treatment Foster Care, 122
Family-based prevention
   "adolescent outcome" orientation, 20
   empirical evaluation, 129–130
   information, 134–135
   programs (*see* Family programs)
   skill development, 128
Family-based research. *See also* Models
   adolescents, stepfamilies, 143
   analysis issues
      dyad/two-person system, 18

"family level" variables, 18–19
  intergenerational dyad and, 19–20
  parent–adolescent dyad, 19
  reciprocal relationships, 20
empirical work, 15
"happiness" and "unhappiness", 14
theory classification, 14
unit of analysis, 14–15, 18, 146
Family conflict
  adolescent depression levels
    alleviation, 96–97
    mother-adolescent affection, 16
    symptoms, 15
  internalizing and externalizing
    problems, 16
  and problem-solving
    adolescent adjustment, 85
    alliances and adolescent age, 86
    demographic variables, 86–87
    disagreements and differences,
      members, 85–86
    parents handling, 85
    race/ethnicity and community
      variables, 86
    social learning theory, 85
Family development theory
  autonomy, 28
  boundary flexibility, 29
  conventional issues, 25–26
  developmental tasks, 26–27
  "emptying nest", 29
  "epigenetic principle", 26
  families with adolescents
    criticisms, 31
    descriptive and sensitizing function, 30
    family-oriented ideas, 32
    microtransitions, 31
    and real world experiences, 30
  life course status, 29
  life cycle stage, 27
  "sandwich generation" term, 27
  "second-order changes", 27
  sexually oriented topics, 28
  timing, sexual activity, 30
Family distance regulation
  bi-dimensional structure, 83
  differentiation levels, 83
  functioning levels, 39
  parental and marital conflict, 84
  parentification, 84
  relative balance, individuality and
    intimacy, 39
  sibling relationships and fathers
    protective role, 84
  social relations model, 82
  tolerance intimacy and individuality, 82
  triangulation, 83–84
Family intrusiveness scale (FIS), 78
Family problem-solving
  adolescent depression, 96
  and family conflict, 85–87
  units of analysis, 146–147
Family programs
  The Bridges to High School Program, 130
  CHAMP, 130–131
  characteristics
    advanced training opportunities,
      128–129
    audiovisual instructional material,
      use, 128
    best practice and promising
      approach, 130
    categories, principles, 129
    cultural specificity and developmental
      appropriateness, 128
    dosage and follow up, 128
    literature and professionals, 129
    principles, 127
    skill development, attention, 128
  Familias Unidas/United Families, 131
  The Families and Schools Together
    Program, 131
  The Families in Action Program, 131–132
  Families with Adolescents Surviving and
    Thriving Program, 132
  The Home and On Your Own Program, 132
  initiatives, 127
  The Preparing for the Drug Free Years
    Program, 133
  The Strengthening Families Program, 133
  The Strengthening Families Program
    (parents and youth 10–14), 133–134
  web-based resources, 134–135
Family systems theory
  complementary types, moderate family
    differentiation levels, 36
  concept of circularity, 37
  differentiated family, 33–34, 36
  differentiation levels, 36
  distance regulation and boundary
    maintenance, 35–36
  equifinality and multifinality, 38
  families with adolescents
    explanatory function, 39

integrative function, 39
  sensitizing function, 38
  value function, 39
  wholeness and hierarchy, 38
 family members, 35
 under functioning and over functioning
    behaviors, 37
 GST, 34–35
 homeostasis, 35
 human development and family
    science, 13
 individuality and intimacy tolerance, 36
 interaction, parts, 34
 mistranslation, 35
 separateness and connectedness, 37
Family therapy
 AAMFT, 155
 adolescent conduct disorders and
    treatment, 116
 adolescent-oriented problems, 115
 family development theory, 31
 intervention models
    BSFT, 116–117
    family-based, 122–123
    FFT, 117–119
    MDFT, 119–120
    MST, 121–122
 Journal of Marital and Family Therapy,
    115–116
 parental coalitions and boundary
    maintenance, 53–54
 services, 115
FFT. *See* Functional family therapy
FIS. *See* Family intrusiveness scale
Functional family therapy (FFT)
 adolescent recidivism rates, 118–119
 constituent, 118
 description, 117–118
 prevention indicators, 118

G
General System Theory (GST), 34–35
Global risk assessment device (GRAD), 6, 93
GRAD. *See* Global risk assessment device
Growing Up FAST program
 Families with Adolescents Surviving and
    Thriving Program, 132
 successful adult, 126
GST. *See* General System Theory

H
The Home and On Your Own Program, 132

I
Integration
 families with adolescents
    crime, 157–158
    empirical treatment, 158
    leadership ability, 157
    "triple threat" model, 157
 linkages creation, 152
 "natural overlap", 153
 "triple threat"
    authentic life situations, 154
    bridging theory, 153
    favorable contributions, 154
    theory, research and application
      efforts, 153
    therapeutic efficacy, 154
    "win–win" relationships, 155
 unification barriers
    AAMFT, 155–156
    "both/and" approach, 157
    "ghettoization", 156
    graduate training programs, 156
    pressures, graduate school, 156
    "split" perceptions, 155

M
MDFT. *See* Multidimensional family therapy
Mental health
 adolescent, families impact
    attachment theory framework and
      friends, 98
    depressed *vs.* non-depressed, 96
    gender and race, influence, 98
    internalizing and externalizing
      problem behaviors, 97
    males *vs.* females, 97–98
    parenting behaviors, 97
    psychological distress, 96
    race, 99
    variables association, 96–97
 CHAMP, 130–131
 systems, services, 149
Models
 BSFT (*see* Brief strategic family therapy)
 child effects, 44
 family-based research
    "complex mediated family effects", 16
    "direct family effects", 15
    "family as mediator", 16, 17
    "family as moderator", 16–17
    "transactional family effects", 17–18
    types, 14
 family-based treatment, 154

Models (*cont.*)
  FFT (*see* Functional family therapy)
  internal working
    attachment theory, 52
    types, 51
  MDFT (*see* Multidimensional family therapy)
  MST (*see* Multisystemic therapy)
  PPCT, 46, 47
  secure attachment, 51
  social development
    The Families in Action Program, 131–132
    integrative function, social learning theory, 62
    The Preparing for the Drug Free Years Program, 133
  social learning, family process, 62
  SRM, 146–147
  transactional, 38
  triple threat (*see* Triple threat model)
  "value orientation", 47
MST. *See* Multisystemic therapy
Multidimensional family therapy (MDFT)
  vs. cognitive behavioral therapy, 120
  description and targets, 119
  "multidimensionality", 119–120
  outpatient substance abuse treatment, 120
  parent-adolescent relationship, 119–120
  substance-abusing adolescents, 120
Multisystemic therapy (MST)
  criminal behaviors and marijuana use, 121
  description, 121
  Drug Court groups, 121–122
  family empowerment component, 149
  home-based service delivery model, 121
  vs. usual community services, 122

P

Parent–adolescent dyad
  authoritarian, 69
  behaviors
    competence level, 71–72
    cultural relevance, 74–75
    dimensionality, 72–74
    insider *vs.* outsider perspectives, 72
    mothers and fathers contributions, 70–71
    uniformity, parenting styles, 71
  communication, sex, 144
  "intergenerational nurturing" definition, 19
  law and factors, 69–70
  parenting
    styles, 68
    two-dimensional view, 68
  permissive parents, 69
  responsiveness and demandingness, 68–69
  style consistency, 75–76
  trends, 70
Parenting behaviors
  competence level, 71–72
  cultural relevance
    behavioral and psychological control, 74
    demandingness and responsiveness combination, 75
    equivalency, 74–75
  dimensionality
    connectedness and behavioral regulation, 73
    monitoring and supervising, 74
    observational techniques, 73
    parental knowledge, 74
    responsiveness and demandingness, 73
    strengths, parenting styles, 72–73
  insider *vs.* outsider perspectives, 72
  mothers and fathers contributions, 70–71
  uniformity, parenting styles, 71
Polyadic research
  attachment theory, 52
  conflict and problem-solving, 85–87
  distance regulation, 82–85
  family-based application efforts, 20–21
  family processes
    adolescents comparison, 80
    compelling, 79
    definition, 79
    disruptive, 80
    distance regulation, 81
    scholars conflict, 81
    sibling relationship, 81
    supervision and caring, 79
  family system and FIS, 78
  general systems theory, 79
  siblings influence
    "differential parenting", 87
    differential treatment, 88
    interparental incongruence, 87–88
    parental psychological control, 89
    relational aggression, 88
  units of analysis, 79
The Preparing for the Drug Free Years Program, 133
Process-Person-Context-Time (PPCT) model, 46, 47

S

Sexual activity
  adolescent, families impact
    initiation and interaction quality, association, 102
    parenting factors, 101–102
    siblings role, 103
    timing/initiation, 101
    unsafe practices, pregnancy and teen parenthood, 102
  CHAMP, 130–131
  timing, adolescents, 30
Social competence
  emotional and cognitive dimensions, empathy, 107
  enmeshment styles and reciprocal influences, 108
  parenting styles and self perceptions, 109
  prosocial and parental behaviors, relationship, 108
Social learning theory
  cascade effect, 61
  coercive family processes, 60
  components, 59
  and families, adolescents
    dyadic relationships, 63–64
    functions use, 61
    integrative function, 62–63
    level factors, 62
    Multidimensional Treatment Foster Care, 62
    psychological mechanisms, 63
    social development model, 62
    substance use and abuse, 63
    triangulation processes, 62
  irritable exchanges, parents and adolescents, 61
  mixed verbal and nonverbal messages, 59–60
  peer group, coercive adolescent behavior, 61
  reciprocal determinism, 60
  reinforcement and parental responses, 59
  threats and out-of-control behavior, 60
The Strengthening Families Program, 133
The Strengthening Families Program (parents and youth 10–14), 133–134
Substance use
  adolescents
    BSFT, 116–117
    FFT, 117–119
    internet use, 45
    MDFT, 119–120
    MST, 121–122
  families impact
    alcohol use and parenting behaviors, association, 99
    environment, 99
    peer and protective factors, 100
    sibling effects, 100–101
    social learning and control theory approach, 99–100
    structure and process variables, 100
  social learning approach, adolescent, 63

T

Triple threat model
  family-based interventions, 157
  favorable contributions, 154
  relationship
    theorist–practitioner, 155
    theorist–researcher, 154–155
    "win–win", 155
  theory, research and application efforts, 153
  therapeutic efficacy, 154

U

Unification barriers
  AAMFT, 155–156
  "both/and" approach, 157
  "ghettoization", 156
  graduate training programs, 156
  pressures, graduate school, 156
  "split" perceptions, 155

W

Web-based resources, family programs, 134–135

LaVergne, TN USA
06 April 2011

223147LV00007B/1/P